SEEING THROUGH CHRISTIANITY

SEEING THROUGH CHRISTIANITY

A Critique of Beliefs and Evidence

Bill Zuersher

Copyright © 2014 by Bill Zuersher.

Library of Congress Control Number:	2014908789
ISBN: Hardcover	978-1-4990-1848-6
Softcover	978-1-4990-1849-3
eBook	978-1-4990-1845-5

All rights reserved. No part of this book may be reproduced or transmitted in any form or by any means, electronic or mechanical, including photocopying, recording, or by any information storage and retrieval system, without permission in writing from the copyright owner.

Print information available on the last page.

All Scripture quotations, unless otherwise indicated, are taken from the Holy Bible, New International Version®, NIV®. Copyright ©1973, 1978, 1984, 2011 by Biblica, Inc.™ Used by permission of Zondervan. All rights reserved worldwide. www.zondervan.com. The "NIV" and "New International Version" are trademarks registered in the United States Patent and Trademark Office by Biblica, Inc.™

Cover consultation: Holly A. Jones
Photo credits, left to right: Lauren Simmons, vician, Steven Frame / Shutterstock.com

Christianity, Religion, Atheism, Separation of church and state, Skepticism, Apologetics.

Rev. date: 01/21/2016

To order additional copies of this book, contact:
Xlibris
1-888-795-4274
www.Xlibris.com
Orders@Xlibris.com
605065

ABOUT THE COVER

The collage of crosses represents the three main branches of Christianity—Roman Catholic, Eastern Orthodox, and Protestant. While the instrument of Jesus's execution is the religion's unmistakable symbol, it appears in a variety of formats.

Catholics usually depict the cross including the *corpus* (Latin, "body"), as in the photo on the left. Only when the corpus is included is it correct to call it a crucifix (Latin, "fixed to a cross").

The Eastern Orthodox churches have their own diverse traditions. The corpus is sometimes painted on or represented in low relief but more often, as in the middle photo, not included at all. Many Eastern Orthodox crosses have three crossbars. The topmost represents the mocking sign said to have been posted over Jesus's head, and the lower represents the bar to which his feet were nailed.

Most Protestants favor a plain cross with a single crossbar, as in the photo on the right. The inclusion, or not, of the corpus reflects a traditional interpretive emphasis. While the Catholic crucifix emphasizes the passion of the atonement, the empty cross of Protestantism emphasizes the triumph of the resurrection.

The good life is one inspired by love and guided by knowledge.

—Bertrand Russell

CONTENTS

About the Cover 5
Acknowledgments 11

Introduction 13

Part 1: Beliefs

1. The World 19

Doctrinal Core
2. The Fall 23
3. Original Sin 26
4. The Satan 30
5. Atonement 34
6. Afterlife 41

Revelation and Response
7. Revelation 48
8. Faith 53
9. Judgment 59
10. Hell 63

Nature of the God
11. Trinity and Mystery 68
12. The Incarnation 72
13. Holy Spirit 78

Guidance
14. Morality 82
15. Purpose 94

Interaction in History
16. The Church 99
17. Prayer 105
18. Miracles 109
19. Prophecies 115
20. Second Coming 120

Part 2: Evidence

21. Baseline 127

The Evidence of Scripture
22. Paul 136
23. Oral Tradition 144
24. Canon 151
25. Gospel Composition 159
26. Gospel Preservation 169
27. Misrepresentation 174
28. Contradiction 181
29. Corroboration 190

The Evidence of the Early Church
30. Resurrection 198
31. Legend 208
32. Growth 215

Conclusion 221

Appendix 1. Christianity's Jewish Roots 229
Appendix 2. Historical Outline of Ancient Israel 231
Appendix 3. The Suffering Servant of Isaiah 53 233
Appendix 4. Descents and Resurrections 252
Appendix 5. Canon 256
Appendix 6. Corroboration 263

ACKNOWLEDGMENTS

I want to thank Michael Todor for his many insights, suggestions, cautions, and corrections. I also owe a debt to the writings of Barton Ehrman and Richard Carrier. They are two scholars who, while they may not always agree with each other, never fail to enlighten me. Most importantly, thank you to my wife, Linda, for her patience and encouragement.

INTRODUCTION

Polite company, we are told, refrains from discussing religion and politics. This is probably good for digestion, but not so good for religion and politics. Ideas about these subjects have important consequences, and for that reason they should not be exempt from challenge.

This essay consists of two parts. The first addresses Christianity's beliefs, and the second, evidence for them. I find the difficulties with the beliefs on the one hand and the limitations of the evidence on the other to make a compelling case for rejecting Christianity.

By numbers, Christianity is the world's most successful religion, claiming about 32 percent of the population.[1] But not all Christians believe the same things. There are three main branches with a worldwide distribution as follows: Roman Catholic, 50 percent; Eastern Orthodox, 12 percent; and Protestant, 37 percent. (The remaining 1 percent consists of "other Christians," including Mormons and Jehovah's Witnesses.)[2]

While sharing many beliefs, the three main branches—and there are many subdivisions—disagree on others. For the most part, this essay addresses a "common denominator" Christianity: some of the details important to certain subsets of Christians are omitted, and some generalizations are made, in an effort to describe what most Christians would agree upon.

Many religions have apologists, people who explain the belief system to outsiders or defend it from critics. Developing with little power on the margins of society, first as a dissident Jewish sect in Palestine and then as a foreign cult imported into Rome, Christianity was a religion of apologists from the beginning. The New Testament's 1 Peter 3:15 counseled, "Always be prepared to give an answer to everyone who asks you to give the reason for the hope that you have."

In this essay, I ask Christianity to "give the reason" for its beliefs, challenging them in each case. Of course, defenders of the faith have had two thousand years to practice and a knowledgeable apologist will have a set of ready responses, many of which I have included in my discussions. Nevertheless, in some cases, it is very difficult to see how the Christian position can be maintained. In others, the issue boils down to competing points of view. The question for the reader is which point of view is more plausible.

What's coming?

Part 1 surveys Christian beliefs or doctrines. Each chapter contains a short summary of a belief followed by a critique. Many of the issues overlap. The chapter groupings in the table of contents are intended merely to make the discussions easier to follow.

Chapter 1 sets the stage by describing the problems that Christianity, like most religions, seeks primarily to address, namely, suffering and death. Chapters 2 through 6 review Christianity's doctrinal core, the story used to reinterpret the world as a temporary state of affairs in an unfolding cosmic drama. Chapters 7 through 10 discuss the expected human response to the Christian god's revelation. Chapters 11 through 13 review that god's nature, one necessarily complicated by the demands of the drama. Chapters 14 and 15 discuss guidance for living, and chapters 16 through 20 discuss divine interaction in human affairs.

Part 2 surveys the evidence for Christianity. This evidence consists of two types: religious writings, particularly scripture, and the emergence of the early church itself. There is, of course, overlap since scripture and church coevolved; but for clarity, they are treated in sequence.

Chapter 21 sets the stage by describing aspects of Christianity which appear to derive from the broader religious milieu of the ancient Mediterranean and reflecting upon how this might inform our attitude toward the evidence. Chapters 22 through 29 discuss the written record, including canonical and noncanonical Christian writings, along with non-Christian sources. Chapters 30 through 32 discuss the emergence of the early church, with an emphasis on the origin of the resurrection belief.

Many of the issues have roots in Jewish history and theology because Christianity developed from Judaism. Readers who find this to be new information are urged to glance at appendix 1, "Christianity's Jewish Roots," before proceeding. Most readers would also benefit from the brief refresher provided by appendix 2, a "Historical Outline of Ancient Israel."

Conventions

The words "god" and "goddess," along with the names given to events in their lives, are not capitalized, unless they are capitalized in text being quoted. Of course, the proper names of gods and goddesses are capitalized.

The masculine pronoun is generally used, not to convey gender bias but for economy of expression.

CE stands for "common era" and BCE for "before the common era." In referring to historical individuals, I generally provide a single date of flourishing rather than the dates of births and deaths, which tend to be less relevant.

There are many Bible translations from which to choose. Unless otherwise indicated, quotations are from the New International Version (NIV). In three instances, Ezekiel 18:21-22, Mark 8:35, and James 2:24, I have corrected the text so that a singular noun is accompanied by the singular pronoun "he" rather than the plural "they." In one instance, Luke 12:47, I have shown the Greek word δουλος as "slave" rather than "servant." "Slave" is the more common translation, and substitution of the word "servant" appears to be an inappropriate attempt to downplay the harshness of the situation.

PART 1

Beliefs

1

THE WORLD

Christianity teaches that the world was created by an omnipotent god who loves it. "For God so loved the world . . ." (John 3:16). In fact, "God is love" (1 John 4:8).

These are surprising assertions since every man, woman, plant, and animal dies, often following great suffering. Why would a loving deity create a world in which the only way animals can feed themselves is to kill and devour? One animal's horrific death is another's life-sustaining meal. A gazelle's throat is torn off by a lioness with hungry cubs; a rabbit thrashes desperately as a snake begins to swallow and digest it; a caterpillar is eaten alive from the inside because a wasp has injected its eggs into it. Is this how a creator-god manifests love?

Carnivores are not the only killers. Herbivores kill plants, or parts of plants, as they eat them. All food was alive until recently. The basic requirement of animal life is killing and eating. And plants? Plants draw nutrients from dead plants and animals. They too live on death.

Human beings are at the top of the food chain, but this provides only partial, and only temporary, relief. Why do human babies suffer and die of leukemia or malaria? Malaria kills a child every minute.[1] Is this how a creator-god manifests love?

Not only is the scale of suffering immeasurably vast, but its distribution appears blind at best, if not perverse. It often seems that good people suffer the most, and bad, the least. While human beings are certainly capable of creating many of their own problems, they do not create all of them. Much of the suffering appears to be undeserved and completely pointless.

We would expect any loving human being to try to mitigate the suffering of others. If he possessed superpowers, we would expect him to be successful. And yet the Christian god is supposed to be both more loving and more powerful than any superhuman.[2] Nevertheless, pointless suffering continues. The evidence from the world we observe appears inconsistent with a loving and all-powerful creator-god. Is there any way to reconcile the two?

One approach is to argue that suffering exists to teach us or to build character. Unfortunately, this is not persuasive. Animals and human babies suffer all the time, but their learning is severely constrained by their ability to understand what is happening. Even for adult humans, suffering is often disproportionate to learning. It is not necessary for someone to be raped and tortured to learn something.

A second approach is to argue that suffering exists because humans have free will. If the god who created them wants people to choose the good freely, then they must be free to choose the bad too. As a result, people sometimes make poor choices and suffering ensues. This too is unpersuasive. Human free will does not cause natural disasters, such as earthquakes or tsunamis. And there is another problem, one rooted in Christian doctrine. Many Christians believe that they will retain their personalities and free will in heaven. But they also believe there is no suffering in heaven. If those two things are true, then free will cannot be the cause of suffering. If a deity can make a place where there is free will and no suffering, then why did he make this world instead?

A third approach is to argue that mere humans cannot understand their creator's reasons for allowing suffering; some larger good is being served, even if we cannot see it. This type of argument is what philosophers sometimes call a retreat to the possible. It is indeed possible. But there is not much evidence for it. Proponents of the "larger good" position believe that a loving deity allows some bad in order to maximize good. But it is equally possible that an evil deity allows some good in order to maximize bad.

Which of these is more likely? If some larger good were really being served by our suffering, then it is difficult to see why we would be kept ignorant of that fact. If a child needed a painful operation, a caring parent would explain to him why it was necessary. If the child were too young to comprehend, the parent would at least comfort him. But we see neither of these behaviors from the god in question.

A fourth approach is to argue that life's suffering will be undone or compensated for in something called an "afterlife." In fact, some believers reduce all of life to a mere tryout for this alleged afterlife.

The idea of an afterlife is discussed further in chapter 6, but two preliminary observations can be made here. First, it fails to address the suffering of animals. They do not participate in the Christian afterlife and are consequently deprived of its compensations. Second, insofar as it addresses human suffering, this argument is yet another retreat to the possible. But it is equally possible that there is no afterlife, simply oblivion. It is also possible that an afterlife exists but that it consists merely of more suffering. It is possible that an afterlife is restricted to special groups only, such as children who died before they grew to adulthood. Perhaps an afterlife consists of punishments and rewards allotted according to the caprice of a council of gods and goddesses. Then again, this life itself could be the afterlife of some prior life, or it could simply be one in a long series of lives. Lots of things are "possible."

Since Jesus appeared in this life, it is fair to ask why he did not eliminate suffering in this life. The defeat of suffering, at least for his own followers, would be the type of thing we might expect if Jesus were really an all-powerful deity. The problem with such a belief, of course, is that it would be obvious if it were true or false. On the other hand, deferring the defeat of suffering into an alleged afterlife that no one can investigate would be the type of thing we might expect if Jesus were simply a human and Christianity simply another human-made belief system.

If a god were omniscient, he would know about the pointless suffering in the world. If he were omnipotent, he could change it. If he were benevolent, he would want to change it. It appears that a deity with these three qualities does not exist.

On a rational level, all of this suffering and death is significant evidence against the existence of a loving god. But on an emotional level, it provides the impetus for wanting to believe in precisely that. The tension between the rational and emotional responses can be resolved only through some creative storytelling. Christianity exonerates its god by contriving an elaborate story to explain how suffering and death are actually the fault of human beings.

In this story, humankind deserves to suffer, not just in life but for all eternity as well. And yet, while humankind does not deserve it, the Christian god has provided an escape route. Those eligible, a fortunate fraction of humanity, will not only avoid suffering in the afterlife, but will enjoy such bliss there that they will be more than compensated for their former terrestrial troubles. This story simultaneously explains suffering and provides hope for its defeat. In order to do so, however, it shifts responsibility for the state of the world from a god to humankind. In making this shift, Christianity resembles a victim of domestic abuse who puts the blame on herself in order to protect her abuser.

2

THE FALL

    Christianity teaches that a perfect, all-powerful deity created the world, and yet the world is not what he wanted. According to the Jewish creation story in Genesis, which Christians retained, a god created the world, including two prototype humans: Adam and Eve. He placed a "tree of the knowledge of good and evil" near them, instructing them not to eat from it, but they disobeyed because they were tempted and deceived. Their act of disobedience brought suffering and death into existence.

    This constellation of beliefs has serious difficulties. First, there is no reason to believe that the ancient Israelites' story of Adam and Eve is historically accurate. Second, the story itself is logically and morally flawed.

    Many cultures have creation stories that include explanations for suffering and death. Compare the Israelite creation story with the Native American Iroquois creation story. Twin sons of the Sky People created the world. One twin named Sapling created all the good things, including useful plants and animals. The other twin named Flint created harmful animals, put thorns on plants, and created winter. Eventually, the twins fought. Sapling won, but the influence of Flint persists.[1]

There are no good reasons for believing that either the Israelite story or the Iroquois story is more historically accurate than the other. And there are many more to choose from. Religions were humankind's earliest attempts to explain the world, and we should not be surprised that, though their explanations are as varied as any other aspect of culture, they address universal concerns.

The Israelite story presents logical difficulties, not only for those wishing to take it literally, but also for anyone seeking a coherent message.

First, why would a creator-god withhold from humans the knowledge of good and evil? Knowledge of good and evil is the basis of morality. This knowledge would have been essential if the god wanted humans to be "in his own image," as the story claims.

Second, having decided to withhold the knowledge, why would the god choose to create a magic fruit that confers upon its eater, of all things, that very knowledge? To compound this strange behavior, he then elected to plant a tree bearing the magic fruit conspicuously in the center of "the garden." If such a tree existed, monkeys, squirrels, and birds would certainly have eaten the fruit. Did this god intend to endow humans with reason but no morality, reserving the latter only for frugivorous animals?

Third, before they ate the fruit, Adam and Eve did not know the difference between right and wrong. They could not have known, therefore, that it was wrong to disobey the god's command to refrain from eating it. How then could it be fair to punish them for disobedience?

Finally, any creator would bear responsibility for the nature he gave his creatures. If this god were omniscient, he would have anticipated Adam and Eve's vulnerability to deception and temptation. If he were omnipotent, he could have created them with a different nature. For example, he could have made Adam and Eve more like Jesus. Why did he endow them with a nature that was incapable of meeting his standards? Either this god chose to make Adam and Eve vulnerable or he did so by mistake.

Their god had instructed them to "be fruitful and increase in number" (Genesis 1:28). But even before Adam and Eve had embarked upon this happy assignment, they broke the world. In addition to the problems of internal coherence outlined above, this story lacks features that would commend its historical authenticity beyond that of other creation stories. It is just one of many myths produced by humankind's prescientific mind. This story was told by Hebrew tribes three thousand years ago, yet it is the foundation of the entire Christian worldview. Through it, Christianity asserts that an omnipotent deity created the world but that he is not responsible for anything bad that happens in it. We take the fall for that.

3

ORIGINAL SIN

Christianity teaches that human beings have an inescapable tendency to wrongdoing. Adam and Eve's disobedience was humanity's "original sin." As a result, all of us, their descendants, inherit wickedness. We are not deemed guilty of Adam and Eve's transgression, but we inherit from them a predisposition to transgress ourselves. In other words, because of their transgression, we will inevitably be guilty of our own. "Through the disobedience of the one man the many were made sinners" (Romans 5:19).

Not all Christians accept the term "original sin" or the elaborate rationale behind it. Some simply say humans inherit a sinful nature. But the general idea is similar, and the term original sin is used here to designate all of these perspectives.

This doctrine is indispensable to Christian explanations for suffering and death. A difficulty noted in chapter 1 is that the innocent suffer along with the wicked. Original sin neatly disposes of this difficulty because it teaches that no one is innocent. Everyone deserves punishment, and any relief from that fate is unmerited upside. Though it had been in gestation for some time beforehand, the doctrine of original sin received its most elaborate and influential exposition from the early church leader Augustine (circa 400 CE).

Original sin, however, ill accords with the Old Testament. Even if we put aside the problems noted in chapter 2 and take the Adam and Eve story as we find it, there is no reason to accept the original sin interpretation that Christianity wishes to impose upon it. In fact, there is an excellent reason to reject that interpretation: the god of the Old Testament, Yahweh, is completely ignorant of original sin.

For example, angered by human misconduct, he floods the world, saving only Noah's family. But according to Christian doctrine, Noah and his descendants were just as polluted by original sin as anyone else. If Yahweh had known about original sin, he would have known that it was necessary to kill Noah and his family too. He would have known that he had to start over completely. Instead, he perpetrated a massive slaughter of men, women, and children, not to mention animals, and accomplished nothing because original sin survived through Noah's family.

Furthermore, it is clear that the god of the Old Testament believes humans are capable of living morally. He established "the law," a set of rules to help his chosen people live properly with him and one another. Consisting of 613 commandments, of which the "ten commandments" are the best known, the law is scattered throughout Genesis, Exodus, Leviticus, Numbers, and Deuteronomy. Yahweh states plainly that people are able to follow the law, telling the Israelites through Moses, "Now what I am commanding you today is not too difficult for you or beyond your reach" (Deuteronomy 30:11). The Old Testament even celebrates the success of some individuals in obeying the law. King Josiah lived "in accordance with all the Law of Moses" (2 Kings 23:25). Job "was blameless and upright" (Job 1:1).

How could an all-knowing god be ignorant of what would someday become the Christian doctrine of original sin? The answer is simple: the collection of writings that Christians call the

Old Testament is the Jewish Bible, which was written long before Christianity. Anomalies such as this arise because Christians attempt to project their newer doctrines back onto older Jewish scripture.

The traditional interpretation of the Adam and Eve story, accepted for centuries before Christianity, is that Adam and Eve were punished for disobedience but that their disobedience was a single act. It did not result in an ongoing condition for them and certainly not an ongoing condition transmitted to future generations. Prior to Christianity, the idea of original sin did not exist. The phrase itself does not appear in the Old Testament (or even in the New Testament, for that matter). Wrongdoing had always been a problem, of course, but it was condemned precisely because people recognized that they were free to choose between right and wrong.

Then Jesus came along, and some people believed that he was the son of Yahweh. But they had a problem: why would a divine son die? The answer they eventually developed was that Jesus had died to heal a rift between humankind and its creator. For this to make sense, they had to identify the cause and nature of this rift. Put differently, if Jesus was the solution, what was the problem?

The problem would have to be big. Nothing would do, in fact, short of the universal problems—suffering and death. According to this thinking, Adam and Eve's transgression corrupted human nature. Wrongdoing, consequently, is not merely an act but a condition into which all are born. This corrupt condition can be remedied only with supernatural assistance, that is, through Jesus. His death healed the rift that Adam and Eve's transgression had opened between humankind and its creator.

How Jesus's death might have accomplished this is explored in chapter 5. The question here is whether the doctrine of original sin makes any sense. By what mechanism is the alleged corruption of human nature transmitted from generation to generation?

Apologists generally explain it in one of two ways. The first is that all human beings were mystically united with Adam and Eve when they transgressed. The second is that Adam and Eve's sinfulness is passed to each human being at the time of his or her conception.

Neither of these explanations seems particularly persuasive. In fact, there is absolutely no evidence that either mechanism was, or is, at work. These explanations are nothing more than assertions, backfilling rationales for a conclusion to which Jesus's followers were already committed. The only evidence for original sin is human nature itself.

It is a matter of common experience that human beings are not morally perfect. But is this really evidence of original sin? Or is it simply the nature of things? Imperfection does not appear to require an elaborate backstory; it is exactly what one would expect of ordinary beings. We are not physically perfect. We are not mentally perfect. Why would anyone expect us to be morally perfect?

Apologists might reply that perfect beings are precisely what their god had created. Before the fall, Adam and Eve were perfect in all of these ways. But here, the apologist is caught in the coils of a circularity: If Adam and Eve were morally and mentally perfect, then they would not have succumbed to temptation and deceit. If they had been perfect, they would not have fallen.

So the apologist fails. Imperfection appears to be a natural state, and as such, hardly needs original sin to explain it. Why then was the doctrine invented? Original sin was invented specifically for the purpose of justifying, after the fact, Jesus's otherwise humiliating execution.

Christianity did not start with a problem (original sin) and work toward a solution (Jesus). Rather, it began with the solution (Jesus) and then worked backward to identify a problem (original sin).[1] The sought-after problem was manufactured through a reinterpretation of the old Jewish Adam and Eve story, making wrongdoing an inescapable condition rather than an act. Its corollary is the disgraceful dogma that a newborn baby is corrupt.

4

THE SATAN

Christianity teaches that its god created a multitude of supernatural beings called "angels" to protect and bring messages to humankind. In fact, many Christians believe that each human being is assigned his own guardian angel. Tragically, one of the angels, Satan, rebelled against his creator and took some of the others with him. His greatest treachery was to tempt and deceive Adam and Eve into disobeying their god, as discussed in the previous chapters.

Once again, these ideas suffer from both internal flaws and a lack of consistency with the scripture from which they allegedly arise.

First, if one were to accept the traditional characterization of the Christian god as omnipotent, the obvious question cannot be ignored. Why would an all-powerful god need helpers? He could perform all of the angelic duties directly and effortlessly. Not only would this be simpler, but it would eliminate the drawbacks of under-performing and even mutinous helpers. Angels do not quite fit within monotheism. Their presence in Judaism and Christianity seems best explained as a vestige of a primitive spirit religion, elements of which were later imperfectly absorbed into a monotheistic system.

Second, if a god made them, how did Satan and the other angels become bad? Were they tempted and deceived just as Adam and Eve were? By whom? If their god were omniscient, he would have anticipated the angels' disaffection. If he were omnipotent, he could have created angels with a different nature. Christians believe it is possible for a being to possess free will and still be completely good. After all, they believe this to be true of their god. He could have created angels with a nature more like his own. Either he chose to make them as he did or he made a mistake.

The scriptural problem arises because, as with the doctrine of original sin, Christianity is trying to overlay newer beliefs onto preexisting scripture. The Jewish Bible/Old Testament does not teach that any of the angels oppose their god. The few times Satan appears there, he is working under Yahweh's instructions. For example, in Job 1:6-12, Satan requests permission to test Job, and the god agrees but gives him strict limitations, which Satan observes.

According to Christianity, the talking snake or serpent in Genesis is Satan. But the text does not say this. It never gives a name. It is simply a talking snake, an animal of fable. The snake's identification as Satan is a later invention, and it creates an amusing problem for those who believe it. The Bible says that snakes slither on their bellies to this day because that was Yahweh's punishment for them (Genesis 3:14). But why did the god punish snakes? If the culprit was in fact Satan impersonating a snake, why didn't the god punish Satan? Did he aim for Satan, miss, and hit the snake instead?

The term satan (שטן) means adversary or opponent. It is used in 9 passages in the Jewish scriptures, but never in the sense of an opponent to Israel's god.[1] Purely human interactions provide the setting for 5 of these 9 passages. For example, Solomon explains that a respite from war will enable him to build the temple: "Now the Lord my God has given me rest on every side, and there is no adversary (satan) or disaster" (1 Kings 5:4). See also 1 Samuel 29:4, 2 Samuel 19:22, 1 Kings 11:14, and Psalm 109:6.

The supernatural realm is the setting for the remaining 4 passages in which the term satan is used. Here, the activity is personified or formalized as a title. In 1 Chronicles 21:1, Satan induces King David to conduct a census. That contradicts 2 Samuel 24:1, which states that Yahweh induced David to conduct the census. From a Jewish standpoint, this apparent contradiction can be explained as a decision made by Yahweh but implemented by his underling, Satan. No such explanation is available to Christians, however, because they claim that Satan opposes Yahweh. For Christianity, these verses constitute only an embarrassing contradiction, and they are generally ignored for that reason.

In Job 1:6-2:7 and in Zechariah 3:1-7, the term is השטן, pronounced "hasatan" and translated as "the satan." The definite article "the" indicates that this is a role or title, not a name. In this capacity, the satan serves Yahweh by challenging some human endeavor. In fact, the Greek word *diabolos*, later translated into English as "devil," means "one who throws something across one's path."[2]

This is nowhere better illustrated than in the story of Balaam and his talking donkey. In Numbers 22:21-35 a man named Balaam tries to travel to a place Yahweh had told him not to go. Suddenly, his path is blocked by an otherworldly being. This is an angel acting in the capacity of a satan sent to obstruct (לשטן, pronounced "lesatan") Balaam's path. Explications of the text intended for Christian audiences seldom draw out the satan connection here. To do so would contribute to the understanding that the Christian Satan, who is evil and opposes his creator, was a late invention not supported by the Old Testament.

How did Christianity find itself with a belief that is so much at odds with the Jewish Bible/Old Testament, the scripture in force at the time and place of its founding?

During and after the Babylonian exile (see appendix 2) the Israelites became exposed to Persian thought, a conspicuous feature of which was cosmic dualism, the notion that the universe contains two warring principles: one good and the other evil.[3] In Zoroastrianism, the dominant Persian religion of the time, the god Ahura Mazda personifies goodness, and the god Ahriman personifies evil.

During the postexilic period, ideas about an evil principle evolved within Judaism, particularly among a group of thinkers known as apocalypticists.[4] (For more on apocalypticism, see chapter 20). The evil principle was named variously—Azazel, Belial, Mastema, or Satan—with the latter eventually emerging as the most common.

Satan resembled the Zoroastrian Ahriman in many ways. Both Ahriman and Satan were cast out of heaven, both operate via seduction or accusation, both are associated with snakes, both lead ranks of lesser evil spirits and war against the forces of light, and both are prophesied to increase their power toward the end of the age before they are destroyed.[5]

The Christian Satan, the notion of a satan who opposes his creator, was a late development, heavily influenced by Zoroastrianism and never part of mainstream Jewish thinking. But for some Jews of the last few centuries BCE and for Christianity, which adopted their apocalyptic outlook, this satan came to personify evil. His opposition to their god was then read back into prior scripture, such as the book of Genesis, whose author(s) had never contemplated such a being.

5

ATONEMENT

Christianity teaches that Jesus's death atoned for humankind. Atonement (from Middle English, meaning literally "at one-ment") is an act undertaken by someone who has transgressed so that he can be reconciled with his god. As discussed in chapter 3, the need for atonement arose because Adam and Eve's disobedience had created a rift between humankind and its creator. Healing this rift is the reason the god's son had to die.

How does atonement work?

Over the past two thousand years, Christian thinkers have proposed numerous explanations for how atonement works; and even today, consensus is elusive. While some theologians and clerics have articulated variations or combinations, the following table summarizes, in very simplified form, the main theories of atonement:

Ransom	Because of its sins, humankind is the rightful property of the devil. God exchanged his son for us, but the devil was unable to possess Jesus.
Victory	Because of its sins, humankind is under the control of the devil. Jesus liberated humankind by defeating the devil and hence sin and death.
Moral	Jesus's death demonstrated god's love for humankind and serves to awaken in us love and goodness in return.
Recapitulation	Jesus lived a sinless life in contrast to Adam's, and Christians are mystically united in Jesus. Consequently, humankind's fall is reversed.
Satisfaction	Humankind's sins insult god's honor, but god accepts Jesus's sacrifice as restitution on humankind's behalf.
Penal	Humankind's sins must be punished because god is just, but god accepts Jesus's sacrifice as punishment on humankind's behalf.

Because the satisfaction theory (emphasized by the Catholic church) and the penal theory (generally favored by Protestants) are the most common, the discussion below focuses on them.

Both the satisfaction and penal theories are built around the idea of substitutionary sacrifice. With ancient sanction in the story of Abraham's slaughter of a ram as a substitute for his son, Isaac, substitutionary sacrifice had been institutionalized in the ritual observance of the Israelites. According to the satisfaction and penal theories, humankind, because of its wrongdoing, owed an infinite debt to its creator. But mere humans are unable to discharge an infinite debt, so Jesus substituted for us. Because he was both fully human and fully god, he represented humankind in infinite sacrifice—as "a sin offering" (Romans 8:3).

A close look at blood sacrifice

Despite centuries of learned study and debate among Christian scholars, the satisfaction and penal theories are beset with theological difficulties. The following are a half-dozen:

First, the confusion surrounding how atonement works and the late vintage of the most popular theories to explain it suggest human construction rather than divine disclosure. Notice that after two thousand years, Christianity still lacks agreement on which theory is correct. The satisfaction theory, though it had precursors in earlier thought, is typically associated with Anselm (circa 1090 CE), and the penal theory came hundreds of years later with the Reformation. In other words, over a thousand years after Jesus, Christian writers were still trying to backfill the logic for his death. Far from suggesting privileged access to the ways of the divine, this raises the suspicion that church leaders have been making all this up as they go along.

Second, the satisfaction and penal theories imply contradictions with traditional views of the Christian god. The satisfaction theory argues that the restoration of his honor was required. But this belief ascribes to the god personality traits unworthy of a morally perfect being. It is not as if human sin harmed him; at worst, it wounded his pride. While Zeus may have been thin-skinned, the god of Christianity is supposed to be above umbrageous scorekeeping.

The penal theory, on the other hand, argues that this god cannot let transgressions go unpunished. But such a belief constrains an allegedly all-powerful deity. To argue that justice requires the god to do something is to concede that justice exists independently of the god himself, a concession Christianity is loath to make. How could a god give Adam and Eve free will if he didn't have it too?

Some insist that "a price must be paid" for transgressions. But a god could simply forgive them. Forgiving, after all, is not equivalent to condoning. If humans are capable of forgiving one another, wouldn't an all-powerful deity be capable of doing the same? In fact, a scriptural case could be made that "a price does not have to be paid" because the god in question would prefer not to punish people. "Do I take any pleasure in the death of the wicked? declares the Sovereign Lord. Rather, am I not pleased when they turn from their ways and live?" (Ezekiel 18:23).

Third, if human misdeeds offended the god, then the execution of the god's son by humans constituted a further injury to the god, not recompense. If Jesus possessed, as Christian doctrine insists and indeed requires, a fully human nature, then his sacrifice was a fully human sacrifice. But that is murder, an act prohibited (Exodus 20:13 and Deuteronomy 5:17) by the very same scripture that Christians believe Jesus to have been fulfilling.

The murder of a god's son by humans increases the tally of human wrongdoing rather than decreases it. That Jesus is alleged to have died willingly does not excuse his executioners. In claiming that the sacrifice of Jesus was required to atone humankind, Christianity would have us believe that its god's instructions were, "Thou shalt not kill . . . but you have to kill my son."

Fourth, Christianity characterizes Jesus's death as the culminating sacrifice, fulfilling all of the Old Testament atonement requirements in one act. But this understanding can be achieved only through an abusively selective reading of those requirements. A sacrifice for humankind was not necessary. And even if it were, Jesus's execution did not qualify.

According to the Old Testament, sacrifice is neither the only nor the most important way to atone for sins. In fact, sacrifice is prescribed primarily for unintentional sins (Leviticus 4:1-6:17). The more important means of atonement are repentance and prayer. "If my people . . . pray and seek my face and turn from their wicked ways, then . . . I will forgive their sin" (2 Chronicles 7:14). "Through love and faithfulness is sin atoned for" (Proverbs

16:6). "You do not delight in sacrifice, or I would bring it; you do not take pleasure in burnt offerings. My sacrifice, O God is a broken spirit; a broken and contrite heart" (Psalm 51:16-17). "I said, 'I will confess my transgressions to the Lord.' And you forgave the guilt of my sin" (Psalm 32:5). "If a wicked person turns away from all the sins he has committed and keeps all my decrees and does what is just and right, that person will surely live; he will not die. None of the offenses he has committed will be remembered against him" (Ezekiel 18:21-22).

Some alight upon the phrase, "It is the blood that makes atonement" (Leviticus 17:10-12) and interpret it to mean that only blood, i.e., sacrifice, can make atonement. But as we have already seen, that is not the case. Leviticus 17:10-12 does not say that only blood makes atonement; it says that, in the case of a sacrifice, the blood makes atonement. For that reason—and this is the main point of the passage—blood must not be consumed. Rather, it must be handled according to strict rules.

Note that these rules create yet another problem for those wishing to interpret Jesus's execution as a sacrifice. The sacrificial victim's blood must be sprinkled and his fat burned upon the altar (Leviticus 4:1-10 and 17:6). Neither of these procedures was followed in the case of Jesus. Consequently, even if a sacrifice for humankind were necessary, Jesus's execution failed to meet the stated requirements for one.

Note also that there is a doctrinal conflict between the belief that Jesus's death was a sacrifice and the belief that he was resurrected. If his death were truly a sacrifice, then he would have had to stay dead. But according to Christian doctrine, he did not. If the resurrection is true, then the sacrifice was counterfeit.

Fifth, Christian doctrine maintains that Jesus's execution constituted a once-and-for-all sacrifice. After Jesus, sacrifice is no longer necessary. "We have been made holy through the sacrifice of the body of Jesus Christ once and for all" (Hebrews 10:10). But there is no Old Testament provision for a once-and-for-all sacrifice. In fact, numerous Old Testament prophecies indicate that precisely the opposite is true: the coming of the messiah does not end blood sacrifice but ensures its continuation.

The Old Testament god tells Jeremiah, of the days of the coming messiah, that "David will never fail to have a man to sit on the throne of Israel, nor will the Levitical priests ever fail to have a man to stand before me continually to offer burnt offerings, to burn grain offerings and to present sacrifices" (Jeremiah 33:17-18). Ezekiel describes his vision of the final temple in which there "were two tables on each side, on which the burnt offerings, sin offerings and guilt offerings were slaughtered" (Ezekiel 40:38-43). His god tells him, "These will be the regulations for sacrificing burnt offerings and splashing blood against the altar when it is built: You are to give a young bull as a sin offering to the Levitical priests . . ." (Ezekiel 43:18-27). Describing the day of Israel's vindication against her enemies, Zechariah wrote, "Every pot in Jerusalem and Judah will be holy to the Lord Almighty, and all who come to sacrifice will take some of the pots and cook in them" (Zechariah 14:21). Third Isaiah added, of the foreigners who will someday turn to Israel's god, "Their burnt offerings and sacrifices will be accepted on my altar" (Isaiah 56:7).

According to these prophecies by Jeremiah, Ezekiel, Zechariah, and Third Isaiah, blood sacrifice will flourish forever after the coming of the messiah. Christians, however, are required to ignore these prophecies in order to maintain the doctrine that Jesus was a once-and-for-all sacrifice.

Sixth, the doctrine that a third party's suffering can atone for the guilt of others is immoral. The satisfaction and penal theories envision Jesus standing in lieu of human beings for the consequences of their actions. For one moral agent to assimilate the guilt of another and thereby shield him from its consequences undermines individual accountability.

A superior moral principle was already in place. "The one who sins is the one who will die . . . The righteousness of the righteous will be credited to them, and the wickedness of the wicked will be charged against them" (Ezekiel 18:20). Even temple sacrifice did not break completely the moral bond between action and consequence because the person seeking atonement had to relinquish something of value to him, either a blemish-free animal or a quantity of the finest flour (Leviticus 4:1-5:13). That may not be an infinite payment, but at least it's something. By contrast, the Christian relinquishes nothing.

If the moral bond between action and consequence is broken, the traditional term "substitutionary sacrifice" may be inappropriate. The Christian transaction in which a god accepts the punishment of one moral agent on behalf of another is better described as "vicarious sacrifice." This offensive idea appears to have been first suggested by the prophet known as Second Isaiah (see appendix 3), and while it remained peripheral to Judaism, it became the very cornerstone of Christian theology.

The bigger picture

In summary, the Christian theories of atonement are incoherent. Moreover, while this discussion has trod into the theological morass, there is a larger point to be observed from a distance. Like the people of many other primitive cultures, Christians believe that a blood sacrifice can win favor with the spirit world. Yet, as shown above, even the ancient Israelites believed that repentance was superior to sacrifice. The idea that the ritual slaughter of Jesus was necessary to propitiate a god is a savage step backward in the moral and intellectual development of the human species. It is an idea that, frankly, would embarrass most witch doctors. That educated men and women of the present day could actually entertain such a belief should require no further comment.

6

AFTERLIFE

Christianity teaches that after death, individuals have a continued existence, something popularly called an "afterlife." The catechism of the Catholic church reads, "In death, the separation of the soul from the body, the human body decays and the soul goes to meet God, while awaiting its reunion with its glorified body."[1] Similarly, the Westminster Confession, a touchstone for many Protestants, reads, "At the last day, such as are found alive shall not die, but be changed; and all the dead shall be raised up with the self-same bodies, and none other, although with different qualities, which shall be united again to their souls forever."[2]

We return to the problems with which we began: suffering and death. The true heart of Christianity, as of most religions, is the fact that human beings are terrified of death. Escaping it is the wellspring of the religious imagination. Thousands of gods and goddesses have been invented and discarded over the millennia as humans have taken flight from the primal horror of realizing that they will die and be consumed. The problems of suffering and death, discussed in chapter 1, constitute a powerful argument against the existence of a benevolent creator. Ironically, these very problems impel many people to crave just such a being so that death can be defeated.

The Christian afterlife presupposes a two-part human: a physical body and a magical part called a "soul." All animals have bodies, but only humans have these soul parts. At some future point, the body, glorified (i.e., immortal), will be resurrected, and the soul will be reunited with it. The combined package will then be assigned to an afterlife in one of two special places: "heaven," a happy place for Christians, or "hell," an unhappy place for all others. This enables believers to engage in double wishful thinking: comfort that they can continue to exist in heaven and satisfaction that others will be punished in hell.

Judgment and hell are discussed in chapters 9 and 10. Our concern here is the Christian notion of afterlife personhood. As will be shown, both parts, the body and the soul, are problematic.

The body

The notion of a physical self that survives death is replete with absurdities. The promise of a bodily resurrection is modeled on that of Jesus. But while Jesus had been dead only briefly at the time of his alleged resurrection, the vast majority of Christians will have been dead a long time. Their bodies will be fully decomposed, and the atoms of which they had been comprised long since scattered and incorporated into other bodies. To decompose is to be consumed by plants and animals. Those plants and animals also die and are, in turn, consumed by other plants, animals . . . and humans. Because of this endless chain of consumption, every atom in our bodies previously belonged to other bodies—plant, animal, human—and will, in the future, belong to yet others. If a given atom has belonged to multiple people, who gets it at the resurrection?

Moreover, we have different bodies and different atoms when we are young than when we are old. In fact, the atoms which constitute our bodies are in constant flux. At which point in our lives do we possess specifically those atoms that make us us? Given the flux, a god could choose to resurrect many versions of the same person's body, the five-year-old, the ten-year-old, the twenty-year-old, and so on. Which will it be? Perhaps it does not matter if we receive exactly the same atoms that we formerly possessed. After all, one carbon atom is identical to any other carbon atom. But if they are not the same atoms, then is the body really the same body or just a replica? And again, there would be no limit to the number of such replicas that a god could choose to manufacture.

There are additional difficulties. Why should people who suffered with birth defects get the same body? What about people who donated or received organ transplants? Will they share? By number, though not by mass, the majority of the cells in the human body are not human, but bacterial. Since many of these bacteria perform beneficial functions, will they be conscripted into the reconstituted body? If in the afterlife we do not eat, then what use is there for teeth or a stomach? If we do not procreate, what use is there for reproductive organs? This list could be expanded until virtually nothing of the body remains.

Given these difficulties, why resurrect the old body? Why not simply issue a new body or dispense with the body altogether? The answer is simple: Jesus must remain relevant. If in the afterlife we have new bodies or are bodiless, then the resurrection of Jesus's former (flogged, crucified, and speared) body was different. And if Jesus's resurrection were different, then it would not be relevant or applicable to us. What would its point have been?

If we say that our resurrections will be bodily like Jesus's, then we encounter absurdities like those described above. If we abandon the notion of bodily resurrection, then we avoid those absurdities but render Jesus's resurrection irrelevant. Some Christians are understandably embarrassed by the idea of a bodily resurrection. But if they do not believe in it and think instead in terms of souls only, then they are not really Christians; they are New Agers.

The soul

That brings us to the other part of afterlife personhood—the soul. Are there any good reasons to believe that souls even exist, let alone reunite with their former bodies after death? The most common argument for the existence of souls is that they explain the difference between living and nonliving things. But this argument does not work for Christianity. Christianity teaches that animals do not have souls. But since animals are clearly living, the existence of souls cannot, in the Christian view, account for the difference between the living and the nonliving.

The best argument for the existence of souls is that they explain consciousness. It is easy to see how a brute body can walk or digest, but how can it have thoughts? Compared to the body, the mind seems both different and superior. It is the engine of a consciousness that discerns patterns in cause and effect, represents abstractions through symbols, and imagines realms where the body cannot follow. Does this sense of duality between mind and body require a supernatural explanation, a soul? While there is much we do not yet know about consciousness, it appears to be tied inextricably to the physical brain.

For example, when parts of the brain are killed as a result of trauma, the mental faculties with which those parts are associated also die. Suppose a person suffers a head injury and loses the ability to remember names. If the capacity to remember names were housed in a soul, then why should a head injury make any difference? He cannot remember names because that part of his brain has died. Is it reasonable to expect, as those who are enamored of the soul thesis do, that when he dies (and the rest of his brain dies), his mind will reacquire the ability to remember names? If the soul is the seat of consciousness, then why should the ingestion of alcohol, a completely physical substance, have any impact on an individual's decision-making process? If the soul is the seat of consciousness, then how could general anesthesia, induced by completely physical substances, result in the elimination of pain and the absence of memory during surgery? It is evident from these examples that consciousness depends upon the physical brain.

The physical brain is necessary; but is it sufficient? Present day science cannot explain how the activities of a physical brain—electrochemical events located in time and space—can produce mental experiences, such as thoughts and feelings. This is known as the hard problem of consciousness. A related challenge arises from our sensation of possessing free will. If the brain is subject to physical laws, then all of the things it does, including thinking and feeling, may be nothing more than law-governed consequences of prior biological facts. How then could we have free will? Someday, it may be shown that consciousness is an emergent property of brains, but for now, we must admit ignorance.

Might souls solve the hard problem of consciousness? They do not appear to provide a satisfactory solution. The only way a soul could be free of the laws governing material matter would be to be completely immaterial itself. But if the soul were completely immaterial and the body completely material, it is unclear how the two could interact. How could a wholly immaterial soul perform an executive function, or get any traction at all, upon a wholly material body?

The case for the existence of a soul is inconclusive at best. And even if there were a soul, there is no reason to believe that it would survive the death of the body. If it comes into existence with the body, then it seems reasonable to assume that it ceases to exist with the body too. Put another way, there is no reason to believe that consciousness after death is any different from consciousness before birth. As Mark Twain allegedly remarked, "I do not fear death. I had been dead for billions of years before I was born and never suffered the slightest inconvenience from it."

For the sake of argument, suppose that souls exist and suppose further that they survive bodily death. The continuation of individual personality through them raises another issue. Many personalities seem unsuited for an eternity of bliss. Why retain the old errors, prejudices, addictions, neuroses, fears, and resentments? In fact, their elimination might be necessary for heaven to operate as advertised—full of human beings and yet astonishingly devoid of human troubles, such as boredom, jealousy, and conflict. But here is the problem: if all of the negative aspects of our personalities are erased, to what extent is what remains truly us, or even truly human?

Finally, the notion of heaven itself might bear some scrutiny. Communion with a god and reunion with loved ones are the common expectations, but if we inquire into the details, things fall apart quickly. Each person has a different view of heaven, and these views are not all compatible. Perhaps someone wants to be reunited with a beloved grandmother. But the grandmother wants to be twenty-five and play golf. The only way to make this work would be for the grandmother to play golf and all those wishing to spend time with her doing other things to be issued replica grandmothers.

Of course the problem of incompatible heavens arises only within the confines of an anthropomorphic understanding of what heaven is like. Perhaps there is no golf in heaven and no such condition as being twenty-five, only an ecstatic embrace of the divine, whatever that means. But this non-anthropomorphic understanding leads to a different problem. It eliminates the problem of incompatibility at the expense of individuality. If our only activity were embrace of the divine, then how would we retain our unique personalities? Would we even still exist independently, or would we be absorbed into a larger consciousness?

In summary, neither a resurrected body nor a retention of personality through the soul makes much sense. The same can be said of heaven itself. Despite its illogicalities, however, the notion of an afterlife assuages the fear of death. As a result of this common fear, men and women claiming to possess revelations from the presiding deity can set the rules for admission and, by doing so, appoint themselves gatekeepers. Ironically, if they paint the afterlife alluringly enough, people can even be willing to die in their service.

7

REVELATION

Christianity teaches that its god has revealed himself and his message through the life of Jesus, the words of the Bible, and the church (though some Protestants may disagree with the last of these). In other words, Christianity is a "revealed religion," one whose doctrines rely on a god's deliberate communications.

Problems with revelation

There are serious problems with the notion of revelation in general and with the plausibility of the Christian version in particular. First, one person's revelation is just as valid as another's. Any person, at any time, can have a revelation that revises or overturns previous revelations. When does it stop? Determining which revelation is the true one is unavoidably a political process. Men fight and kill for the authority to speak for the gods and thereby exercise power over other men.

Second, neither the Bible nor a church can constitute revelation for any person living today. Unless a person receives communication directly from a deity, he does not have revelation.

He has merely the hearsay, in the form of books or a priesthood, of one group of humans or another.

Many religions claim to safeguard the revelation of this or that deity. But if there were only one god, why would he permit so many false reports of revelation? The ensuing confusion diverts believers from the true message and virtually guarantees violent conflict between competing ethnic or religious groups, each of which believes it is absolutely right and all the others are absolutely wrong. One might respond that the true god does not prevent false revelations because he does not want to interfere with people's free will. But if that is the case, he could have made his own revelation, the real one, so overwhelmingly convincing that the others would pale by comparison.

That a book might contain communication from a deity is an idea whose strangeness is disguised only by its familiarity. An omnipotent god could communicate with anyone or everyone, with perfect clarity, anytime he wants. Books, on the other hand, are how humans communicate with one another. Surely, an infinitely inventive deity could come up with a better communication technique than one that just happened to be invented by our own species.

Even if one were to seek revelation in a book, the Bible hardly seems qualified. A communication of the highest importance, intended for all humankind by an omnipotent deity would be distinguishable from other books that make similar claims; reflect a global, if not cosmic, perspective and therefore be equally accessible to every culture; be so unambiguous that no confusion about its meaning would be possible; remain unchanged over time; be internally consistent; and possess the highest-quality scientific and moral content. The Bible fails all of these tests.

For example, reckoning generations from the Bible, it can be shown that the earth is approximately six thousand years old. Modern science, on the other hand, indicates that the earth is approximately four billion years old. The difference between these two estimates is not due to anyone's miscalculation. It is due to a choice about how knowledge is obtained. Does knowledge come from revelation, or does it come from evidence and the reasoning process? This choice has huge practical consequences.

Thoughtful Christians try to reconcile revelation and science. The literal-minded Christian will argue that if science indicates that the earth is four billion years old, then that is because god—for reasons satisfactory to himself—created it six thousand years ago to appear four billion years old. On the other hand, the metaphorically minded Christian will concede that the earth is in fact four billion years old and argue that the Bible's chronologies are intended to be symbolic rather than literal.

Even if either of these attempts to reconcile science and scripture were persuasive, Christianity would still have the problem that an all-powerful deity was unable to make himself clear. Two groups of Christians, each eager to follow him, have very different understandings of what his revelation was. That alone is reason to reject the assertion that the Bible is an omnicompetent god's attempt to communicate.

In addition, neither of the above-described efforts to reconcile the sources seems honest. The literal-minded Christian makes his god a trickster, but a morally perfect being would not be deceitful. The metaphorically minded Christian claims the Bible is literal where it is convenient to do so but that it is metaphorical where it is convenient to do that. As a result, he creates his own personal revelation by picking and choosing. Both of these strained attempts at reconciliation lead to a loss of integrity. If one is honest, a choice between science and revelation must be made.

Problems with hiddenness

The flip side of revelation to a few is hiddenness from the many. People are unlikely to seek closeness to a god that they don't believe exists. Therefore, if the Christian god were real and loving, he would let us know that he exists. But the majority of the world's people do not believe in the Christian god. Given this majority—people who worship other gods and goddesses or none at all—it is difficult to avoid the conclusion that the Christian god is either not real or not loving.

If a supernatural realm existed and any one of its occupants wished to make his presence known, it seems reasonable to assume that he would be successful. This holds true particularly for any of the monotheistic gods who are allegedly all-powerful and infinitely resourceful. If such a deity wanted me to know something, I would know it. Period.

The evidence for the existence of the Christian god is insufficient. To go one step further, it has to be. If there were sufficient evidence, we would not need faith. But as discussed in the next chapter, Christianity teaches that faith is required. In other words, acknowledgment that the evidence for its claims is insufficient is built into Christianity's core.

Apologists have tried to justify their god's hiddenness in several ways. One is to argue that irrefutable proof of his existence would interfere with people's free will. "God maintains a delicate balance between keeping his existence sufficiently evident so people will know he's there and yet hiding his presence enough so that people who want to choose to ignore him can do it. This way, their choice of destiny is really free."[1]

This argument is an apologetic attempt to spin a lack of evidence into an asset. But the reasoning is plainly wrong. Even with irrefutable proof of a god's existence, people would still possess free will to embrace him or not. For example, Adam and Eve knew that their god existed; they talked with him. And yet according to the story, they disobeyed him. From this, Christians can see that proof of a god's existence would not interfere with free will. On the contrary, it would highlight free will by eliminating the information excuse. A god who wanted people to make free decisions about their salvation would provide them with the necessary information—so that a lack of information could not be an excuse—and then let them exercise their free will.

Another attempt to justify the hiddenness of the Christian god is to argue that his existence is obvious but that many people simply refuse to accept the fact because they are stubborn or rebellious. The failure of this argument can be seen in the fact that there are many sincere seekers in the world, many people who ardently want to believe in and embrace a god; and they do, but somehow they get the wrong one. Billions of Muslims and Hindus are eager to submit to a god. But with the information they have, they see no reason to worship the Christian one.

The hiddenness of a god from sincere seekers constitutes a credibility problem for any religion. But the problem is particularly acute for Christianity because its god explicitly promises that sincere seekers will find him. "You will find him if you look for him with all your heart and with all your soul" (Deuteronomy 4:29). "Those who seek me find me" (Proverbs 8:17). "Seek and you will find" (Matthew 7:7 and Luke 11:9). The fact that the god of the Bible does not make himself known to billions of sincere seekers is a straightforward disconfirmation of Christian teaching.

In summary, a god who gives revelation to one person could, if he were omnipotent, give the same revelation to everyone. It is not plausible to claim that instead of communicating clearly, a loving deity would choose to play cat and mouse with prospective followers. In addition, by linking faith with reward and punishment in an afterlife (see next chapter), Christianity has increased the stakes of revelation not only for humans but also for its god. If he existed, his hiddenness would be morally inexcusable. The argument can be stated formally: if the Christian god existed, then he would make himself known to sincere seekers. The Christian god has not made himself known to billions of sincere seekers. Therefore, the Christian god does not exist.

8

FAITH

Christianity teaches that its followers must possess a thing called "faith." Faith is defined as "confidence in what we hope for and assurance about what we do not see" (Hebrews 11:1). It is the central characteristic of a Christian because "whoever believes in the Son has eternal life" (John 3:36).

These quotations showcase the two ways Christianity uses the notion of faith: as a substitute for evidence and as a credential for admittance to heaven. The origin of these beliefs is discussed in chapter 22. Here, the focus is on the beliefs themselves. As will be shown, the first usage is arbitrary and the second is immoral.

Substitute for evidence

The definition of faith above, "confidence in what we hope for and assurance about what we do not see," means accepting that something is true despite insufficient grounds for believing it to be so. Faith replaces the rational basis for holding a belief, namely, evidence and reason, with a mere desire to believe it.

By definition then, faith is arbitrary. Precisely because faith does not require evidence, a person could have faith in anything.

And his faith would be just as legitimate as anyone else's. People can and do have faith in the Indian god Vishnu or in the Nigerian god Olorun just as fervently as they do in the Middle Eastern god Jesus.

What determines a person's faith? Despite the large number of religions in the world, most people in any one place tend to follow the same religion or family of religions. This demonstrates that faith is generally not an individual decision but rather the result of social conditioning. The religion people consider to be true is determined by the arbitrary accident of where they grew up and consequently what they were conditioned to believe as children. If America's Christians had been raised in India or Iran, most would have faith in what some other group of humans had told them.

These are arbitrary allegiances and, as such, scarcely deserve to be celebrated as universal truths. The dominant role played by faith in Western civilization has gone so long unchallenged in mainstream culture that few people see the perversity of complimenting someone by saying, "He's a man of faith," as if believing things without sufficient evidence were a commendable trait in a human being.

There is one sense in which all human beings accept the unproven. In everyday life, as in science, we cannot proceed without assuming that our sensory experiences are reliable and that nature will continue to behave consistently. We make these basic assumptions instinctively and yet they cannot be proven. Is this faith? Notice that it would be impossible to function without these assumptions; we accept them because we have no choice. Faith, by contrast, extends beyond what is necessary; it is a matter of choice. Indeed that is why religious leaders praise it. Because faith is unnecessary, its embrace is arbitrary—a point underscored by the wide variety of faiths from which to choose.

Apologists might complain that this description paints an inaccurate picture of faith. There is some evidence, they claim, even if it is not enough to warrant certainty. Faith is not a substitute for evidence; it fills the gap between the evidence and belief. Yes, of course, to the extent that evidence exists, then belief is warranted. But even if there is some evidence, there is no justification for, and certainly no praiseworthiness in, going beyond it. The cult of faith, however, transforms a lack of evidence into something positive. Christians are taught that believing despite a lack of evidence is praiseworthy. And then, to debase our epistemic standards further, they are taught that the faith itself *is* evidence.

Faith is an odd thing for a deity to reward. The influential Christian writer Tertullian (circa 210 CE) is reputed to have written, "The Son of God died; it is by all means to be believed, because it is absurd. And He was buried, and rose again; the fact is certain, because it is impossible."[1] Few Christians stop to consider what an even-handed application of this thinking would entail. There are many religions in the world that make claims Christianity would deem ridiculous. But that turns out to be a problem . . . for Christianity. To the extent that these other religions' claims are less believable, then they require more faith. That means that the followers of these other religions possess even more faith than Christians and should, according to Christian logic, be rewarded even more richly.

According to the gospel of John, Thomas lived with the other apostles for three years, and yet he did not believe them about the postmortem appearance of Jesus. He had to see and touch for himself. Do we not deserve equally compelling evidence? Instead, we are expected to be satisfied with hearsay of a god who revealed himself to a small group of semiliterate people in the Middle East. If he were in our position, would Thomas be satisfied with this?

Credential for heaven

While the arbitrariness of faith empties it of virtue, its use as a credential for admittance to heaven is downright offensive.

Christianity teaches that, the blood sacrifice having been made, humans must possess faith that Jesus is their savior. This is the primary—and for some Protestants, the only—demand of a Christian life.

Faith is linked in Christian theology to something called "grace." Because all human beings transgress, all deserve to be punished. Some, however, are spared through grace—god's mercy and undeserved favor. While the blood sacrifice extended grace to humankind, faith is the response required of individuals. "For by grace are you saved through faith" (Ephesians 2:8-9). Some denominations teach that grace was extended to all humankind; others, that it was extended only to a subset known as "the elect."

The assertion that faith constitutes a salvific credential is immoral because it elevates belief above conduct. According to this doctrine, a person can live a wicked life, but as long as he passes the faith-in-Jesus test, he will be rewarded in an afterlife. By contrast, someone like Gandhi, who lived virtuously but never passed the faith-in-Jesus test, will be tortured in an afterlife.

Apologists defend the elevation of belief above conduct by arguing that no matter how decently someone lives, he will fall short of moral perfection. "Whoever keeps the whole law and yet stumbles at just one point is guilty of breaking all of it" (James 2:10). But this is a deeply flawed position to adopt. In fact, it would be difficult to think of a better recipe for moral confusion.

Falling short of perfection is no excuse for failing to distinguish between good and bad conduct. To say that what matters is perfection or nothing is to say that conduct does not matter at all. This makes it all too easy to commit a crime and excuse oneself on the grounds that "we are all sinners" anyway. Do Christian apologists want to argue that their god cannot or should not distinguish between the murderer and the humanitarian? Admission to heaven based on the test of faith trivializes this distinction.

To turn a mere profession of a belief into a salvific credential while disregarding a person's conduct is morally repugnant. If a just and loving god existed and wanted to test us, that test would be: do we live in a just and loving way? That is the only test relevant to a moral being.

Pascal's Wager

The marriage of faith as a substitute for evidence and faith as a salvific credential produces a further problem: it corrodes our standards of knowledge and truth. Not content with advancing arguments that people can evaluate disinterestedly, Christianity resorts to offering people an inducement to believe it, an afterlife prize. Responding to this incentive program, some reckon that it is best to bet on Christianity. After all, life is short but eternity is long. This train of thought, known as Pascal's Wager, has at least four serious flaws.

First, it assumes there is no cost to believing. But if there were really no cost to acting as though a possibility were true, why stop here? We cannot disprove the existence of vampires, so we'd better wear garlic around our necks, just in case. You may not believe there's a car bomb in your car or that the waiter poisoned your food, but can you take the chance? Wouldn't it be better to act as if these things were true, just in case?

Second, it assumes that if there were a god who is seeking allegiance, he would be satisfied by a professed belief in him based on a cynical and self-interested calculation as opposed to a heartfelt conviction. If this deity knows people's thoughts, then wagering on him because of a prudential calculation will not impress him and may, in fact, insult his intelligence.

Third, it assumes that this god's intention is to torment, or allow to be tormented, those who fail the faith-in-Jesus test. But such a test would be illogical and immoral. Why would a loving god punish me for using the limited intelligence he gave me? It would seem more likely that he gave it to me to protect me from false beliefs, including the thousands of religions that human beings have invented. Would you be persuaded by the assertions of a two-thousand-year-old Cambodian tradition that a certain medicine man was divine and that you would be punished in another world if you failed to believe it in this one?

Fourth, it does not inform us which of the many gods or goddesses to believe in. It is unclear whether a god who is jealous enough to inflict torment would prefer us to worship no god at all or to take a guess and worship the wrong one(s). Hindus believe in reincarnation, but Jews do not. Christians believe their god had an offspring, but Muslims do not. Hinduism teaches there are many gods while Islam teaches there is only one god and Buddhism does not teach about any gods. Because these religions contradict one another, only one—at most—can be right. How can we avoid a mistake? The most prudent course of action may be to survey all of the world's religions and identify the cruelest, most vicious god available. Worship that god because he is the one you least want to offend. If a loving god existed, is this the conclusion he would want us to reach?

Faith is a tragic invention. It is arbitrary by its very nature; if evidence and reason are inoperative, then all faiths are equal. Even worse, its use as a qualifying test for an afterlife rewards some simply for affirming a belief while it relegates good people who happen to lack that particular belief to an eternity of torture. Pascal's Wager is the misshapen offspring of these two errors.

9

JUDGMENT

Christianity teaches that divine judgment will determine each person's afterlife destination. Those few judged favorably will go to heaven while the majority will go to hell. Jesus said, "No one comes to the Father except through me" (John 14:6) and "Small is the gate and narrow the road that leads to life, and only a few find it" (Matthew 7:14).

The Christian god's judgment, it would appear, will not excessively tax his powers of discernment. As explained in the previous chapter, it is primarily a matter of whether the individual passed the faith-in-Jesus test. If one were to accept, for the sake of argument, the existence of an afterlife, the doctrine that only a few will be rewarded and that the majority will be punished there is unfair and cruel. The faith-in-Jesus test puts certain groups of people at a considerable, and, in many cases, insurmountable disadvantage. First, many people lived and died before the time of Jesus; second, others, though born later, lived in places where they had never heard of him; third, still others lived or live today in areas where other religions predominate.

Those who lived and died before Jesus obviously could not have had faith in him. As a result, they are consigned, through no fault of their own, to an eternity of hellfire. Some apologists argue that before the gospel, humankind possessed the law that the Old Testament god had given to the Israelites. But the Israelites constituted only a small fraction of a percent of the world's population. This embarrassingly provincial argument suggests that the people of China were either subject to the Jewish law, news no doubt to them, or that they were simply unimportant to the Christian god.

Members of the second group, those who never heard the gospel because of where they lived, are also consigned, through no fault of their own, to an eternity of hellfire. For most of the two thousand years since Christianity's inception, travel and communication were very limited. While Christianity claims to be universal, its foundational story neglects to mention the vast majority of the human beings on the planet. Then as now, the world's two great population centers were China and India. Why didn't Jesus appear in Han Dynasty China or the Guptan Empire in India, or at least indicate an awareness of their existence? Instead, the Bible recounts tiresome parochial squabbles among Mediterranean peoples.

Two thousand years ago, the philosopher Celsus noted this problem. Lampooning the notion that Jesus's brief career in a patch of the Middle East was intended to convey a message to all humankind, he wrote, "If God, like Zeus in the comic poet, woke up out of his long slumber and wanted to deliver the human race from evils, why on earth did he send this spirit that you mention into one corner? He ought to have breathed into many bodies in the same way and sent them all over the world."[1]

Finally, those who have heard the gospel but live in parts of the world where other religions predominate do not have the same likelihood of embracing it as those who live in heavily Christian areas. Faith, as noted already, is largely a product of social conditioning. Even after two thousand years of proselytizing, Christianity today claims only 32 percent of the world's population. The other 68 percent will be sentenced to everlasting torment.

A judgment based on faith in Jesus is unjust. Stung by this criticism, apologists have offered some creative replies.

One reply is that the Christian god can use his omniscience to arrange people's births so that the time and place do not matter. This argument is based on the idea that an omniscient god knows in advance whether a person, were he to hear the gospel, would embrace it or not. With this foreknowledge, he arranges for those people who would not embrace the gospel if they heard it to be born in one of the times or places where they don't. In other words, we do not need to worry about people who never heard the gospel because they are the ones who would not have embraced it anyway.

This is another retreat to the possible, and it seems a bit far-fetched. If it were true, then what would be the point of preaching the gospel? Jesus instructed his disciples to spread the word (Matthew 28:19-20), but this would be unnecessary if he had already acted upon foreknowledge of everyone's responses. More fundamentally, why would the Christian god allow those he already knows will fail his faith-in-Jesus test to be born at all? It would be more benevolent simply to refrain from creating them in the first place.

A second apologetic reply is that people can be judged on the basis of their response to "the information they had" or to "general revelation," knowledge of a god arising from his handiwork in nature and humankind's innate morality. If everyone has access to this knowledge, then they can be judged on the basis of whether they conducted their lives in accordance with it.

This second reply, in contrast to the first, is refreshingly reasonable. According to this viewpoint, individuals do not need to know anything about the gospel. They need to live morally and, possibly, to recognize a creator. Well, if that's the case, why can't this god judge everyone on that basis? Why discard such a sensible criterion only to replace it with the arbitrary faith-in-Jesus test? If one were to grant, for the sake of argument, that there is such a thing as salvation, then it it would be easier to understand, fairer to diverse populations, and more closely predicated upon moral conduct *without* Jesus. The claim that general revelation is an avenue to salvation serves only to demonstrate that Jesus was, at best, utterly superfluous.

10

HELL

Christianity teaches that those judged unfavorably, the majority of humankind, will be punished in an afterlife of perpetual fire. Jesus says, "Fear him who, after your body has been killed, has authority to throw you into hell" (Luke 12:5) "where the fire never goes out" (Mark 9:43).

This doctrine enters the Bible only in the New Testament. It is never mentioned in the Old Testament. The god of the Old Testament is vengeful, and if you anger him, he will kill you; but the god of the New Testament is far more vengeful, and if you anger him, he will torture you for eternity.

Hell is a peculiar idea, and its prevalence is almost accidental. In traditional Jewish thought, the afterlife was not differentiated into separate places for reward and punishment.[1] That idea most likely came into Palestine from Zoroastrianism.[2] It was slow to gain currency in mainstream Judaism, but it became popular among Jewish apocalyptic thinkers during the last centuries BCE. Jesus incorporated this idea into his teachings, and through him, it infected the whole of Western civilization.

For the ancient Israelites, heaven was god's abode, not an afterlife destination. The spirits of the dead, they believed, occupied a realm called Sheol, where they existed in a disembodied and semiconscious state. Sheol differed from the afterlife of Christianity in two fundamental ways. First, it was the end of any meaningful experience, consisting of neither suffering nor pleasure. Second, it was the end of the line for everyone, the virtuous and the wicked alike. There was no differentiation based on prior conduct in life; life itself was where one received divine rewards and punishments (Deuteronomy 28:1-68). Job is a perfect example. He suffered greatly yet remained loyal to his god. After all of that, it is nowhere suggested that he would be compensated in an afterlife. Instead, his fortune was restored in life. "The Lord restored his fortunes and gave him twice as much as he had before . . . and so Job died, an old man and full of years" (Job 42:10-17).*

But during the postexilic period, under Persian influence, a different conception took root. Zoroastrianism teaches that human conduct is part of the cosmic war between the forces of light under Ahura Mazda and those of darkness under Ahriman. Every human decision with a moral dimension contributes to one side or the other of this titanic struggle. Consequently, Zoroastrianism places a high value on moral conduct. When Ahura Mazda eventually triumphs, everyone will be judged. The good will be welcomed to paradise and the bad hurled into a pit of torment.

Jewish apocalyptic thinkers adopted the notion of a coming judgment that would determine everyone's afterlife destinations. They developed the belief that the righteous would be resurrected but that the rest of Israel would remain in Sheol. In fact, the only reference in the Old Testament to a differentiated afterlife comes

---

* Some versions of the Bible, most notably the King James, incorrectly translate the Jewish Bible/Old Testament word Sheol as Hell. This error has the effect of disguising the fact, for English language readers, that the Old and New Testaments have very different conceptions of the afterlife.

in the only apocalyptic writing to be included in it, the book of Daniel, written circa 165 BCE.[3] For these thinkers, Sheol began to be associated with Gehenna, an actual place where one of Israel's enemies had sacrificed children in fire to propitiate the god Moloch.[4]

The association with Moloch may be the origin of Christianity's odd notion of hellfire. Humans generally regard fire positively as a source of light and warmth and as a means of protection and cooking. In the Greek world, Prometheus was revered because, at great personal sacrifice, he brought the gift of fire to humankind. In Zoroastrianism, the good forces of light battle the bad forces of darkness. Accordingly, that religion venerates the two main sources of light: the sun and fire. Fire does not figure prominently, if at all, in the Zoroastrian pit of torment. While Christianity also conceives of forces of light battling forces of darkness, it does not view fire positively, focusing instead on its destructive aspects. This may be due to the coalescence of Sheol and Gehenna in Jewish apocalyptic thought and the subsequent transmission of this prejudice to Christianity.

Does the idea of hell make sense? It appears to be incompatible with a god of love and justice. First, as discussed in the previous chapter, people are not sent to hell for being evil; they are sent to hell for failing to believe in Jesus. Billions of devout Muslims, Hindus, and others live decent lives and worship a god (or even several of them). As a reward for their piety, they will be devoured ceaselessly in a lake of fire. The author of such a plan might well tremble at the prospect of a judgment himself.

Second, if people are guilty of crimes, even real ones rather than simply failing the faith-in-Jesus test, they are finite crimes. Infinite punishment for finite crimes is unjust. After burning for, say, a billion years, wouldn't the point have been made? Because there is no chance of release from the Christian hell, its purpose cannot be rehabilitation but only retribution. By contrast, in Zoroastrianism, no soul remains in torment for eternity; all are ultimately admitted into paradise.[5] Anything less would detract from the triumph of the good.

If a deity actually sent people to a hell permanently, he could not be described as either loving or just. Would a loving parent torture his children for misbehaving? Even if one argues that those failing the faith-in-Jesus test are not true children of god, the question becomes whether a loving parent would torture someone else's children. Uncomfortable with reflections of this nature, many Christians adopt either a hard-line or a soft-line perspective.

The hard-line is to argue that people in hell deserve to remain there forever because they continue to sin. For example, in their agony, they curse the god who put them there. This is not persuasive in the least. Individuals sent to hell would have, at that point, ample evidence of the existence of this god and of the behavior he requires. It is implausible in the extreme to believe that not a single one of them would ask for forgiveness and promise to correct his behavior if given a chance to do so.

The soft-line is to argue that the Christian god is not too keen on the idea of hell either. Apologists say things such as, "He offers people a way out of hell" or "He won't force anyone to go to heaven against his will." But this is really a dishonest argument, an attempt to insulate the Christian god from Christianity's own teachings. It implies that hell is a natural default destination, that the god has nothing to do with its occupancy, and that his paramount concern is to respect free will.

The soft-line argument fails both scripturally and logically. As shown in the quotations with which this chapter began, Jesus is not describing a default mechanism; the god is proactively throwing people into hell. And free will is clearly not his priority. The Bible recounts numerous instances of this god interfering with people's free will.* Logically, if a just god really wanted to respect people's free will not to go to heaven, then he

---

*   See Exodus 7:3, 9:12, 10:1-27, 12:36, 14:4; Deuteronomy 2:30; Joshua 11:20; 2 Samuel 24:1; 1 Chronicles 5:26; 2 Chronicles 36:22; Romans 11:7-10.

could simply provide an alternative to eternal torture, a neutral place—not heaven but not hell either.

Finally, a bizarre hybrid argument is to claim that by sending people to hell, the god is being merciful because for them, being with god in heaven is even more unbearable than being in hell. This makes no sense. Hell is customarily defined as the worst possible torment. A god bestowing mercy would not put anyone there. Moreover and once again, why should this god be constrained to only two alternatives? He could provide a neutral place or simply oblivion rather than confining himself to an unimaginative two-tiered afterlife.

Apparently without noticing the irony, Christians routinely thank their god for saving them. Saving them from what? He is saving them from eternal torture, something that he himself created or allows to exist. That is like thanking a firefighter for putting out a fire that he himself started.

11

TRINITY AND MYSTERY

Christianity teaches that there is one god who exists in three persons: a father; a son, Jesus; and something called a "holy ghost." The doctrine of the trinity, so it is claimed, allows for a plurality of three persons within the unity of one god. The persons are consubstantial, that is, of the same essence.

How did this belief come about? Very briefly, the early Christians had a problem: They were devout people who already believed in a god, but then Jesus came along, and they wanted to believe he was a god too. They were torn between pride in their traditional monotheism and the polytheism required to believe that Jesus was a divine offspring. They wanted it both ways, and in the end, they fudged it.

The trinity does not mean that each of the three persons is one-third of the god. Each person is god. The father is god. Jesus is god. The holy ghost is god. But there is only one god. This is a logical impossibility. It's like saying, "I play the clarinet. I play the piano. I play the guitar. But I play only one musical instrument."

Are the three persons simply different names for the same thing? No, because each has unique experiences. For example, Christians believe that Jesus died, but the father continued to live.

The one god was both dead and alive at the same time! Are the three persons simply different modes in which the god reveals himself—like water, which can change from gas to liquid to solid? No, the three persons do not change into one another. All three persons exist as themselves all the time.

Some apologists have argued that the trinity constitutes only one god, not three, because multiplication, not addition, is the relevant arithmetic operation: $1 \times 1 \times 1 = 1^3 = 1$. This is interesting, but normally, when we want to know how many of something there are, we count them. Using their logic, we could prove that the United States has only one state: $1^{50} = 1$.

Other apologists have tried to rescue the doctrine by arguing that one god in three persons is like one soul endowed with three minds. But this too fails. If one mind were omniscient, what would be the point of the other two? If one of the three omniscient minds decides something, can either of the other two omniscient minds disagree? If they cannot, then they are redundant. If they can, then the one soul is prevented from having a single belief. It is like three men in a horse costume trying to go in different directions.

The doctrine of the trinity is illogical. Each person is either a complete god or not. If each person, considered independently, possesses that set of attributes sufficient to be a god, then each must be a god. If any one of them, considered independently, does not possess that set of attributes, then that person is not a god. In sum, if each person is a complete god, then there are three gods. If each person is not a complete god, then the father is not god, or Jesus is not god, or the holy ghost is not god.

In addition to illogicality, the trinity flatly violates scripture. "The Lord is one" (Deuteronomy 6:4). "There is no God besides me" (Deuteronomy 32:39). "I am the first and I am the last; apart from me there is no God" (Isaiah 44:6). The reader is invited to try to devise a clearer statement of this god's singularity.

The word "trinity" does not appear anywhere in the Bible nor is the doctrine explicitly taught anywhere therein (see chapter 26 for more on this). But the trinity enables Christianity to have it both ways. When it is convenient to have only one god, such as when discussing *"God's will,"* Christianity wears monotheistic clothing. When on the other hand it wants to enact a cosmic drama in which a god's son is sacrificed and an expanded cast of characters is required, Christianity wears polytheistic clothing.

Confronted with the illogicality of the trinity, the religion retreats to its last redoubt: *"It's a mystery. Man cannot fully understand God."*

But there are problems with the mystery defense. First, the humility is exaggerated. Christian theologians do in fact claim to know a lot about their creator. Insisting that, *"God is a mystery,"* they nevertheless teach that, *"God exists in three consubstantial persons, one of whom reconciled humankind to himself."* These are bold metaphysical and moral claims. True humility is to acknowledge that we know little about this world, let alone realms beyond it.

The second and more fundamental problem with the mystery defense is that someone *could tell us anything* and then, when the statement is shown to be illogical, simply shrug and say, *"It's a mystery."* If we put ourselves in the business of accepting illogical statements as mysteries, then we have no way of choosing among the infinite number of illogical statements that might be made. All utterances become equal. In such a situation, people simply believe the things that feel right because they have been exposed to them since childhood.

Christianity characterizes mystery as a good thing, a reminder of our limitations. It is certainly true that an acknowledgment of what we don't know is the beginning of wisdom. But there are plenty of things that we genuinely don't know. We don't need to manufacture mysteries where there are none.

Is it wrong to insist upon an explanation that makes sense? Surely, it is appropriate to apply reasoning to the most important questions of life. Many Christians do so reflexively when they think about other people's religions. They conclude that the difficulties they see in other religions are due to false beliefs, but they accept Christianity's mysteries as the legitimate by-products of true ones.

Anyone who asks us to accept a mystery instead of an explanation obviously doesn't know anything more about the topic than we do. For all any of us know, there is no good explanation. The mystery is simply a contradiction, and we are being asked to disregard one of our most precious faculties, that of reason, by accepting it.

12

THE INCARNATION

Christianity teaches that the second person of the trinity took on the form of a human. He was incarnated (made flesh) as the man Jesus. According to this doctrine, Jesus was fully man and fully god at the same time. He was not half and half. He had all the attributes of both simultaneously: 100 percent human and 100 percent god. The doctrine that the one person of Jesus comprised two complete natures is called dyophysitism.

Christianity needs dyophysitism for its various theories of atonement, discussed in chapter 5. Only if Jesus were fully human could he represent humankind; but only if he were fully divine could his sacrifice be sufficient to save it. So Christianity needs the doctrine that Jesus was 200 percent of a person. But does it make any sense?

Humans are fallible. The Christian god is allegedly not fallible. With his two natures then, the one person of Jesus was both fallible and not fallible. This is a contradiction. Therefore, the premises cannot be true. The same argument can made about some other characteristics commonly attributed to the Christian god, such as omnipotence and eternality. Dyophysitism is illogical.

The notion that a god could be a man is also refuted by scripture. "God is not human, that he should lie, not a human being, that he should change his mind" (Numbers 23:19). "For I am God, and not a man" (Hosea 11:9).

Unsurprisingly, there was a lot of confusion among early Christians over Jesus's nature, a subject that would become known as christology. In many cases, controversies arose not because people wanted to dissent from doctrine, but because doctrine had not yet been established.

Over time—in some cases, centuries—many of these issues were resolved. The winners enjoyed thereafter the right to label the losers "heretics" (Greek, *hairetikos*, meaning "able to choose"). Heretics stood in contrast to those who followed the church-approved line, the "orthodox" (Greek, *orthodoxos*, meaning "having the right opinion"). But these controversies could have turned out differently. If they had, then what we today call Christianity would have been labeled heresy instead. Discussed briefly below are three of the most prominent christological controversies: gnosticism, Arianism, and monophysitism.

Gnosticism

One of the oldest and most persistent competitors to that strain of early Christianity that would eventually triumph was gnosticism. From the Greek *gnosis*, meaning "knowledge," gnosticism was a family of ideas that generally shared two basic beliefs. First, matter is evil but spirit is good. It followed that since Jesus was unequivocally good, he must have been pure spirit. If so, his physical body and his death were illusory. Second, Jesus's role was primarily that of a teacher. Human beings, or at least some of them, can liberate their inner divinity from the matter in which it is imprisoned through a special knowledge (gnosis). Salvation is the reunification of one's inner divinity with its creator, and it comes not from faith, but from this knowledge.

The nature of this knowledge was some type of inner mystical awareness of the self, but it was kept secret because only the spiritually mature were eligible for it. In accordance with these basic beliefs, most gnostics did not believe in a physical resurrection of Jesus but rather in a spiritual one that symbolized the insight that the kingdom of god was in fact a transformed consciousness.[1]

These views found some scriptural warrant in writings that would eventually be included in the New Testament. John's Jesus suggested that he had a purely spiritual nature, saying, "I am not of this world" (John 8:23). In Mark 4:11 and Matthew 13:11, Jesus reminded the disciples that he had told them secrets not intended for others.

The most extensive documentation of gnostic influence, however, comes from Christian writings that were eventually excluded from the New Testament. These include the gospels of Thomas, Philip, Truth, and Mary. For example, in the gospel of Thomas, Jesus hinted that salvation comes through knowledge, saying, "Whoever finds the interpretation of these sayings will not taste death" (1). Suggesting that the kingdom is a transformed consciousness to be discovered within oneself, Jesus mocked literalists, saying, "If those who lead you say to you, 'See, the kingdom is in the sky,' then the birds of the sky will precede you. If they say to you, 'It is in the sea,' then the fish will precede you. Rather, the kingdom is inside of you, and it is outside of you. When you come to know yourselves, then you will become known, and you will realize that it is you who are the sons of the living father" (3).[2]

It is easy to see why the early church reacted so negatively to gnosticism. In addition to opposing the physicality of the resurrection and salvation by faith, it taught people to look within themselves rather than to the authority of the church. Under Constantine, the first Christian emperor, possession of the gospels of Thomas, Philip, Truth, or Mary was made a criminal offense.[3]

Arianism

Arius was a church leader who believed that Jesus was divine but not on the same level as the father. Since Jesus was a begotten son, he must, in some manner, be subsequent or subordinate to the father. This argument made sense, and it enjoyed support in the New Testament. "'Why do you call me good?' Jesus answered. 'No one is good—except God alone'" (Mark 10:18). "About that day or hour no one knows, not even the angels in heaven, nor the Son, but only the Father" (Matthew 24:36). "The Father is greater than I" (John 14:28).

Arianism, as this view came to be known, attracted a following large enough to threaten the cohesiveness of the church. Because church unity facilitated political unity, Constantine wanted the issue resolved. In 325 CE, he convened and personally presided over the Council of Nicaea, at which the doctrine of consubstantiality (that the father and son are of the same essence) was officially established.[4] Constantine outlawed all of Arius's writings and commanded that anyone hiding them be put to death.[5]

Monophysitism

Constantine's desire for unity notwithstanding, the notion that Jesus was simultaneously wholly divine and wholly human continued to trouble people who thought about it. Monophysitism was another christological interpretation ultimately declared heretical. In direct opposition to dyophysitism, it was the belief that Jesus had a divine nature only, not a human one, or that the two natures had been fused into one in which the divine predominated.

In 449 CE, a rogue Second Council of Ephesus endorsed monophysitism. Only two years later, in 451 CE, the Council of Chalcedon overruled that decision and endorsed dyophysitism.[6]

Dyophysitism has since been the dominant doctrine, but to this day, some Eastern Orthodox churches continue to maintain a version of monophysitism.

Bandages

As seen so far, the doctrine of the incarnation violates the law of non-contradiction and flies in the face of scripture. But when it encounters the doctrine of original sin, it descends into farce. In order to be morally perfect, Jesus had to be born without original sin. But according to the story, he had a human mother. He would therefore have inherited original sin from her.

The Catholic church, in what appears to be an afterthought, addressed this problem through the doctrine of the "immaculate conception of Mary." Although it had been discussed for centuries beforehand, it was not declared dogma until 1854. It states that at the time Mary's parents conceived her, her god made a one-time intervention to prevent the transmission of original sin. Consequently, Mary didn't carry it, and Jesus didn't inherit it.

The obvious question: if Mary's god could prevent the transmission of original sin for her, why could he not do that for everyone? All of us, not to mention his son, could have been spared the whole incarnation-crucifixion rigmarole.

There is more. According to Christian doctrine, death exists because of sin. In that case, since Mary never sinned, she could not have died. She would have been indestructible! In 1950, in another apparent afterthought, the Catholic church established the doctrine of the "assumption of Mary." Without any scriptural basis, the church declared the dogma that Mary did not die. She was, at the end, simply taken into heaven, whatever that means.

All of this seems like an example of someone making up something, and then finding he must make up other increasingly elaborate things in order to justify the first made-up thing.

Some Protestants do not accept the doctrinal bandage of the immaculate conception, preferring a different explanation for Jesus's alleged moral perfection. They claim that while both males and females inherit a sinful nature, only males transmit it. According to this view, since there was no human male involved in Jesus's conception, he was free of original sin.

This approach has its own difficulties. First, it is scripturally questionable: "Adam was not the one deceived; it was the woman who was deceived and became a sinner" (1 Timothy 2:14). According to this verse, woman is more polluted by sin than man. Second, if the absence of a male circumvents original sin, then it would be possible to create morally perfect people, people in no need of Jesus's atonement, by cloning women.

Yet another indignity for the incarnated body concerns this god's immutability. By incarnating his second person at a specific point in time, he changed. He thereby contradicted his own declaration: "I the Lord do not change" (Malachi 3:6).

In fact, he may have changed a second time. Christians believe that Jesus was resurrected *bodily* and that a short time later, he "ascended" to heaven. Did Jesus retain his human part, including his body, when he ascended? Presumably, the 100 percent god part of Jesus reunited with the other two persons of the trinity after depositing the 100 percent human part somewhere else. This would suggest that there is not one Jesus in heaven, but two. The alternative is that Jesus retained his human part, in which case the trinity is now a foursome: the preexisting three persons plus the 100 percent human part still bolted to the 100 percent god part of Jesus.

These christological difficulties highlight the fact that Christian doctrine was hammered out by church leaders, human beings, over a long period. Modern Christians have inherited only the views of the winners in these controversies. Moreover, these doctrines still have logical problems, as identified above. There do not appear to be any good reasons for believing that the men who created these doctrines were any more qualified to speak for the gods than anyone else.

13

HOLY SPIRIT

Christianity teaches that the third person of its trinity is a holy ghost or holy spirit. It is purported to be the person of the trinity most active in human affairs, guiding individuals inwardly just as it guided humankind outwardly by speaking through the Old Testament prophets and Jesus's apostles. Most spectacularly, the holy spirit effected the impregnation of the human virgin Mary (Matthew 1:18-20, Luke 1:35) bringing the enfleshed god into the world.

The ancient Israelites had spoken of their god's spirit but meant it as an effect Yahweh could have upon human attitudes and behaviors. Fiercely monotheistic, most Jews would never have characterized this spirit as an independent agent. But some Christians began to do just that; they personified it. The discussion below touches upon a few highlights in this personification process and then considers the psychology of its enduring appeal.

Personification

The personification of the spirit was by no means obvious to all early Christians. It developed slowly. Even some church leaders were confused, thinking the spirit was another term for Jesus. The anonymous author of 2 Clement (circa 150 CE) wrote, "If we say that the flesh is the church and the spirit Christ, then it follows that he who shall offer outrage to the flesh is guilty of outrage on the church. Such a one, therefore, will not partake of the spirit, which is Christ."[1] Justin Martyr (circa 160 CE) wrote, "It is wrong, therefore, to understand the Spirit and the power of God as anything else than the Word, who is also the first-born of God."[2]

The Council of Nicaea had focused primarily on the relationship between Jesus and the father. It was not until the First Council of Constantinople in 381 CE that the church officially expanded the scope of consubstantiality to include the holy spirit as well.[3]

This was not the end of the confusion. If Jesus was begotten, then where did the holy spirit come from? In 451 CE, the Council of Chalcedon declared that the holy spirit emanated from the father. But a fresh controversy ensued. In the Western church, leaders began to insist that the holy spirit emanated from both the father and the son. This addition, known as the *filioque* (Latin, "and the son") was formalized at the Council of Toledo in 589 CE.[4] The Eastern church did not agree with the filioque innovation, holding instead to the original Council of Chalcedon position. To this day, the filioque remains a bone of contention between the Roman Catholic and Eastern Orthodox churches.

The appeal of anomalous experiences

The adherents of many religions have had personal experiences that they describe as direct encounters with a god or with the divine realm. These experiences are of many sorts and of varying degrees of intensity. They range from seeing blinding lights or hearing voices to a feeling of oneness with everything or simply a deep sense of well-being. Within the Christian tradition, these experiences are generally considered to be the work of the holy spirit.

Do such experiences provide us with evidence that one or more gods exist? Or that the Christian god in particular exists? There are reasons to be skeptical.

A natural basis for these experiences seems plausible. Much about the brain is not yet understood, but it appears to be a complex system of electrochemical processes. It is not difficult to imagine a temporary anomaly in these processes caused by illness or duress, or even one induced deliberately through such brain-addling practices as prolonged fasting, chanting, meditation, or prayer. Supernatural explanations for anomalous experiences are unnecessary.

It is not uncommon for a Christian to claim that he felt the holy spirit "come upon" him. But people in many religions have powerful, even transformative, experiences. Buddhists and Hindus have these experiences, but that does not mean that Buddhism or Hinduism is true. The potential to undergo these experiences appears to be a universal feature of human psychology rather than the work of a deity.

Reports of anomalous experiences coincide suspiciously with the prevailing expectations of the local culture. Any claim to a direct encounter with the divine comes to us through the interpretive lens of the individual reporting it. And these individuals typically see the experiences as confirmation of the religions in which they were raised. Hindus tend to see Vishnu and Christians tend to see Jesus, not the other way around. This is because the individual's religious background shapes his expectations, the way he makes sense of the experience, and the vocabulary with which he describes it afterward. For most people, there would simply be no question as to the source of these experiences. They would be attributed to whatever gods or goddesses the people grew up believing in.

Finally, many of us, probably a majority, have not had anomalous experiences. Do our lives not provide data? If an anomalous experience is an argument for the existence of a god or a holy spirit, then the lack of such an experience is an argument for the nonexistence of that god or holy spirit.

In summary, while neuroscience is still young, there appears to be little reason to conclude that anomalous experiences are the work of a deity, much less of a specifically identifiable one. Given plausible naturalistic explanations, supernatural ones are unnecessary.

Because claims of anomalous experiences are supported only by the subjective reports of the faithful, an empirically verifiable test would be helpful. And Christianity actually provides something close. Some Christians believe the holy spirit descends upon people and endows them with the ability to "speak in tongues." According to Acts 2:1-4, the holy spirit descended upon the apostles at the Feast of the Pentecost, enabling them to preach to all of the visiting foreigners despite language differences.

As this story shows, speaking in tongues means being able to speak a foreign language instantaneously. To be useful for preaching, it must be a human language. If a person is speaking gibberish, he is not speaking in tongues. He is just embarrassing himself.

A specialized vocabulary makes the distinction clear. The term for speaking gibberish when ostensibly in the thrall of the holy spirit is "glossolalia." This is reported regularly. The term for speaking a known human language, without any prior exposure to it, is "xenoglossy." This is not reported regularly.

If a holy spirit performed the sort of miracles described in Acts 2:1-4, we would possess empirically verifiable evidence of its existence. The ability of a god's spokesmen to preach, without prior training, in any language that the occasion demands is exactly the type of thing we would expect to see if there really were a holy spirit. The fact that people speak gibberish rather than a human language is a strong hint to the contrary.

14

MORALITY

Christianity teaches that its god is the source of morality. Indeed, it inherited from Judaism the presumption that morality is first and foremost a religious matter. This stood in contrast to the predominant view within Graeco-Roman society that morality and religion were two separate spheres, where morality dealt with how to live, and religion dealt with paying proper respect to the gods.

But is morality derived from a religion superior to morality derived from other sources? And is their religion really the moral recourse of most Christians? The discussion below is in three parts. First, Christian moral guidance is shown to be deficient. Second, the secular alternative is shown to compare favorably, as can be seen in its frequent adoption by Christians. Finally, a discussion of Christianity and morality would be incomplete without addressing a special problem born with the religion itself.

Does the god of Christianity provide morality?

While different denominations have their own emphases, most would include one or more of the following as avenues of moral guidance: first, direct instruction from the Christian god;

second, inspiration from humankind's share in his goodness; third, reciprocation of his love, and; fourth, the operation of conscience. Let's consider each in turn.

The first and most obvious avenue is direct instruction or example. The Bible contains some sound moral principles, such as the golden rule, discussed further below. But these sound principles are outnumbered by those which are quite simply appalling. If a man works on the Sabbath, "the man must die. The whole assembly must stone him" (Numbers 15:35). If a man discovers that his bride is not a virgin, then "the men of her town shall stone her to death" (Deuteronomy 22:21). Christians who disregard these teachings claim that the law of the Old Testament was superseded by Jesus. But then they contradict themselves by claiming that the Old Testament's ten commandments are the foundation of Christian morality.

The ten commandments, incidentally, could easily be improved upon. The second, third, and fourth commandments prohibit graven images of competitive deities, prohibit misusing the deity's name, and reserve a special day to honor the deity each week. These precepts would not approach a top-ten list under any rational analysis. Far better ones readily suggest themselves: do not enslave your fellow humans, do not allow children to starve to death, do not rape. The primary purpose served by the originals is nothing more than the perpetuation of the belief system itself.

The Old Testament is packed with divine endorsement of violence. Its god commands the Israelites to exterminate the Midionites (Numbers 31:7-18), the Amorites (Deuteronomy 2:33-34), and the Amalekites (1 Samuel 15:2-3). "Do not spare them; put to death men and women, children and infants, cattle and sheep, camels and donkeys" (1 Samuel 15:3). On another occasion, he even removes people's free will in order to feel better about butchering them: "For it was the Lord himself who hardened their hearts to wage war against Israel, so that he might destroy them totally, exterminating them without mercy" (Joshua 11:20). In case the soldiers needed extra motivation: "Kill all the boys. And kill every woman who has slept with a man, but save for yourselves every girl who has never slept with a man" (Numbers 31:17-18). Christians might mock some Muslims for seeking virgins in paradise, but what enticement was their own god offering here?

In the New Testament, Jesus said he came not to abolish, but to fulfill the law (Matthew 5:17); but he violated at least two of the commandments personally. One commandment requires that people honor their parents. Jesus rudely spurned his own mother (Mark 3:31-35) and taught that to be his disciple, a man must "hate father and mother, wife and children, brothers and sisters" (Luke 14:26). When a follower asked for time to bury his deceased father, Jesus said, "Let the dead bury their own dead" (Luke 9:60). Another commandment prohibits working on the Sabbath. Asked why he picked crops on that day, Jesus replied, "The Sabbath was made for man, not man for the Sabbath" (Mark 2:27). That's like getting pulled over by the highway patrol and arguing, "The speed limit was made for man, not man for the speed limit."

The Old and New Testaments are fully aligned in their endorsement of slavery. "Your male and female slaves are to come from the nations around you . . . You can bequeath them to your children as inherited property and can make them slaves for life" (Leviticus 25:44-46). "Slaves, obey your earthly masters with respect and fear" (Ephesians 6:5). "Slaves, obey your earthly masters in everything" (Colossians 3:22). "All who are under the yoke of slavery should consider their masters worthy of full respect" (1 Timothy 6:1). "Slaves, in reverent fear of God submit yourselves to your masters" (1 Peter 2:18). Jefferson Davis, the president of the Confederacy, was able to observe that slavery "was established by decree of Almighty God, that it is sanctioned in the Bible, in both testaments, from Genesis to Revelations."[1]

Despite his alleged moral perfection, Jesus never condemned the widespread slavery of his time. He even compared divine judgment to whipping slaves, apparently without it ever occurring to him that there was anything wrong with either. He said, "The slave (Greek, δουλος, written in English as "doulos") who knows the master's will and does not get ready or does not do what the master wants will be beaten with many blows. But the one who does not know and does things deserving punishment will be beaten with few blows" (Luke 12:47-48). How could Jesus and his closest followers be so blind to the moral outrage of slavery? Part of the answer was their preoccupation with god's kingdom, where everything will be made right. It may be the case that the more a society emphasizes an afterlife, the more it is willing to tolerate injustice in life.

One could continue feasting on the buffet of barbarism spread out in the pages of these ancient Middle Eastern writings, but the point will by now have become clear. Neither the instruction nor the example of the Bible's god provides a consistent moral compass. If readers claim to find guidance in these pages, something else is going on.

A second possible avenue of moral guidance is the belief that humankind shares in its creator's goodness. "God created man in his own image" (Genesis 1:27). As a result, everyone has an equal moral worth, and moral conduct can fairly be expected of us.

These teachings can certainly be uplifting. It is difficult, however, to credit Christianity with them. They can be distilled from a reading, albeit selective, of the Jewish Bible/ Old Testament, and they constitute the heart of modern Jewish morality.

What has Christianity contributed? That, as a result of Adam and Eve's disobedience, humankind is depraved and deserves not merely to die, but to be tortured for eternity; and that those possessing faith in the efficacy of Jesus's scapegoating will escape this deserved punishment.

Immoral aspects of these Christian beliefs have been touched upon already, but they bear repeating here because they are directly relevant to any claim that the religion is moral. Vicarious sacrifice is immoral because it deflects guilt from the transgressor onto an innocent scapegoat, thereby breaking the bond between action and consequence. Salvation by faith is immoral because it rewards people for holding a belief rather than right conduct. Eternal punishment is immoral because human transgressions, even if real crimes, are finite.

Jesus's career, that is, the entire incarnation-atonement-resurrection drama, was a creative response to the problems of suffering and death. It had little to do with morality. In fact, it dulled the moral strength of its Jewish origins by positing that humankind is depraved and deserves to suffer yet can escape through the suffering of another. This is the very negation of mutual respect and individual accountability.

God's love is a third possible avenue of moral guidance. "For God so loved the world that he gave his one and only Son" (John 3:16). Some Christians claim that this is the key, not only to salvation, but to morality as well. Because through his sacrifice, Jesus gave humankind the gift of atonement, humans will naturally want to reciprocate by treating others well.

The idea that Jesus gave humankind a gift makes sense, however, only if one believes humankind is depraved and needs to be atoned to begin with. As discussed in chapters 2 and 3, the doctrine of the fall and the consequent depravity of humankind were Christian innovations developed by early church leaders in order to legitimize retroactively Jesus's otherwise humiliating death.

Furthermore, according to Christianity, the majority of humankind will not be reconciled with its god but will be tortured in hell for eternity. For a god who is supposed to be both infinitely powerful and infinitely loving, it is difficult to see this as anything but a colossal failure. Contrast this with the thoroughgoing triumph of Ahura Mazda in Zoroastrianism. After his victory over the forces of darkness, he will throw the wicked into the pit to be tortured for their misdeeds; but eventually, all will be redeemed and admitted to paradise. The Christian god, who supervises the perpetual torture of the majority of his creation, fares poorly by comparison and is hardly a model of love to be emulated.

A fourth possible avenue of moral guidance is conscience. Some Christians believe that their god implanted a conscience in humankind and may even guide it on occasion. Indeed, a conscience, or moral sense, is widely observed. After all, most people agree about most moral questions most of the time.

The existence of a conscience does not, however, require a supernatural explanation. In fact, if an all-powerful deity had created it, it would probably work better. Wouldn't our moral intuitions be clearer and more universal and more insistent in that case? The conscience is better explained naturalistically. Individual reason and empathy on the one hand and societal norms on the other are constantly informing each other. Both are sources of conscience; neither requires a deity. This brings us to the next question.

Where do Christians really get their morality?

Most Bible readers do not learn morality from the Bible. They pick and choose from the text which lessons to follow and which to ignore. Therefore, their morality does not come from the Bible but rather from the criteria they use to pick and choose. Which criteria are these? For the most part, they are the same moral standards respected by non-Bible readers.

True morality is conduct that aims to reduce suffering or increase well-being. It comes from empathy and the reasoning process. We do not want to suffer, and we can generalize that to others. Because human nature is an amalgam of good and bad impulses, humans need moral instruction to guide their decisions and actions. We can follow and teach the golden rule without attributing it to a supernatural authority. One of the world's most influential belief systems, Confucianism, does precisely this. Confucianism has no deity, but it has extensive moral teachings.

Confucius taught the golden rule five hundred years before the time of Jesus.[2]

Some believers labor under the impression that unless values such as morality come from a god, they are merely opinions. But even if we assume that a god exists, how would we know that his values are anything more? Consider why a god would enshrine one set of values as opposed to another. If the god had good reasons for choosing the values he did, then we could access those reasons ourselves, and the god would be unnecessary. If, on the other hand, the god lacked good reasons, then we, as responsible moral agents, would have to ask whether it is appropriate to obey him. The only moral authority left to him at that point would be that he is bigger and stronger, that "might makes right."

For example, if a god said that it was morally necessary to torture and kill all left-handed people, would that make it moral? If we answer yes, then we collude in an absurdity. If we answer no, then we acknowledge that moral judgments can and must be made independently of any god. Finally, if we answer, "God wouldn't say that," then again we acknowledge that moral judgments can and must be made independently of any god (because the only way we could answer in this manner would be if we had formed precisely such a judgment in order to predict what the god might or might not say).

This exercise demonstrates that moral judgments must be made by those acting and that they cannot abdicate this responsibility to another.

Is morality subjective or objective? Begin by noting that moral judgments are relevant to humans precisely because they arise from human experience. Morality is not objective in the sense that it exists independently of human judgment; so it is, in that sense, subjective. The definition of morality given above—conduct that aims to reduce suffering or increase well-being—is a declaration of values. It cannot be derived or proven from prior principles. Once this definition is accepted, however, morality can be objective in the sense that claims about suffering or well-being are amenable to rational analysis and subject to empirically verifiable facts.

Moral judgments are not necessarily easy and it may be difficult to prove moral truth. After all, someone can always disagree. Call this the problem of disagreement. Note, however, that religion does not eliminate the problem of disagreement. To take an extreme example, suppose religion A teaches that child sacrifice is necessary and religion B does not. From the point of view of each of these religions, the other one is immoral. And there is no *religious criterion* for saying that one is right and the other is wrong. One faith is just as valid as another. The only way to resolve the disagreement is to examine the consequences of the disputed practice—in other words, to discard the religions and use reason. The consequences can be seen and understood by anyone, regardless of his religion. Whereas faith divides people along ethnic and historical lines, reason can be shared by all.

It is also worth observing that even people within the same religion do not necessarily agree about its god's moral instructions. The god of the Bible commanded, "Thou shalt not kill," and Catholics oppose the death penalty for this reason. Many Protestants, however, favor the death penalty. The problem of disagreement exists with or without religion.

Note further that, with religion and the certitude it tends to foster, the problem of disagreement is aggravated. Those who believe they have a god on their side are capable of suppressing empathy and committing atrocities because they believe themselves accountable to a god instead of other humans. Good people do not need a deity to do good things; they would do those things anyway. But good people almost always need a deity to do horrible things. The Bible story in which Abraham shows his unquestioning willingness to butcher his son, Isaac, and is rewarded for it, neatly illustrates how religious faith can suffocate natural, widely shared morality.

It may be difficult to prove moral truth without a god, but as this exercise has shown, it is equally difficult *with* a god. Christian and secular moral reasoning can be summarized side by side as follows:

Christian Approach	Secular Approach
Assumption 1: There exists a personal god who cares about human behavior.	Assumption 1: Morality is behavior that aims to reduce suffering or increase well-being.
Assumption 2: Morality is what this god says it is, and humans are able to understand his instructions.	Assumption 2: Humans can determine, or approximate, what reduces suffering or increases well-being.
This god's instructions say X is moral.	X reduces suffering or increases well-being.
Therefore, X is moral.	Therefore, X is moral.

It might be argued that the difficult thing about morality is not knowing what it is, but getting people to follow it. In other words, why behave morally? The table can be extended as follows:

Christian Approach	Secular Approach
Behave morally out of love of god and fear of his punishment.	Behave morally out of empathy with, and respect for, humankind.

Some people genuinely fear that anarchy is the only alternative to religion. For them, the threat of a god's punishment is the linchpin of any possible morality; without it, everything would be permitted. But even if this fear were well-founded, it would not be an argument for the truth of a religion, only for its usefulness. And it does not, upon examination, appear very well-founded.

First, most religious people, if asked whether they would rape and murder in the absence of a god, acknowledge that they would not. This demonstrates that reason and empathy, and the societal norms that spring from them, are more powerful factors than they realize. Second, the anarchy concern could be entertained only by someone with an impoverished understanding of other cultures. Many societies in the past have observed predominantly nontheistic moralities (for example, ancient Greece and Rome and Confucian China). And today, the countries that lead the world in most indicators of societal well-being (for example, the Scandinavian countries and Japan) are those with the highest rates of organic (that is, not politically imposed) atheism.[3] Finally, let's not forget that Christian doctrine itself devalues divine enforcement: salvation is not dependent upon morality but upon faith in Jesus. Christians will enjoy heaven, the majority of humankind will suffer hell, and neither outcome is based on moral conduct.

A last and dispositive point is this: Christians frequently disown Christian teachings and adopt the secular approach instead. One example is Jesus's prohibition of divorce except in cases of adultery (Matthew 19:4-9). Many Christians ignore Jesus's instruction because they understand that remaining unhappily married can cause more harm than good. Another example is the biblical sanction of slavery, discussed above. If they really took moral guidance from the Bible, Christians would be obliged to maintain that slavery is moral. Instead, they ignore the offending passages. In both of these cases, Christians choose to override Christianity with secular morality.

Christianity's special moral problem

The birth of Christianity created a special moral problem. Its need to define itself as distinct from its mother religion had an ugly by-product. The anti-Semitism that pockmarks European history—ghettos, blood libel, pogroms, and Holocaust—has few antecedents in the pagan world.[4] It comes largely from Christianity.

As discussed in appendix 1, devout Jews charged Jesus's followers with blasphemy, and the latter countercharged blindness. In its earliest phase, the Jesus movement was outnumbered, and the Jewish establishment persecuted it. But with Christianity's growth, it was the Jews who found themselves outnumbered and who, throughout most of European history, were the persecuted. The stakes were high; and they remain so. If one side is right, then the other is wrong. Anti-Semitism is a result of the credibility problem Judaism poses for Christianity, a problem with both evidential and interpretive dimensions.

Consider the evidence for Christianity. The Jews were there to see and hear firsthand Jesus's teachings, his miracles, and his resurrection. Why weren't more of them Christians? The fact that the Jews of first-century Palestine were those closest to the events, and at the same time, those least impressed by them is an embarrassment to Christianity.

Consider Christianity's interpretation of the Jewish Bible/Old Testament as a text whose meaning can be understood only retroactively through the lens of Jesus's career. The Jews' refusal to interpret their own scripture the way that Christians want to interpret it constitutes a challenge to the Christian interpretation. For Christianity, a viable alternative interpretation is a source of insecurity. A healthy and vibrant Judaism living that alternative interpretation imperils the entire Christian worldview.

The Jews had to be discredited, and the men who wrote the gospels obliged. The author of Matthew put into the mouth of a Jewish mob the preposterous cry, "His blood is on us and on our children" (Matthew 27:25). The gospel of John refers to the Jews repeatedly without distinguishing between the laity and the priests, to whom Jesus says, "You belong to your father, the devil" (John 8:44). From traditions such as these arose the popular refrain that the Jewish people as a whole were "christ killers."

Early church leaders repeated this message. Tertullian wrote, "Though Israel may wash all its members every day, it is never clean. Its hands . . . are always stained, covered forever with the blood of the prophets and of our Lord himself."[5] Eusebius wrote, addressing the Jews directly, "From being the Elect of God you became wolves, and sharpened your teeth upon the Lamb of God. Hell . . . shall imprison you with your father the devil."[6] Augustine likened the Jews to the murderer Cain, noting that "the Jews will be a proof to believing Christians of the subjection merited by those who, in the pride of their kingdom, put the Lord to death."[7]

In his book, *On the Jews and Their Lies* (circa 1540), Martin Luther wrote, "Be on your guard against the Jews, knowing that wherever they have their synagogues, nothing is found but a den of devils in which sheer self-glory, conceit, lies, blasphemy, and defaming of God and men are practiced most maliciously."[8] He concluded with policy prescriptions: "What shall we Christians do with this rejected and condemned people, the Jews? . . . First, to set fire to their synagogues or schools . . . Second, I advise that their houses also be razed and destroyed . . . Third, I advise that all their prayer books and Talmudic writings, in which such idolatry, lies, cursing, and blasphemy are taught, be taken from them . . ."[9]

Long before the twentieth century and the Third Reich, anti-Semitism had been deeply ingrained throughout European culture.[10] While the proximate cause of the Holocaust was a flagitious totalitarian regime, it was also an outgrowth of this centuries-old and religiously instilled hatred. Adolf Hitler inherited and continued the tradition of accusing the Jews of being god's enemies when he wrote in his book, *Mein Kampf*, "I believe that I am acting in accordance with the will of the Almighty Creator: by defending myself against the Jew, I am fighting for the work of the Lord."[11]

15

PURPOSE

Christianity teaches that humankind's purpose comes from its god. He made human beings "to know and love God" and "to share in his own blessed life"[1] or "to glorify God" and "to enjoy him forever."[2] Questions of purpose (or meaning) are difficult, but every story needs a "why." Taking a cue from the above quotations, let's explore some of the reasons the god posited by Christianity might have created humankind and what they might mean for our purpose.

Did he create so that humankind could know him? No, that is illogical. Humankind's ignorance of its god could not have been the reason for creating human beings because it was not a problem until *after* human beings were created. Before then, human beings had no ignorance that needed to be remedied. (Of course it is sensible to argue that once a god had created humans, their purpose might include knowing him. But that does not explain why he created humans in the first place.)

Did he create to glorify himself? To glorify means to "reveal or exhibit the magnificence of." A popular minister wrote, "The ultimate goal of the universe is to show the glory of God."[3] This makes no sense either. To whom was it necessary to reveal or exhibit the god's magnificence? Before the creation, there was no one around to be awed by the creation. (The glorification motive might be apt if the god intended to outshine other gods who had created less impressive universes, but that would entail polytheism.)

These considerations signal a problem for Christianity. Its god is allegedly perfect, and a perfect being would not need to create anything. Nor would he even desire to do so. Either a need or a desire would indicate a state of discontent or deprivation, in short, some manner of imperfection. We cannot say that he created because it gave him pleasure; that would indicate that he was lacking pleasure beforehand, which would make him less than perfect. If a perfect god existed, he would not create. He would have no reason to do anything at all. He would abide in an eternal perfect stasis.

One possible work-around to this problem is to argue that he created simply as a by-product of his overflowing love and inventiveness. In other words, it just sort of happened, like an unplanned pregnancy. This does not seem very persuasive. First, if it were true, the result would more likely be a large number of universes rather than just one. While modern cosmologists consider this a possibility, it is not the position of Christianity. Second and more fundamentally, an all-powerful god ought to be able to bring by-products of his own nature under the control of his conscious will.

Perhaps the god created so that humankind could enjoy him and share in his life. A creation motivated by benevolence is at odds, however, with life's suffering, discussed in chapter 1. Even if a heaven were to outweigh suffering, that compensation would accrue only to a minority of humankind. As discussed in chapter 9, the majority will be punished for eternity in hell, and—worse—an omniscient god would have known this even before creating it. That a god created humankind out of love, only to torture the majority for eternity, would be a curious position to adopt.

A version of the loving creator idea might be rescued if we contemplate the possibility that a god created not for humankind but for some other species that does not suffer at all. This prospect helps us shed the egotistic assumption that earthlings are at the center of the universe. Perhaps humankind's purpose is to be food for this other species, which presently resides in a distant galaxy and has not yet found us. In this case, would the worshipful among us be so eager to fulfill their god's plan?

If the world were indeed created by a god, his purpose in doing so is not readily apparent and we are thrown back upon our own resources. Many Christians believe that their purpose is simply to know their god or to prepare themselves for an afterlife. But what do these things actually mean?

Given the Christian god's hiddenness, discussed in chapter 7, knowing him would be a challenge. Many Christians believe that through prayer and reflection, they develop a "relationship" with him. But there do not appear to be any good reasons for believing that they are doing anything other than talking to their own projections.

Preparation for the afterlife presumably means that we are expected to learn and grow. But there are problems with this view. How does it apply to those who die young? Are they finished learning and growing? How does it apply to the majority earmarked for hell? What preparation is necessary for residence there?

While we share a common humanity, we have unique personalities. How are we to find unique purposes? To argue that a god gives each of us a unique purpose is merely to defer the question: instead of asking, "What is my purpose?" we ask, "What purpose does my god have for me?" Not only is this unhelpful on a practical level, but it is also logically questionable.

How can a purpose be assigned by someone else? Whose purpose would that be then? If I built a robot for the purpose of washing cars, that would be my purpose, not the robot's. Would we consider the robot lucky because he had a purpose given to him by his maker? Similarly, if a god created a man for some purpose, that would be the god's purpose, not the man's.

It seems that there is no way to avoid the conclusion that humans must make their own purposes. This can be difficult. One of the reasons religion is attractive is that it provides the illusion of relieving us of this responsibility. But we can give our lives purpose by developing and using our talents in service of the people and things we love. No gods or goddesses are necessary to do that. Nor are souls, immortal or otherwise.

A possible objection to the conclusion above is to complain that temporary existence cannot have value. What does it matter in a billion years what we do today or that we even existed at all? Only a god and immortality can offer ultimate meaning. But this argument does not withstand scrutiny. The assertion that a god is needed in order for values to exist was rejected in the previous chapter. What about the assertion that immortality is needed?

This too is easily refuted. Through the use of the word "ultimate," the apologist plants the premise, subtly but unjustifiably, that meaning requires permanence. But if nothing in life has value, then what would be gained from an infinite extension of it? Conversely, if something is valuable when it exists forever, then a short bit of it would have some value too. The apologist's logic would tell us that Bach's Brandenburg Concertos have no more value than the sound of a raccoon toppling and rummaging through a trash can because, after all, they both come to an end. The apologist's logic would tell us not to feed the hungry because, after all, they'll just be hungry again later.

It is possible that a god created humankind, but that does not appear to change the fact that we must create our own purposes.

To love, to learn, to help others, to raise a family, to express a creative impulse, to develop an athletic talent, or to cultivate any other worthy excellence—we do these things because they bring satisfaction in their own right, here and now. These experiences are meaningful now. They don't have to last forever to have value.

At best, belief in a god does not equip people any better for the difficult questions of purpose than the lack of such a belief. More likely, belief in a god is a distraction because it fixates people on hypothetical afterlives rather than on making the most of the lives they have. Values, such as goodness and beauty, come not from a god but from human experience in life, and purpose derives from putting those values back into it.

16

THE CHURCH

Christianity teaches that Jesus brought to human beings a vital message through his instruction and life example, the "good news" of the gospel. But what exactly is the gospel? And who gets to say so? While the Jews had held a notion of national salvation, Christians saw salvation as an individual matter. It was not long, however, before individual salvation became dependent on membership in the church.

The word typically translated as "church" in the New Testament is the Greek *ecclesia*, which has the general meaning of an "assembly" or a "society." The first Christians lived communistically, sharing all of their goods without hierarchy (Acts 2:44-45). Writing a couple of decades after Jesus's death, Paul addressed his letters to church members generally rather than to any leaders. This is because there were no leaders, at least not formally. The church structure of priests, bishops, and pope evolved slowly.

Despite attempts at organization, Christian doctrine and practice were and continue to be marked by confusion. The lack of agreement among those wishing to follow him is strong evidence that Jesus was not a competent instructor, much less an all-powerful deity. An all-powerful deity could have documented his teachings in an unambiguous form, perpetually accessible in every existing and future language.

Instead of this, we have multiple branches of Christianity, each teaching different things about very fundamental questions. Some disagreements (theories of atonement, filioque, immaculate conception) have already been touched upon. Other disagreements are even more profound. Most of them can be traced back to the question of the church's authority, and that is the appropriate place to start.

Authority of the church

The fount of church authority is often held to be Jesus's pronouncement, "I tell you that you are Peter, and on this rock I will build my church" (Matthew 16:18). Roman Catholics interpret this to mean that Jesus was bequeathing leadership of the movement to Peter and by extension to his successors, the bishops of Rome, i.e., the popes. The Eastern Orthodox reject the understanding that one individual rules the church, insisting instead that all of the bishops are equals. In fact, it was largely this political issue that triggered the Great Schism of 1054, which split Christendom into the Roman Catholic and Eastern Orthodox churches.

The Protestant Reformation, conventionally dated from 1517, created Christianity's most violent fault line, that between Roman Catholic and Protestant. Protestants came to reject nearly all of the traditional church hierarchy. This radical view was based on the conviction that believers could understand the Bible for themselves without the mediation of clergy or tradition, a view encapsulated by the catchphrase *sola scriptura* (Latin, "scripture alone"). The Reformation had complex causes, ranging from the venality of the clergy to rising nationalism; and while the desire for independence was understandable, sola scriptura was not without its own difficulties.

One difficulty was that Protestants retained some beliefs from the church despite a lack of scriptural warrant for them. The Nicene doctrine of the trinity, for example, finds no support in scripture (see chapter 26), but most Protestants nevertheless continued to accept it. In this regard, only the Unitarians applied sola scriptura consistently and scrapped the trinity. Another even more fundamental issue is the identity of the scripture itself. As discussed in chapter 24, it was the church that decided which writings to include and which to exclude from the New Testament. In other words, it was the church that Protestants reject that picked the scripture that Protestants embrace. This is circular. Anyone familiar with the dependence of Christian doctrine and scripture on the church would be tempted to agree with Cardinal Newman, himself a former Anglican, when he observed, "To be deep in history is to cease to be a Protestant."[1]

A second difficulty was that, like any text, scripture needs to be interpreted. As a result of its rejection of church authority, Protestantism splintered into a Babel of denominations. Without a central authority to interpret scripture, any number of interpretations is possible. Without a central authority, in fact, there is no one to arbitrate new revelations that might supplement existing ones and add to scripture. Mormons, for example, accept not only the Old and New Testaments, but also the Book of Mormon, which constitutes a third testament. Without it, from the Mormon perspective, other Christians are handicapped by incomplete information. If Joseph Smith had published the Book of Mormon in 1430 instead of 1830, the church would have burned him at the stake as a heretic, and few would ever have heard of him. Instead, a new branch of Christianity flourishes. Mormonism—Latter Day Saints, buried gold plates, the angel Moroni, and the rest—is a reductio ad absurdum of the Reformation.

Means of salvation

Doctrinal confusion brought to the surface by the Reformation goes to Christianity's very heart. For Christians, there is no subject more important than the means to saving the soul. But only a short time after Jesus died, even close followers could not agree upon what he taught regarding salvation. Paul wrote, "we maintain that a man is justified by faith apart from the works of the law" (Romans 3:28). But the author of James, contradicting Paul, wrote, "a person is considered righteous by what he does and not by faith alone" (James 2:24).

Both Catholics and Protestants believe that Paul replaced the Jewish law with faith in Jesus. But they disagree about what that means. To Catholics, the law is overthrown, but actions still matter; specifically, one must partake in the church's sacraments. While Jesus's sacrifice made grace available to humankind, the church's sacraments confer that grace upon individuals. The Council of Trent (1545 to 1563) formalized seven of them: baptism, confirmation, eucharist, penance, extreme unction, matrimony, and orders.

It might appear from this that Catholicism resolves the Paul-James contradiction: Paul is correct that the law is overthrown, and James is correct that actions matter. But a careful reading of James makes this conclusion a highly unsafe one. Its author displays little interest in rituals such as those Catholicism calls sacraments. When he endorses "works," he means primarily moral conduct, especially helping the poor and disadvantaged. This sounds more like Jewish morality than Catholic sacrament.

By contrast, most Protestants interpret Paul's teaching to be that faith is all that really matters, that an individual receives grace through faith. This gave rise to the other principal catchphrase of the Reformation, *sola fide* (Latin, "faith alone"). Accordingly, Protestants de-emphasize sacraments. Many observe at most two, baptism and eucharist, and believe that even these do not confer grace but are merely external signs of it.

Protestants attempt to resolve the Paul-James contradiction in a different way. They insist that salvation brings improved moral conduct as a consequence. The belief here, as discussed in chapter 14, is that humans will treat others well because of what Jesus did for them. Hence, good works follow faith. But even if this were true, it misses the point: the disagreement between Paul and James is not about what one does after being saved but how one is saved in the first place.

It is instructive to contrast the Catholic and Protestant views of salvation with a third view, that of Jesus. When asked by a wealthy man how to inherit eternal life, Jesus began by naming some of the Jewish laws. Then he added that the man must give all he had to the poor and follow him (Mark 10:17-21, Matthew 19:16-21, Luke 18:18-22). Because Jesus's response does not accord with the doctrines later developed by church leaders—righteousness through the Jewish law would be rejected and there is scant mention here of a requirement to have faith in Jesus—some scholars believe this may be an instance of the Bible accurately capturing something the real Jesus actually said.[2] John, the last of the four gospels to be written and consequently the most theologically evolved, omits this episode, probably because Jesus was being too Jewish and not adequately Christian.

Jesus's teaching that salvation comes from living justly is also communicated in his "parable of the sheep and the goats" (Matthew 25:31-46). In this parable, humanity will be divided into two groups at the judgment. One group will be rewarded, "for I was hungry and you gave me something to eat." The other will be punished, "for I was hungry and you gave me nothing to eat." Once again, there is no mention here of a faith-in-Jesus test.

Route to the afterlife

Confusion over the means of salvation extends to its nature. Catholics believe in a temporary, intermediate state called "purgatory," where the dead destined for heaven but not yet ready for admittance undergo a process of purification. Closely connected with purgatory are "prayers for the dead." Through prayer, those still living can help those in purgatory along their way.

Protestants reject all of this, maintaining instead that, following judgment, individuals go directly to heaven or hell. They argue that neither purgatory nor prayers for the dead enjoys an adequate basis in scripture. Of course, part of this disagreement is due to the fact that Catholics and Protestants have different Bibles (see chapter 24). Purgatory and prayers for the dead are based primarily on passages that Catholics find in their Bibles, but Protestants do not. "He also took up a collection, man by man, to the amount of two thousand drachmas of silver, and sent it to Jerusalem to provide for a sin offering . . . Therefore he made atonement for the dead, so that they might be delivered from their sin" (2 Maccabees 12:40-46).[3]

How could an all-powerful deity, or his chosen human intermediaries, create so much confusion about such fundamental questions? Obviously, no deity has taken effective steps to ensure his message has been received and understood by all members of his target audience. If Jesus had intended to establish a single church with a single message, he failed. The resulting confusion and antagonism, which embroiled Christendom in centuries of internecine bloodshed, is strong evidence that the belief system is nothing more than a human invention.

17

PRAYER

Christianity teaches that, through prayer, believers can communicate directly with their god. While prayer can serve the purpose of thanking or praising, it is often used to ask for forgiveness or for some favor. Jesus said, "Whatever you ask for in prayer, believe that you have received it, and it will be yours" (Mark 11:24) and "If you believe, you will receive whatever you ask for in prayer" (Matthew 21:22).

These promises are incoherent because, if true, they would be tantamount to the doctrine that any Christian can cause his god to do things he would not otherwise do. This plunges the believer into immediate difficulties. First, wouldn't an omniscient god already know what a person wants? Second, shouldn't a fair god do what is right, irrespective of a person's petitions? And third, it simply cannot be true. Equally devout believers can pray for contradictory things: the French Christians prayed for victory against the Germans, and the German Christians prayed for victory against the French. Above all, the claim that prayer works is demonstrably false. It is, as shown below, disconfirmed by the evidence of common experience and scientific study.

One might well respond that the purpose of prayer is not to reduce the Christian god to a wish-granting genie but to see his will be done: "Our Father in heaven . . . your will be done" (Matthew 6:9-10). But what exactly does this mean? It cannot mean that the individual offers to help an all-powerful deity achieve his objectives since such a deity would not need any help. A more reasonable interpretation is that the individual requests help in aligning himself with his god's will. But if that is the meaning of Matthew 6:9-10, then it contradicts Mark 11:24 and Matthew 21:22, cited above. In those passages, Jesus's promises about prayer's power to deliver "whatever you ask for" are unambiguous and unqualified.

Many people insist that prayer has worked in their lives. There are other explanations, however, for the patterns they believe they see. It is not difficult to understand, for example, how prayer might appear to bring answers to troubling questions. It combines quiet reflection with a positive mental attitude. A person in this state will be receptive to ideas that have formed in his or her mind. And because the prayerful, by definition, believe they are communicating with a supernatural agent, they will assume that agent was the source of any new ideas.

Some people contend that prayer has actually altered events around them. But this perception is easily explained by "confirmation bias." A phenomenon extensively studied by psychologists, confirmation bias refers to the tendency to seek, interpret, or recall information in a manner which supports one's preconceptions. Humans respond selectively to the vast amount of information they encounter. Evidence that confirms our beliefs tends to get noticed and remembered more than evidence that disconfirms them. Confirmation bias is the engine behind the enduring popularity of horoscopes, whose readers routinely convince themselves that events in their day are fulfillments of that morning's prophecies.

Confirmation bias can cause people to remember the times that they prayed for something and received it, but forget the times they prayed for something and did not. Alternatively, they might reinterpret the failure of prayer as a lesson from their god, reading his beneficence into outcomes that are different from those for which they had prayed. This is illustrated by the cliché about the Christian who prays to find a good parking space. When he finds a parking space directly in front of the store, he thanks Jesus. When he is obliged to park a mile away, he also thanks Jesus—this time for teaching him patience.

The realms of science and religion overlap when religions make claims about the world. Unlike metaphysical claims regarding heaven or hell, claims about prayer can be put to the test. "The prayer offered in faith will make the sick person well" (James 5:15). Like Jesus's promises cited above, this promise is unambiguous and unqualified. It can be tested. And it has.

Numerous studies have found that prayer has no effect on the health of those named in the prayer. One well-known example is the Therapeutic Effects of Intercessory Prayer (STEP) study. Christian groups prayed for patients recovering from coronary artery bypasses at six U.S. hospitals. They prayed for some patients, but not others. The test was double-blind, which means that neither the patients nor the medical staff knew which patients were the targets of the prayers. The study found that there was no statistically significant difference in complication rates between those patients for whom prayers were said and the others.[1]

Apologists may try to excuse their god's failure by citing Jesus's admonition, "Do not put the Lord your God to the test" (Matthew 4:7). But the only rationale suggested there (and in its antecedents, Deuteronomy 6:16 and Exodus 17:2) is the general sense that doubt itself is a weakness. To follow this rule would be to shut down rational inquiry. A religion confident of its god ought to relish opportunities to showcase his steadfastness.

Yahweh, in fact, had not always shied away from tests. In a competition with rival god Baal, he responded to Elijah's supplications by incinerating a sacrificial bull and ending a drought (1 Kings 18:19-46).

There is no evidence that those who pray to a particular god heal better or more quickly than those who pray to other gods. Given comparable medical treatment, Christians do not heal better or faster than Hindus or Muslims. If any one of the gods to whom people pray actually provided the slightest therapeutic advantage, there would be a medical stampede to his banner.

Christians with vague illnesses sometimes claim to be cured by prayer. This should come as no surprise given the well-known power of suggestion to alleviate symptoms, at least temporarily. But there is no case where an unambiguous illness has been cured by prayer. For example, the Christian god has never caused a human amputee's limb to grow back. Why not?

The efficacy of Christian prayer is tested every day and every night. Thousands of devout amputees pray in vain to the god who promised them "whatever you ask for in prayer." And not only amputees. Prayerful Christians suffer and die from traumatic injuries or terrible diseases every day and every night. This massive, systematic, globally observed failure of prayer tells us that Jesus was wrong and Christianity is proven false.

18

MIRACLES

Christianity teaches that Jesus performed miracles, that he altered the normal operation of natural laws. The authors of the gospels adorned his career with these feats, ranging from the private and compassionate to the public and conspicuous. Jesus's miracles are important because they serve to demonstrate, for some Christians at least, that he was indeed who he said he was.

There are serious difficulties, however, with accepting the gospel miracle stories at face value. (While this chapter discusses miracles generally, the resurrection, the most important miracle, is examined further in chapter 30.)

First, other religions make miracle claims too. Why should we believe those of Christianity and disbelieve the others? Second, if miracles are meant to foster belief, then why do we not have any in our own time? Instead, we are expected to content ourselves with secondhand reports from prescientific Middle Easterners. Third, the lack of originality in Jesus's miracles reinforces the suspicion that they are simply tall tales consistent with and indeed emerging from the local culture. Let's review each of these points in greater depth.

The first difficulty is that many religions celebrate miracles. What makes those of Christianity special or true? Consider some of the miracle claims of Buddhism and Islam.

According to The Divyavadana, a brutal king ordered his soldiers to cut off a man's hands and feet. The Buddha dispatched one of his disciples, Ananda, to heal him. In front of a large marketplace crowd, Ananda uttered the words the Buddha had given him, and the man's hands and feet were restored.[1]

At Sravasti, the Buddha touched the ground with his foot and created a great earthquake, following which the sun and moon blazed simultaneously, and lotuses fell from the sky. He levitated and emanated a rainbow of light from his body. Then he shot flames from one part of his body and at the same time issued a shower of water from another. He sat upon a lotus and multiplied himself so that his many selves formed a chain skyward that could be seen from anywhere in the world. Some of these selves sat while others stood or walked about; some created fire and rain; others instructed the open-mouthed onlookers in the four noble truths.[2]

The foundational miracle of Islam is Mohammed's dictation of the Koran. An unlettered man, Mohammed was visited by the angel Jibrael, who commanded him to recite. Over the following years, he was periodically inspired anew, and his followers committed his words to writing.

Mohammed engaged in at least one other miracle. According to the Koran, Allah took him for a journey by night from Mecca to Jerusalem.[3] The hadith, collections of oral traditions about Mohammed, add the details that he rode the winged steed Buraq to Jerusalem, where he met the other prophets, including Moses and Jesus, and finally ascended to heaven to receive instructions from Allah himself.[4]

Are these stories about the Buddha and Mohammed true? If one is obliged to accept Jesus's miracles as true, then why is one not similarly obliged in the case of the Buddha and Mohammed?

Conversely, if untrue stories about the Buddha and Mohammed could arise without factual basis, then why couldn't untrue stories about Jesus arise in the same manner?

Witnesses do not appear to be the decisive factor. The Book of Mormon, for example, boasts eleven witnesses to its unusual provenance. Allegedly composed by ancient sages and edited by the prophet Mormon on gold plates, it was buried by his son, Moroni. Fourteen hundred years later, Moroni, by that time an angel, appeared to a young farmer named Joseph Smith, told him where to find the plates, and instructed him to translate them into English. (Unfortunately for forensic science, Smith returned the plates to Moroni after translating them.)

Three witnesses, Oliver Cowdery, David Whitmer, and Martin Harris, testified that an angel had shown them the golden plates and, furthermore, that god had commanded them to bear witness that the plates had been translated by his power. Eight other witnesses, Christian Whitmer, Jacob Whitmer, Peter Whitmer Jr., John Whitmer, Hiram Page, Joseph Smith Sr., Hyrum Smith, and Samuel H. Smith, testified that they personally had held some of the plates that Smith was translating.[5]

Despite this cornucopia of named witnesses, most Christians are unpersuaded that the Book of Mormon bears a heavenly imprimatur. Christian belief in certain miracles but not others appears, therefore, to be nothing more than the leg irons of social conditioning and cultural prejudice against other equally valid claims.

Rather than believe that the miracles of one religion are true and those of others are false, it appears that a common factor is at work in all of them: human beings want heroes and are prone to embroider their exploits. When these stories originate in prescientific settings, we should not be surprised to find deeds in which the laws of nature are defied or bent to the will of the hero. The minting of heroes, a universal human practice, constitutes a completely naturalistic explanation for the origin of miracle stories.

The second difficulty with Christian miracles is that they occurred long ago, and we are expected to believe in them without witnessing them for ourselves. It is highly suspicious that miracles would occur in a time of great ignorance and superstition but evaporate in an era of literacy, education, and science.

While the Christian god stopped performing miracles upon his departure two thousand years ago, he could have devised a mechanism by which to continue. In fact, according to Matthew 10:1-4 and John 14:12, Jesus empowered his apostles to carry on performing miracles. This practice could have been extended from generation to generation so that no historical epoch or geographic region was deprived of the necessary demonstrations.

Given our literacy, education, and science, modern people would be even more appreciative of miracles than the people of ancient times, when conjurors and faith healers abounded. We stand ready to put literacy, education, and science in the service of recording, investigating, and publicizing miracles. We stand ready to be awestruck. But the miracles have dried up.

Ironically, Jesus understood this problem. Why didn't he simply tell people that he could perform miracles rather than actually perform them? He told us, "Unless you people see signs and wonders . . . you will never believe" (John 4:48). In other words, Jesus knew that simply telling people would not foster belief. They must see for themselves. And yet, according to Christian teaching, we are expected to believe in these miracles simply because the authors of the gospels told us so.

Why would the Christian god stop performing miracles, knowing as he does that we "will never believe" without seeing them for ourselves? In the absence of the prescribed miracles, contemporary Christian evangelism fails to meet the evidentiary standards set by Jesus himself.

The third difficulty with Jesus's miracles is that they are unimpressive for a cosmic creator. They might be worthy of a minor deity or a demigod at best. Many are simply Jewish hand-me-downs. For example, both of the prophets Elijah and Elisha cured lepers, multiplied food, and resurrected the dead.* One would think that the infinitely inventive creator of the cosmos could have come up with a few miracles that were both original and impossible to counterfeit rather than simply rehash those commonly expected within the local culture. For a cosmic creator, Jesus's miracles are startlingly mundane. Why not appear to all humans, living and dead, simultaneously? Why not show heaven to everyone together or rewind time to demonstrate the creation?

The conformity of Jesus's miracles, or at least some of them, to the expectations of the local culture supports a naturalistic explanation for their origins. If, as appears to be the case, his earliest followers deemed him something less than the all-powerful creator of the cosmos, then the provinciality of his miracles makes sense. Jesus may have established his reputation, commonly enough, as that of a faith healer. This reputation was then embellished as time passed. In fact, the earliest gospel may preserve a shard of precisely this tradition. We are told that Jesus was unable to perform miracles in his hometown of Nazareth: "He could not do any miracles there, except lay his hands on a few sick people and heal them" (Mark 6:5). In other words, those who knew him before he was famous were the least impressed and least inclined to embellish his accomplishments. This is what one might expect to find beneath the progressive development of a legend.

---

* Lepers: 2 Kings 4:13; 2 Kings 5:10-14; food: 1 Kings 17:14-16; 2 Kings 4:3-6, 42-44; resurrecting the dead: 1 Kings 17:21; 2 Kings 4:32.

Jesus's emulation of Elijah and Elisha served the purpose of situating him within the Jewish prophetic tradition. The social context of Jesus's miracles brings out a further point. Compare the positive expectation of miracles in the case of Jesus, discussed above, with the negative expectation in the case of Mohammed. According to the Koran, Mohammed's primary function was that of a messenger, not a miracle worker. "The disbelievers say, 'Why has no miracle been sent down to him by his Lord?' But you are only there to give warning."[6] Nevertheless, the hadith contains stories of Mohammed performing miracles. In one, he issued water from his fingers so that his followers could drink and wash before prayers. In another, he caused the earth to spit up the corpse of a man who had insulted him. In another, he split the moon into two.[7]

These examples illustrate the tendency of uneducated storytellers to ascribe miracles to their heroes. In the case of the hadith, people ascribed miracles to Mohammed despite clear scriptural instruction that he did not perform them. In the case of the gospels, on the other hand, people were encouraged by Jewish tradition to expect miracles. A tendency to ascribe them to Jesus under these circumstances would be unsurprising.

In summary, Christianity celebrates Jesus's miracles but dismisses similarly attested miracles in other religions. It trumpets miracles that occurred long ago, in a time of eye-bulging superstition, but overlooks their convenient absence now, when they can be properly investigated. All of this is as unnecessary as it is unwarranted. The tendency of uneducated storytellers to ascribe miracles to their heroes provides a straightforward naturalistic explanation for the origins of these tales.

19

PROPHECIES

Christianity teaches that Jesus's life and death were prophesied, that is, predicted on the basis of divine disclosure, many years beforehand. Specifically, Jesus is said to have fulfilled Old Testament prophecies regarding a "messiah."

For centuries, Jews had looked back on the reign of King David as a golden age. They longed for the emergence of a hero, a messiah, who would throw off foreign oppression and reestablish Davidic greatness. Some prophets spoke of supernatural events that would inaugurate this era.

All kings and high priests of ancient Israel had ceremonial oil sprinkled on their heads to mark their assumption of responsibilities, a process that became known as anointing. The Old Testament was written (mostly) in Hebrew, and the Hebrew word for "anointed" is *messiah*. The New Testament was written in Greek, and the Greek word for "anointed" is *christ*. While some Jews still await the messiah, Christians contend that this was Jesus. As his movement expanded into the Greek-speaking world, *christ* became the customary honorific.

Before we assess claims about Jesus specifically, there are preliminary difficulties with the belief that the Old Testament, or any book, contains divinely disclosed predictions of the future. First and most generally, why would a god trouble himself with such disclosures? A fascination with prophecies, oracles, and divination is characteristic of many primitive cultures, including that of first-century Palestine. But an all-powerful deity could find a better means to communicate. Divine prophecy entails selecting one individual and communicating with others through him. Such a communication system is slow, open to misinterpretation, and susceptible to skepticism. An omnipotent deity could simultaneously communicate with perfect clarity to all humans whenever he chose.

Second, the Old Testament predicts nothing that could not have been imagined by a member of a 2,500-year-old herding culture. It is silent on the main contours of subsequent human history: the expansion of China during the Han Dynasty, the unification and flowering of India under the Guptas, the Columbian Exchange and the destruction of the Amerindian empires, the scientific method and the industrial revolution, the germ theory of medicine and the doubling of human life expectancy. These are world-changing events, and their omission reveals human rather than divine authorship.

And yet some Christians claim to find numerous prophecies that Jesus fulfilled. How can that be? There are two primary explanations: selective interpretation of the Old Testament by Christian readers and deliberate matching of it by the gospel writers.

Some readers of the Old Testament see patterns that they are predisposed to see, cherry-pick phrases that fit, and ignore those that do not. This is another example of confirmation bias, discussed in chapter 17. For example, Hebrews 10:5-7 asserts that Psalm 40:6-8 is a prophecy of Jesus. But two problems become immediately apparent. The first is that Psalm 40 is not a prophecy at all. It is simply a prayer of thanks for past support and a request that it continue. The second problem is the selectivity of the Christian analysis. The speaker says, "I desire to do your will, my God" (40:8). According to Christianity, this is Jesus speaking. But a few lines later, the speaker says, "My sins have overtaken me" (40:12). According to Christianity, which maintains that Jesus was sinless, this is no longer Jesus speaking.

It is easy to see what is going on here. An Old Testament passage that does not contain a prophecy is excerpted selectively and then paired with something Jesus may have said or done or thought. The pairing is then touted as a fulfillment of prophecy by Jesus. Those who encourage such readings are the architects of a house of mirrors in which the faithful see reflections of what they expect to find, or are told to look for.

The second explanation for the apparent abundance of prophecies is that, in many cases, New Testament writers intentionally fashioned their stories to echo the Old Testament. The gospel writers wanted to tell a story that, as far as they were concerned, conveyed theological truth. But their sources were oral accounts of varying quality and completeness. Each of these accounts probably lacked certain elements and at the same time contained elements that conflicted with those in other accounts. The writers may have responded by selecting those details, and inventing others, that supported their message.

An example is Jesus's entry into Jerusalem. The Old Testament prophet Zechariah had written, "See, your king comes to you, righteous and victorious, lowly and riding on a donkey, on a colt, the foal of a donkey" (Zechariah 9:9). It would have been simple for the author of Mark to read Zechariah and incorporate this humble means of transport into his story. And according to Mark 11:2-7, Jesus entered Jerusalem in precisely this manner. The authors of Luke and John later followed Mark's lead (Luke 19:30-35 and John 12:14).

But suspicion that the detail is based on the prophecy rather than on actual events swells to likelihood upon a reading of Matthew. Its author betrays the fact that he was reading the prophecy because he misunderstood it and tried to correct Mark's version of the story. Zechariah's third line ("on a colt, the foal of a donkey") is a poetic repetition of the second line, not a reference to an additional beast.[1] But the author of Matthew wrote that Jesus instructed his disciples to find him both a donkey and her colt. As a result, the gospel of Matthew contradicts the other gospels, and its Jesus entered the city atop two animals simultaneously, in what one can only imagine was some rodeo-like manner (Matthew 21:7).

For those interested in an additional example discussed in depth, see appendix 3. One of the most celebrated Old Testament prophecies is that of the "suffering servant" of Isaiah 53. While Christianity maintains that this is a prophecy of Jesus, the text better supports a prophecy of triumph for the righteous minority among the exiled Judahites returning to Jerusalem after the Babylonian exile.

While Christianity finds or manufactures convenient prophecies where there are none, it also commits the reciprocal offense of redefining or simply ignoring inconvenient prophecies that really exist.

Biographical details about the messiah may be interesting, but they miss the big picture. What is significant about the messiah is the set of changes he is supposed to bring to the world. These are massive, unmistakable changes, including world peace (Isaiah 2:4, Micah 4:3), universal knowledge of the one true god (Zechariah 14:9, Isaiah 11:9), and the return of all the Jews, including the lost tribes, to Palestine (Isaiah 11:12, Jeremiah 33:7, Ezekiel 36:24, 37:21-22). Notice that none of these events occurred during the time of Jesus. It is no wonder that those who knew the most about Jewish prophecies, the Jews, didn't think Jesus was a messiah.

Christianity claims that the advertised world changes will occur at something called a "second coming." But isn't it convenient that the prophecies that have allegedly been fulfilled (the biographical details) are those we cannot verify and the prophecies that we can verify (the world changes) have not yet been fulfilled? From this it seems likely that the biographical details are not historical fact at all but merely pious invention.

The apologetic assertion that Jesus will fulfill the messiah's tasks upon a second coming is self-parodying. Such an assertion could be made about anyone: George Washington could be the messiah. Sure, he wasn't much bothered by Palestine during his administrations nor was he descended from David, but just wait till next time. He will do all of those things at his second coming. Unfortunately for Christianity, there is nothing in the Old Testament that says the messiah will come twice. Everyone will know when the messiah comes, and he won't need two tries to get it right.

While the house of mirrors distorts the above prophecies into wishes that recede forever before the faithful, it obscures others that flatly contradict Christian doctrine. A clear example of the latter is the set of prophecies by Jeremiah, Ezekiel, Zechariah, and Third Isaiah discussed in chapter 5, which describe animal sacrifice after the coming of the messiah. To maintain the doctrine that Jesus was a once-and-for-all sacrifice, Christianity must either ignore these prophecies or aggressively reinterpret them.

In summary, not only is the idea of prophecy a vestige of humankind's childhood, but Christianity is abusively selective in its application. Apologists find prophecies where they do not exist and ignore real ones where they are doctrinally inconvenient. It is fitting then to close this survey of flaws in Christian doctrine by attending to a promise straight from the mouth of the Christian god himself, the greatest prophecy of them all.

20

SECOND COMING

Christianity teaches that its god will return to planet earth someday. Two thousand years ago, Jesus promised a glorious return—within a generation. He said to his listeners, "Some who are standing here will not taste death before they see that the kingdom of God has come with power" (Mark 9:1) and "Some who are standing here will not taste death before they see the Son of Man coming in his kingdom" (Matthew 16:28).

He was wrong. In an attempt to avoid the obvious conclusion, some Christians have tried to argue that Jesus's return meant his transfiguration or his post-resurrection appearances. Still others have claimed that what Jesus meant by the coming kingdom was the establishment of his church, which occurred at the Feast of the Pentecost, about fifty days after his resurrection.

But these arguments are contradicted by Jesus's own description of his return and the events preceding it. His disciples asked, "When will this happen and what will be the sign of your coming and of the end of the age?" Jesus replied, "Nation will rise against nation . . . the sun will be darkened, and the moon will not give its light; the stars will fall from the sky, and the heavenly bodies will be shaken . . . All the peoples of the earth will . . . see the Son of Man coming on the clouds of heaven with power and great glory. And he will send his angels with a loud trumpet call, and they will gather his elect from the four winds, from one end of the heavens to the other . . . this generation will certainly not pass away until all these things have happened" (Matthew 24:3-34).

These apocalyptic events did not occur prior to the transfiguration or post-resurrection appearances. Nor did they occur during the fifty days preceding Pentecost or at any other time in the two thousand years since Jesus predicted them. In a final attempt to salvage Jesus's credibility, some argue that time has a different meaning to a god and that a thousand years to a human can be like a day to a god. But this is irrelevant because Jesus was not speaking to gods; he was speaking to human beings. If Jesus were an omniscient deity, or even a wise human, he would not have made such an egregious prophecy.

It is only in the context of Jesus's mistaken belief in a looming apocalypse that we can understand some of his more bizarre moral injunctions. Only if the world were ending at any moment would it make sense to say, "Do not worry about tomorrow, for tomorrow will worry about itself" (Matthew 6:34). Jesus's teaching here is the apex of irresponsibility. It means do not plan or prepare, do not save or invest, do not build or plant, do not study or educate. Even most Christians disregard this teaching, knowing as they do that there is no reason to expect the world to end imminently.

As Albert Schweitzer famously pointed out, Jesus's failed prophecy was not an aberrant remark but at the core of his message.[1] The very first words Jesus utters in the first gospel to be written are, "The time has come. The kingdom of God has come near. Repent and believe the good news" (Mark 1:15). When he dispatches his apostles, he tells them, "You will not finish going through the towns of Israel before the Son of Man comes" (Matthew 10:23). Jesus's forerunner, John the Baptist, was possessed by the same idea, teaching, "Repent, for the kingdom of heaven has come near . . . the ax is already at the root of the trees" (Matthew 3:2-10). John the Baptist and Jesus were by no means unique in making such predictions. They were in this respect representative of Jewish apocalyptic thinkers.

The term "apocalypse" comes from a Greek word meaning an "uncovering" or "revelation." Apocalypticism was a current of religious thought circulating among Jews during the last centuries BCE. It was a new response to the old problem of suffering.

Earlier in Israel's history, the explanation for suffering had been straightforward. If there is suffering, then Yahweh must intend it. It is punishment for sin. This applied both to individuals and to nations. Because the Israelites were one people bound to their god by covenant, they tended to assume a notion of "corporate guilt," that if enough individuals transgress, then the society as a whole will be punished. This view was dominant throughout most of the Old Testament. The classical prophets, such as Amos, Hosea, Jeremiah, and Isaiah, had taught that Israel suffered because its god was punishing it for wrongdoing, typically turning away from his commandments or toward other gods.

During the postexilic period, however, many thinkers found this view unsatisfying. They did not think it applied to the current state of affairs. They did not see rampant impiety that deserved to be punished. Why then did Israel suffer?

Imbibing ideas from the dominant religion of Persia, Zoroastrianism, some Jewish thinkers of this era developed an alternative to the classical view of suffering. This was cosmic dualism, mentioned in chapter 4, the belief that good and evil supernatural powers are locked in an all-pervading struggle. On this view, undeserved suffering could be explained as the work of evil powers. Israel suffered not because its god was punishing it for being sinful, but because evil powers resented its righteousness.

But cosmic dualism led to a different problem: if their god were all-powerful, why would he allow evil to exist and even appear to be winning? The solution was to claim that the apparent success of evil is only temporary. God will soon intervene to defeat it, abolish suffering, and inaugurate a new age. His dramatic intervention will be an apocalypse. If cosmic dualism provided an explanation for the existence of evil and suffering, then apocalypticism provided the promise of their ultimate defeat.

Closely allied with the idea of an apocalypse are two other ideas: judgment after death and resurrection. When the apocalypse comes, many will already have died. Where is their justice? A judgment after death provides the opportunity for justice undone in life to be done in an afterlife. But in order to implement this process, individuals must be available for judgment and the meting out of rewards and punishments. Therefore, a resurrection of the dead is needed. At the apocalypse, those who have already died will be resurrected and judged along with those still living. Those judged favorably will gain access to god's kingdom, and the rest will be punished.[2]

Based on his own comments, Jesus believed that the apocalypse was imminent. His prediction of it, quoted above, is almost identical in Mark 13:3-31, Matthew 24:3-34, and Luke 21:7-33. Interestingly, it is completely absent in John. Why? Writing years after the first three gospels, the author of John was obviously aware that the predicted events had never come to pass. The failure of Jesus's personally prophesied second coming is clear disconfirmation of his divinity and of the religion created in his wake.

PART 2

Evidence

21

BASELINE

It is part of the background knowledge of every educated man and woman that humans have a tendency to invent deities. It is appropriate, therefore, to examine historical claims about deities with greater scrutiny than historical claims about more commonplace topics. Religions have a track record of making false claims, and religious people know this because they are often among the most skeptical . . . of the claims of other people's religions.

Elements of the Jesus story were mythological themes common in the ancient Mediterranean world long before Christianity. Did Christianity borrow any of its component beliefs from earlier religions? If it did, then it is, to that extent, a human construction. If it did not, then why would the real god choose to reveal himself in a manner that so closely resembled that of earlier false ones?

This chapter discusses three popular elements of the Jesus story from this perspective: the virgin birth, the winter solstice birthday, and the resurrection. As will be shown, there is good reason to suspect that Christianity borrowed the first two of these from its pagan predecessors. The case of the resurrection is more complicated. It grew out of Jewish apocalypticism, not pagan religion. But pagan ideas would shape the interpretation of what a resurrection might mean.

Divine birth

The ancient Mediterranean world teemed with great men said to have been the offspring of one human and one divine parent. For example, King Minos was the offspring of the god Zeus and the human woman Europa. The Dioscouri twins were the offspring of Zeus and Leda. The Mesopotamian god-man Gilgamesh was the offspring of the goddess Ninsun and Lugalbanda. The Greek hero Achilles was the offspring of the goddess Thetis and Peleus. The Trojan hero Aeneas was the offspring of Venus and Anchises.

In some cases, the divine union involved a human female who was a virgin. This is true of the Greek hero Perseus and the founder of Rome, Romulus. While a divine union and virgin mother were not uncommon, the later and entirely asexual conception of Jesus extended the idea to its logical terminus.

A divine or otherwise miraculous birth is usually found alongside certain additional story elements. Together, they constitute a "hero archetype" in which the protagonist undergoes standard experiences, many of which will be familiar to gospel readers. These include a miraculous birth, prophecy, an attempt to kill the infant, tests or trials at the outset of a career, and ascension at its conclusion. Of course, not every story followed the pattern exactly. Three pertinent examples follow.

The pre-Christian writers Ovid, Cicero, and Dionysius of Halicarnassus tell this story: Romulus was the offspring of the god Mars and the human virgin Rhea Silvia. King Amulius had usurped the throne, killing the rightful king's sons and sequestering his daughter, Rhea Silvia, with the Vestal Virgins in order to prevent the birth of a rival. She nevertheless caught the amorous attention of Mars. He impregnated her and she bore twin sons, Romulus and Remus. Amulius ordered the infants drowned, but their raft floated to safety where they were suckled by a wolf. They grew to manhood, eventually restoring their grandfather to the throne. Romulus founded the city which bears his name, and at the end of his life, he ascended in a cloud. Later, he appeared to a follower with instructions for the Roman people.[1]

The pre-Christian writers Homer, Ovid, and Pindar tell this story: King Acrisius heard a prophecy that a grandson would kill him. To preempt this possibility, he locked up his only daughter, the virgin Danae, in a bronze chamber. But Zeus impregnated her in the form of a golden rain. In due course, Perseus was born. Acrisius ordered mother and son packed into a wooden crate and dropped into the sea. Miraculously, they survived, and Perseus grew to adulthood. His greatest deed, achieved with the aid of Athena and Hermes, was to slay the fearsome gorgon Medusa. Later, he killed Acrisius in a sporting accident, thereby fulfilling the dreaded prophecy.[2]

The pre-Christian writers Ovid, Euripides, and Pindar tell this story: Hercules was the offspring of Zeus and Alcmene (not a virgin in this case). Zeus's jealous wife, Hera, sent two snakes to kill the infant, but he succeeded in strangling them instead. The prophet Teiresias told Alcmene that her son would someday be a hero to all Greece, a prophecy that would be borne out by his remarkable career. When he died, he ascended to Olympus. There, he married Hebe, the daughter of Hera, and lives as an immortal.[3]

These examples of the hero archetype raise a couple of questions. First, why should we disbelieve the stories about these other god-men but believe the stories about Jesus? If their untrue stories could arise in the absence of fact, couldn't untrue stories about Jesus arise in the same manner?

Second, did the Jesus story borrow from predecessors such as these? For example, the earliest Christian writings, those of Paul and Mark, do not mention a virgin birth. This suggests that it was a late addition to Jesus's resume. Might there be some historical explanation for this amendment? During Christianity's early decades, its initial Jewish majority was gradually overtaken by gentiles. These new converts, former pagans, would have been familiar with the virgin births of Perseus and Romulus. They might have expected and insisted that their new god-man boast an equally auspicious beginning.

Winter solstice birthday

Long before Jesus, the idea that a certain time of year is most propitious for the birth of a god had impressed itself upon humankind. The movement of the sun is a fundamental element of the mythic imagination, and the winter solstice, the shortest day of the year (around December 25 in the northern hemisphere), is the most significant marker of seasonal rhythms. On that day, just as the sun and all life that depends upon it seem exhausted, the birth of a solar deity propels a new light. As the days lengthen, life returns to the world.

The Bible provides no date of birth for Jesus. While scholars have tried to calculate it from scriptural clues about the weather or religious festivals, they have not achieved any consensus. Christianity appears to have borrowed the winter solstice birthday (eventually naming it, in English, "Christ-mass") from the solar deities that dominated Roman religion during the second and third centuries. The most prominent of these were the Persian god Mithras and the Syrian god Sol Invictus, "The Invincible Sun." These two gods were sometimes depicted together as companions or alter egos.

Veneration of the sun, deified in various forms, had long been part of Roman religious observance.[4] This tradition flourished under Emperor Aurelian (ruled 270-275 CE), who established the Invincible Sun as the primary god of the Roman state religion and fixed a great public celebration on his December 25 birthday.[5]

Whereas the Invincible Sun enjoyed state sponsorship and was publicly worshipped, Mithras was worshipped privately as a mystery religion. Mithras too was born on December 25.[6] The firmament above, many ancients believed, was comprised of solid ground that held the celestial bodies in place. And so, just as it was believed that sunlight emanates from a solid firmament, Mithras was believed to have been born out of a rock.

Mithras's great deed was slaying the cosmic bull, whose blood fertilized the earth. After the slaying, Mithras feasted upon the bull and then ascended in a chariot. Among the Mithraic rituals was a eucharist in which followers consumed bread and wine, symbolizing the flesh and blood of the bull. This ritual imitation of the god facilitated the salvation of the participant's soul.[7] Interestingly, Tarsus, Paul's birthplace (if we believe Acts 22), appears to have been a center of Mithraic worship in the first and second centuries before the time of Jesus.[8]

Whereas the gospel writers were uninterested in the date of Jesus's birth, it became important to Christians precisely at the time when the worship of solar deities was at its peak in Rome. The first mention of the Christian Christmas in any surviving document is from 336 CE, but it may have originated up to a century earlier.[9]

The adoption of the winter solstice as Jesus's birthday enabled Christianity to assimilate the powerful image of the sun's annual resurrection into its own symbolic narrative. At the same time, it enabled Christianity to compete for popular favor with pagan solstice celebrations, such as the state-sponsored *Natalis Solis Invicti*, "Feast of the Birth of the Sun," and the crowd-pleasing festivals of Brumalia and Saturnalia.

Resurrection

The third element of the Jesus story that was common in the ancient Mediterranean is the resurrection. The question of Jesus's resurrection as an actual historical event is discussed in chapter 30. Here, the focus is on the idea; and once again, it existed long before Christianity.

The Egyptian god Osiris, the Canaanite god Baal, the Babylonian god Tammuz, and the Greek gods Dionysus, Persephone, and Asclepius all either died and rose or travelled to the afterlife and returned.[10] Their stories, documented long before the time of Jesus, are summarized in appendix 4. With the exception of the great healer, Asclepius, these gods began as personifications of natural forces, the annual vegetative cycle in particular. Osiris and Dionysus, for example, associated respectively with grain and grapes, died by being torn to pieces, which symbolizes the threshing of grain and the trampling of grapes.

Some of these gods gave rise to mystery religions. Though much of their practice was secret, their core teaching appears to have been that those properly initiated could hope to imitate or somehow participate in the triumph of the god.[11] Mithraism, discussed above, offered the possibility of the soul's ascent, mirroring the ascent of Mithras himself. Those mysteries grounded in the vegetative cycle—those of Osiris, Dionysus, and Persephone—reinterpreted the god's death and resurrection. Instead of an explanation for seasonal growth and decay, the stories came to symbolize the promise of life after death for humans.[12]

Of the mysteries of Osiris, Herodotus wrote in circa 440 BCE, "On this lake they hold, at night, an exhibition of the god's sufferings, a performance that the Egyptians call the Mysteries. I know more about each element of these, but let me hold my peace."[13] Cicero wrote in circa 50 BCE of the mysteries of Demeter and Persephone (the Eleusinian mysteries), "Nothing is higher than these mysteries . . . They have not only taught us to live joyfully, but they have taught us how to die with a better hope."[14] The mystery cult of Dionysus was not always well received. Alarmed by allegations of impropriety, the Roman Senate in 186 BCE forcefully suppressed its practice in Rome.[15] Nevertheless, a couple centuries later Plutarch would remind his wife that the rites of Dionysus taught the immortality of the soul.[16]

Some of these pagan gods were known to and even worshipped by the ancient Israelites. See, for example, Tammuz in Ezekiel 8:14 and Baal in Numbers 25:3. But the resurrection idea was slow to gain traction among the Jews. The first possible biblical references are prophecies in Isaiah 26:19 and Ezekiel 37:1-14. Read in context, however, both of these references are metaphors for the restoration of the Jewish nation. The prophets were communicating their god's intention to restore it after crushing defeats by the Assyrians in 722 BCE (in the case of First Isaiah) and the Babylonians in 587 BCE (in the case of Ezekiel).[17]

As discussed earlier, the first biblical hint of a resurrection of individuals comes in the apocalyptic book of Daniel. Jewish thought, during the final centuries BCE, when Daniel was written, had been heavily influenced by apocalypticism. Apocalyptic thinkers anticipated a coming judgment in which righteous individuals would be resurrected and the unrighteous left behind in Sheol/Gehenna. By the time of Jesus, some Jews held a feverish expectation that the apocalypse was imminent.

While the original Jewish-Christians almost certainly interpreted the rumored resurrection of Jesus as the beginning of the apocalyptic resurrection of the righteous, this interpretation was reframed over time. Instead of saving only the righteous of Israel, resurrection would come to anyone initiated into the Jesus movement. When the requirement to follow the Jewish law was replaced by the doctrine of salvation by faith (see next chapter), Christianity discarded the least attractive aspect of Judaism and incorporated the most attractive aspect of the mystery religions. Christianity now had the best of both worlds: monotheism uncoupled from the law and the promise of an afterlife for those initiated into the faith.

A Mediterranean heritage

In summary, the virgin birth and winter solstice birthday were almost certainly syncretized into Christianity from earlier paganism. The resurrection probably came from Zoroastrianism via apocalyptic Judaism and was then reframed in terms of a mystery religion. All of this seems completely understandable in terms of stories and doctrine, created by human beings, evolving over time.

When Christianity was young, its followers found it necessary to defend their beliefs by acknowledging that they were not in fact much different from the older pagan traditions. Justin Martyr (circa 160 CE) exemplified this approach, writing for his Roman critics:

> And when we say also that the Word, who is the first-birth of God, was produced without sexual union, and that He, Jesus Christ, our Teacher, was crucified and died, and rose again, and ascended into heaven, *we propound nothing different from what you believe regarding those whom you esteem sons of Jupiter (Zeus).* For you know how many sons your esteemed writers ascribed to Jupiter: Mercury, the interpreting word and teacher of all; Aesculapius, who, though he was a great physician, was struck by a thunderbolt, and so ascended to heaven; and Bacchus (Dionysus) too, after he had been torn limb from limb; and Hercules, when he had committed himself to the flames to escape his toils; and the sons of Leda, the Dioscouri; and Perseus, son of Danae; and Bellerophon, who, though sprung from mortals, rose to heaven on the horse Pegasus (italics and parenthetical clarifications added).[18]

Even if Christianity borrowed nothing from earlier religions, the question remains: Why couldn't an infinitely inventive deity go about his business without resembling so closely all of these mythological predecessors? Why, when the "real deal" came along, did he not do so in a manner that successfully differentiated himself from these imposters?

This problem was not lost on Justin Martyr. Impelled to explain how a resurrected god, along with other elements of pagan religion, such as virgin births and eucharists, could have predated Christianity, he took an imaginative leap. He advanced the eyebrow-raising thesis that Satan had planted these beliefs in earlier cultures in order to create confusion.[19]

Justin's cosmic conspiracy theory is unpersuasive. To begin with, it suggests that the Christian devil outsmarted the Christian god. But an omniscient god would have anticipated Satan's plans and taken effective countermeasures. Moreover, if Justin's argument were true, then all religions, including Christianity, must be suspect. Christianity might be yet another of Satan's deceptions aimed at confusing humans in anticipation of the true god's revelation, which has not yet occurred.

There appear to be no good explanations, other than the obvious one, for why elements of Christianity should so closely resemble those of its pagan predecessors. There are gods and goddesses aplenty, religions routinely borrow from each another, and Christianity was not an exception. Given all of this, a skeptical approach to the evidence seems appropriate.

The heart of Christianity is Jesus's career and its sensational climax, but what we know about these things comes almost exclusively from Christian writings and early church tradition. Of the many contributors to the gradual emergence of a unique Christian scripture and doctrine, one man stands above all others in importance. The next group of chapters, devoted to the evidence provided by Christian writings, begins with him. Uncommonly situated at a cultural crossroads, he was a highly educated Jew, fluent in Greek, and a Roman citizen. Without him, Christianity might have forever remained nothing more than a breakaway Jewish sect.

22

PAUL

Christianity is not principally about what Jesus taught. It is principally about what happened to him and what other people said it meant. Paul's epistles (letters), written circa 50-60 CE, are the earliest surviving Christian writings, and his arguments formed the foundation upon which much of Christian theology was gradually erected.

Saul was his Jewish name and Paul, his Roman name. He never met Jesus, but he persecuted Jesus's early followers. Then suddenly, he underwent a dramatic conversion and became a follower himself. Like Jesus, he was an apocalypticist, preaching that the general resurrection and judgment were near. "Time is short . . . this world in its present form is passing away" (1 Corinthians 7:29-31). He may have expected to see it in his lifetime: "For the Lord himself will come down from heaven . . . we who are still alive and are left will be caught up together with them in the clouds to meet the Lord in the air" (1 Thessalonians 4:16-17).

Paul's most important contribution was the doctrine of salvation by faith. The practical effect of this doctrinal innovation was immense. It meant that non-Jews did not have to convert to

Judaism and follow the Jewish law in order to achieve salvation. While the earliest Christians were Jews, Paul came to see himself as the apostle to the gentiles. He was so successful that within several generations, what had begun as a Jewish sect would become a new religion increasingly unrecognizable to most Jews.

What evidence underpinned Paul's teachings? How did he come to possess the ideas that would prove so revolutionary? He had three sources: first, personal revelation; second, received oral tradition; and third, scriptural reinterpretation. Below is a discussion of each.

The most remarkable of his sources, and presumably the sovereign, was personal revelation. Paul never said how many he had, but it appears to have been quite a few. In this respect, he resembles Mohammed, who is also said to have received multiple revelations over a period of years. Paul's celebrated conversion on the road to Damascus involved some sort of revelatory vision of Jesus. He claims furthermore that his understanding of the gospel came directly from Jesus: "I did not receive it from any man, nor was I taught it; rather I received it by revelation from Jesus Christ" (Galatians 1:12). In other revelations, he apparently received specific instructions. For example, he wrote that he made his second visit to Jerusalem "in response to a revelation" (Galatians 2:1-2). He informs us that he even ascended to heaven on one occasion. There, he "heard inexpressible things, things that no one is permitted to tell" (2 Corinthians 12:1-6).

These revelations in Paul's letters constitute the only first-person eyewitness accounts of Jesus in the entire New Testament. Unfortunately, they are brief and give us little to work with. In his most extensive treatment of the subject, he wrote simply that god "was pleased to reveal his son in me" (Galatians 1:15-16). Later, he wrote, "Have I not seen Jesus our Lord?" (1 Corinthians 9:1) and "he appeared to me" (1 Corinthians 15:8).

His revelations were plainly a source of energy for Paul. They also served as his credentials as an apostle. After all, unlike the other leaders of the early church, Paul had never known Jesus in life. Finally, these revelations would enable subsequent generations of Christians to explain away gaps in Paul's reasoning. When Paul simply asserted something without logic or proof text, the faithful could conclude that it must have come directly from Jesus and therefore be true.

Concerning all of this, one must ask the most basic question: By what authority did Paul write? Or to put it more bluntly, why should anyone believe him? One of his claims was that he received revelations from Jesus. But to use this claim as authentication would be circular. His claim that he received revelations from Jesus cannot be the reason to accept his claims because it is one of those claims itself.

Nor does Christianity adduce reasons to believe Paul, even by its own standards of legitimation. For example, given a long tradition of prophecy, why was Paul's arrival not foretold? Why didn't Jesus tell his disciples that a man would come after him, a fellow Jew who had previously been hostile but who would be able to explain the significance of his imminent death and reinterpret the scriptures accordingly? In the gospels, the disciples often did not understand Jesus. Any one of these instances would have been an opportunity for Jesus to clarify the role he expected Paul to play. But according to Christianity's own source documents, this never happened.

Insofar as revelation was a source for Paul, his letters are on a par with the Koran. Muslims believe that Mohammed received revelation from Allah. Christians believe, in a like manner, that Paul received revelation from Jesus. The Christian belief is no better founded than the Muslim. Paul's claim to divine inspiration was simply one in a long list of unverifiable claims he made.

Paul's second source was received oral tradition. He would probably have heard this tradition from James and Peter during his first visit to Jerusalem, three years after his conversion. Three instances are particularly interesting: first, the list of Jesus's post-resurrection appearances (1 Corinthians 15:3-5); second, the institution of the eucharist (1 Corinthians 11:23-26); and third, the origins of Jesus's divinity (Romans 1:3-4). Many scholars believe that in these verses, Paul was writing down short creeds or hymns that the earliest pre-Pauline Christians repeated.[1]

Many aspects of the familiar Jesus story are missing from Paul's letters. He never wrote anything about a virgin birth, miraculous healings, parables, or an empty tomb. Either these aspects of the story did not yet exist or Paul did not think they were relevant to his purpose. Perhaps his audience already knew these things. Bear in mind also that his letters were written in response to particular problems, and he never aimed to set out a systematic list of Christian beliefs. On the other hand, Paul's silence combined with the absence of a virgin birth in the earliest gospel, Mark, reinforces the suspicion that that particular story element arose after Paul's time.

Paul's third source was scriptural reinterpretation. He articulated a new doctrine of salvation by faith: trusting that the god of Israel will accept Jesus's sacrifice on one's behalf. And he went further, claiming that salvation was available to anyone, Jew or gentile. These were startling conclusions for Paul, a Jew, to reach. Weren't the Jews god's chosen people? And wasn't following the law the path to righteousness?

Paul sought to justify his positions through creative exegesis of scripture. According to Genesis 18:18, "Abraham will surely become a great and powerful nation, and all nations on earth will be blessed through him." This had traditionally referred to Israel's special role in history to lead the rest of the world to the one true god. But Paul was looking for a way to accommodate the newly arriving gentiles within the Jesus movement. He needed a different perspective.

His breakthrough came upon a close rereading of Genesis 15:6. There, Yahweh credited Abraham with righteousness because Abraham believed him (a form of faith). Paul noticed that this was before Abraham was circumcised (a requirement of the law). He argued from this sequence of events that righteousness comes from faith and not from the law (Galatians 2:15-16).

Paul then extended eligibility to non-Jews. Genesis 12:7 and 13:15 state that god's blessing of Abraham extends to his "seed." Paul argued that this meant Jesus (Galatians 3:16). Then he argued that, through faith, Jesus's followers become one with him. As such, whether Jew or gentile, they participate in his blessing (Galatians 3:29).

Paul's conclusion, that righteousness comes from faith, raised an obvious question: if the law did not bring righteousness, then what had been its purpose? His answer: to teach humankind the standard of behavior that was expected and to convict it of an inability to meet that standard. "No one will be declared righteous in God's sight by the works of the law; rather, through the law we become conscious of our sin" (Romans 3:20).

Paul's use of scripture was, to put it politely, misleading. As shown below, his replacement of the law with faith remains difficult to square with common sense. The following are a half-dozen flaws in his argument:

First, a more straightforward explanation for Abraham's righteousness is provided. Yahweh stated that Abraham was blessed because he "obeyed me and did everything I required of him, keeping my commands, my decrees and my instructions" (Genesis 26:5). In other words, it was obedience to Yahweh's instructions, not faith, that made Abraham righteous. In pleading the opposite, Paul is unhorsed by his own cleverness. If his interpretation were correct, then it would *never* have been necessary to follow the law. If Abraham had been righteous simply for having faith in Yahweh, then anyone else could have been deemed righteous by the same standard. Any Jew during the previous one thousand years could have said, *"I have faith just like Abraham. I don't need to follow all these rules."*

Second, contrary to Paul's representations, Israel's god believed that humankind was capable of following the law. "Now what I am commanding you today is not too difficult for you or beyond your reach" (Deuteronomy 30:11). As shown in chapter 27, Paul misleadingly excerpted this verse in order to disguise Yahweh's expectation. Some Christians assume that following the law means being perfect. Since humans are not perfect, they cannot follow the law. But this is not what Israel's god had taught. Yahweh does not expect people to be perfect; the law makes allowance for those who err as long as they sincerely repent. "If my people . . . pray and seek my face and turn from their wicked ways, then . . . I will forgive their sin" (2 Chronicles 7:14). Paul's god loved David, for example, despite the king's crimes. The doctrine that the god of Abraham, Isaac, and Jacob demands perfection is not a message of the Jewish Bible/Old Testament, the scripture that Paul claimed to be consulting.

Third, there was no scriptural indication that the law needed to be nullified or even revised. It was not temporary. "I will establish my covenant as an everlasting covenant" (Genesis 17:7 and Ezekiel 37:26). It was a timeless blessing, not provisional or probationary. Nor was there any indication that it needed an overhaul. "The law of the Lord is perfect" (Psalm 19:7). To argue that Jesus's sacrifice had overthrown the law, Paul had to invert the traditional teaching that "to do what is right and just is more acceptable to the Lord than sacrifice" (Proverbs 21:3).

Fourth, accepting Paul's conclusion requires joining him in an extraordinary conceit. In Exodus 19-20, Israel's god established the law before the entire assembled nation. If it had been his intention to nullify it, why would he not have done so in a similar manner? Jesus's earliest followers certainly did not believe the law had been nullified. They continued to observe it after his death, as is apparent from the "Jerusalem Council" controversy in Acts 15. Paul would have us believe that the god of Israel decided to nullify the law, but that he, Paul, was the only one who was able to figure this out, a quarter century after the fact.

Fifth, the provinciality of Paul's explanation for the law undermines his universal message. He claimed that the thousand-year period during which Israel was under the law constituted tutelage in god's expectations. But why did this god restrict his tutelage to the Jews? Why not give the law to all humankind? After all, Christianity is meant to be universal. If the law were preparatory for the gospel, then according to Paul's logic, only the Jews would have been ready for Jesus. The rest of humankind had yet to satisfy the prerequisite. To make matters worse, his god's tutelary scheme backfired because most Jews did not follow Jesus but remained obedient to the law instead.

Sixth, Paul's argument that Abraham's blessing flowed to Jesus, and then to his followers, is fallacious. The traditional understanding of the term "Abraham's seed" was that of a collective noun, a description of the Jewish people as a whole. In fact, Paul himself used the term in that very manner in Romans 4:13 (Greek, σπερμα, written in English as *sperma*). By arguing in Galatians 3:16 that it referred to Jesus, Paul gave the same term two different definitions.

Finally, Paul's claim that through faith followers somehow become mystically united with Jesus lacks a scriptural basis. He simply asserts it. The belief that a human being could defeat death by becoming one with a god who defeats death is without precedent in the Jewish scriptures and is likely an import from the mystery religions. Paul's description of baptism sounds like ritual imitation of the god's suffering and triumph: "We were therefore buried with him through baptism into death . . . For if we have been united with him in a death like his, we will certainly also be united with him in a resurrection like his" (Romans 6:4-5).

For reasons such as these, Jews familiar with their scripture would not likely have found Paul persuasive. But gentiles who respected the people of Moses constituted a ready market. They were no doubt impressed by this impassioned man who appeared so knowledgeable about his ancient, venerable monotheism and its most recent revelation.

Many gentiles were already attracted to the ethical monotheism of the Jews, as evidenced by the large number of "god-fearers," gentiles who worshipped with the Jews but did not follow all aspects of the law, such as circumcision. One can almost hear the conversation. *"What you messiah-followers say sounds good, Paul. I'd sign up right now, if only I didn't have to chop off a piece of my penis to join."* With his innovative teaching that faith in Jesus had replaced the law, Paul eliminated one of monotheism's highest barriers to entry.

23

ORAL TRADITION

The Christian writer C. S. Lewis, referring to the story that Jesus proclaimed himself divine, famously remarked that this leaves us with three alternatives. We can conclude that Jesus was either a liar, a lunatic, or lord.[1] Unfortunately, he omitted the most obvious choice: legend. If this fourth possibility exists, then we cannot be certain of anything that Jesus is claimed to have said or done.

Where did the gospels come from? They were born of a first-century Jewish oral tradition. Just as Paul's letters can be compared to the Koran, the gospels can be compared to the hadith, the collection of oral stories about Mohammed.

The gospels were composed long after the events they purport to describe. They are anonymous, and they do not claim to be written by eyewitnesses. Let's review each of these facts in turn.

There is a substantial time gap between the gospels and the events they describe. Jesus is said to have died circa 30 CE. The gospel of Mark was written circa 60-75, Matthew and Luke circa 80-90, and John circa 90-100.[2] Generally, the intervention of decades between an event and its documentation permits loss of memory, distortions, and fabrications to enter the record and, for that reason, is cause for skepticism.

All four gospels are anonymous. The earliest manuscripts have no bylines, no signatures, and no titles. The attribution of authorship with which we are familiar was established by the church in the late second century.[3] As a rule, anonymity detracts from credibility because we do not know the qualifications or motivations of the writer.

The gospels do not claim to be written by eyewitnesses. All four gospels were written in the third person, not the first person. And all four were written in Greek, not Aramaic—the language commonly spoken at the time and place of the alleged events.

The traditional Christian view is that Mark was a secretary or translator for the apostle Peter; Matthew was an apostle himself; Luke was a travelling companion of Paul; and John was also an apostle. The following is a discussion of each of these traditional attributions:

The claim that the author of Mark was a secretary to the apostle Peter comes, according to Eusebius (circa 320 CE), from Papias (circa 120 CE), who was quoting an unnamed church elder.[4] In enhancements to this claim, the identities of both the author and the unnamed elder are provided: the author is a character named John Mark, who appears in Acts 12-15, and the unnamed elder is the apostle John.

Both the basic claim and its more ambitious enhancements are doubtful. First, it is unlikely that Papias would have omitted the name of his source had he believed it to be none other than the apostle John. Given that he omitted the name, we are left with an anonymous starting point for our chain of attribution.

Second, the author of Mark appears unfamiliar with Palestine's geography. For example, he says that Jesus left Tyre and went through Sidon to Galilee (7:31). But Sidon is in the opposite direction. A native of Palestine, as John Mark is portrayed to have been, would not likely have confused the location of two of its major cities. The author also writes that a herd of pigs ran down a steep bank into the sea and drowned

(5:11-13). But the location of the episode, Gerasa, is over thirty miles from the sea. (An alternative manuscript reading is Gadara, but that site is still six miles from the sea.)

Third, the author incorrectly describes some Jewish customs. For example, he states that prior to eating Jews gave their hands "a ceremonial washing" (7:3), but that is not accurate.[5] Based on all of this, it seems likely that Mark was composed by someone far removed from Palestine. In any event, even if the attribution were true—the author was a secretary to Peter who wrote down "all that he recalled"[6]—the gospel of Mark would still be secondhand, not written by an eyewitness.

The claim that the author of Matthew was the apostle Matthew also comes from Papias, according to Eusebius.[7] It is extremely improbable. The author of Matthew used the third person to describe the apostle Matthew. Jesus "saw a man named Matthew sitting at the tax collector's booth. 'Follow me,' he told him, and Matthew got up and followed him" (9:9). In addition, there are numerous passages in Matthew based on passages in Mark.[8] Why, if Matthew were an eyewitness, would he borrow passages from a non-eyewitness?

Most scholars agree that Luke and the book of Acts were written by the same individual. The tradition that he was a travelling companion of Paul dates back to Irenaeus (circa 180 CE) at least, and it may be the most plausible of the four attributions. There are several passages in Acts that begin with the pronoun "we." On the other hand, the author sometimes contradicts Paul (see, for example, chapter 25, on Paul's activities following his conversion). But even if the author were, in fact, a travelling companion of Paul's, that would lend little credence to the gospel. After all, Paul was not an eyewitness to any events in Jesus's life. Anything Paul told the author of Luke about them would itself have been secondhand.

The earliest documentation of the tradition that John was written by the apostle John may be found in Justin Martyr and

Irenaeus, including the unverifiable claim that the latter had heard it personally from Polycarp. This tradition is, however, highly doubtful. John was written circa 90-100 CE. If its author had been a contemporary of Jesus, then he would have been in his nineties when he wrote—during an era when life expectancy was much lower than it is today. Moreover, the apostle John is described as unschooled (Acts 4:13). In other words, he could not read or write Aramaic, let alone Greek. It is possible that an illiterate, Aramaic-speaking, nonagenarian wrote the gospel of John, but not very likely.

One might respond that John's age does not matter because the gospels were divinely inspired, i.e., that a god was guiding the writing. Yes, that is possible. But if that is the argument, then what is the need for witnesses at all? A god could communicate through anyone. To make the divine inspiration argument is to give up on evidence. It is simply a faith-based claim and, as such, is no different from the claim that Mohammed's recitation of the Koran was inspired. (See the next chapter for more on inspiration.)

A more likely scenario is that John was written by a second-generation Christian who based it on information, some written, from an individual who had followed Jesus in his lifetime. This would explain the references to the "beloved disciple," someone who appears only in John and who is never named. "This is the disciple who testifies to these things and who wrote them down" indicates that some of the information the beloved disciple provided was in writing. But the next sentence, "We know that his testimony is true" (21:24), indicates that the beloved disciple is not the individual who wrote the gospel itself.[9]

Overall, the picture that emerges is one of an oral tradition that was gradually committed to paper. It is understandable that Jesus's immediate followers did not document their experiences in writing. Most of them were illiterate, and besides, they expected the apocalypse at any moment. Instead of written documentation, an oral tradition was born as stories about Jesus were told and retold. These stories circulated for years among ignorant, prescientific people.

Reading and writing, we must remember, were uncommon talents. The tradition that males should be able to read some scripture arose later, following the loss of the second temple, when Jews needed to develop alternative ways to worship. The literacy rate among Jews in Roman Palestine is estimated to have been between 3 and 15 percent, with the lower end of the range more likely.[10]

A misconception sometimes arises regarding the accuracy of oral storytelling. Some apologists have tried to argue that ancient people or members of societies in which oral tradition is passed from generation to generation have better memories than modern people and are consequently better able to preserve accuracy in oral stories. But there is no evidence that this is the case. On the contrary, it appears that placing a high value on accurate transmission of details, or exact replication, is a characteristic of written cultures in which such transmission is more routinely feasible and details can be checked.[11] Having cleared up that misconception, we can state the obvious without distraction: information transmitted orally is susceptible to error.

Eventually, units of oral tradition were fused and written down. Mark, Matthew, and Luke are called the synoptic (Greek, "seen together") gospels because their outlines are roughly similar, at least when compared to that of John. Most scholars believe that the authors of Matthew and Luke used the gospel of Mark as a source but that they wrote independently of each other.[12] Many scholars hypothesize the existence of an additional written source that no longer exists. It is known as Q, for the German word *Quelle*, meaning "source."

John is very different in content and tone from the synoptics. It includes a lot of new material not present in them, such as changing water into wine, the raising of Lazarus, the woman taken in adultery, the washing of the disciples' feet, and Doubting Thomas. On the other hand, it lacks some of the synoptics' most characteristic elements, such as demon possession and parables. Most significantly, John lacks the synoptics' urgent apocalypticism. To understand why this is important, consider a central motif of the first gospel to be written.

In Mark, Jesus's teachings frequently reverse the reader's (or listener's) expectations. "Whoever wants to save his life will lose it, but whoever loses his life for me and for the gospel will save it" (8:35). "Anyone who wants to be first must be the very last, and the servant of all" (9:35). "Many who are first will be last, and the last first" (10:31). "Whoever wants to become great among you must be your servant and whoever wants to be first must be slave of all" (10:43-44).

Mark's plot also reverses expectations. The act of betrayal is epitomized by a kiss (14:44-46); devotion is prefigured by a thrice denial (14:66-72); the disciples James and John ask to be seated at Jesus's left and right, but Jesus is crucified with robbers on his left and right (10:37, 15:27); Jesus's own people, the Jews, mock him, but the pagan centurion recognizes his divinity (15:39); the empty tomb is discovered not by Jesus's chosen disciples, but by those of the lowest social and legal status, the women (16:1-7); the gospel begins by proclaiming the "good news," but at the end, the women run off saying "nothing to anyone" (16:8).

These subsidiary reversals foreshadow the gospel's primary reversal: the message that a man ignominiously executed is in fact the long-awaited messiah. While most Jews were anticipating a triumphal champion, Jesus's followers had found a different kind of messiah, one who suffered and died instead.

All of these reversals reflect the apocalyptic worldview of Jesus's followers and the synoptic authors. God's imminent intervention will reverse the current state of affairs. Those who are rich and powerful are in that position because they are aligned, consciously or not, with the evil powers that dominate this fallen world. When god's kingdom comes, the present order will be upended, bringing a massive reversal of fortunes. The authors of Matthew and Luke extend the reversal of expectations motif, most famously in "the beatitudes" (Matthew 5:3-11, Luke 6:20-22).

By contrast, the gospel of John does not have this motif. Why not? Unlike the synoptics, John does not emphasize a coming kingdom on earth. As discussed in chapter 20, time had passed when the author of John wrote. He was aware that Jesus had never returned as promised. But Christian leaders could not admit this without a collapse in confidence (and church authority). So instead of emphasizing a future kingdom on earth, the author of John emphasized an ongoing kingdom in heaven. This shift in expectations was manageable in large part because most people were illiterate and could not read scripture for themselves.

This survey of the gospels' origins has highlighted their human authorship. It is appropriate to be skeptical because they were written long after the events, anonymously, and not by eyewitnesses. Furthermore, they are not independent of one another. The fact that there are four versions of the story does not strengthen its credibility because all four versions came from one oral tradition. When no version even claims to be written by an eyewitness, it does not matter how many versions get written down.

Finally, Jewish apocalypticism and its unfulfilled promise shaped the gospel messages. By comparing the synoptics with John, we can see how the passage of time altered the emphasis of the writers. They can, in this light, be seen as shapers of an evolving theology rather than as custodians of a historical record.

24

CANON

The contents of the Bible took human beings a long time to negotiate and assemble. The word "bible" comes from the Greek βιβλια, meaning "books." In other words, it is a collection. From among many writings, some were included and others excluded. How were these decisions made and who made them? The New Testament canon, the collection of books officially accepted as scripture, was not finalized until 393 CE. The Old Testament canon remains disputed to this day.

Old Testament

Each of the three main branches of Christianity has a different Old Testament. The Eastern Orthodox Old Testament contains forty-nine books. The Roman Catholic Old Testament contains only forty-six books because it omits 3 Maccabees and 1 Esdras and it combines the Epistle of Jeremiah with Baruch. The Protestant Old Testament contains a mere thirty-nine books because, in addition to those books excluded by the Roman Catholics, it excludes also 1 and 2 Maccabees, Tobit, Judith, Wisdom of Solomon, Sirach (Ecclesiasticus), and Baruch (see the table in appendix 5). Which Old Testament is correct? At least two of Christianity's three branches have too much or too little.

Within Judaism, the collections of the Law and the Prophets were largely stabilized by the fourth century BCE, though some writings such as Daniel were not written until later.[1] Probably prompted by the loss of the temple in 70 CE, Jewish leaders seemed motivated to firm up the boundaries of their canon near the end of the first century CE.[2]

Many Jews and Christians had become familiar with additional writings originally composed in Greek. Over time, these writings were collected alongside translations of Hebrew books in a compilation known as the Septuagint. Latin for "seventy," the Septuagint takes its name from the story of its composition. In circa 250 BCE, as the increasingly Hellenized Jews of Alexandria and other Mediterranean cities were losing their ability to read Hebrew, a group of rabbis undertook to translate the Jewish scripture into Greek. Legend has it that seventy-two scholars worked independently, and each came up with identical translations.

While Judaism accepted as canonical only those books originally composed in Hebrew, the Catholic and Eastern Orthodox churches came to accept a wider range of Septuagint writings. The Latin-speaking West, however, ultimately accepted fewer than the Greek-speaking Orthodox East.

With the Reformation, Protestants rejected the Catholic and Eastern Orthodox positions and embraced the narrower Jewish canon (though they arrange the books in a different sequence from the traditional Jewish practice). Part of their motivation was that some of the other books provided scriptural foundation for Catholic practices that they rejected. For example, prayers for the dead, and by extension purgatory, derive support from 2 Maccabees 12:40-46 (quoted in chapter 16).

As a result of these disagreements, Christianity's three main branches have different Old Testaments. Who has the word of god, the whole word of god, and nothing but the word of god? And why couldn't that god see to it that they all got the same word?

New Testament

Unlike the Old Testament canon, the New Testament canon is at least agreed upon. The evolution of this agreement, however, reveals a very human and flawed process. Early church leaders disagreed about which books to include, partly because of regional practices and partly because of doctrinal debates. Books considered sacred by some were ultimately excluded. On the other hand, some included books were accepted on faulty grounds.

Christian writings that were excluded from the canon generally fall into the same genres as those included. There were other gospels, such as those of Thomas, Philip, Mary, and Peter; there were other Acts, such as those of Peter, John, and Thomas; there were letters, such as 1 Clement and Barnabas; and there were revelations, such as the Revelations of Peter, Ezra, and the Shepherd of Hermas.

Most of the excluded works were written later than the included ones. For example, the Acts of Peter, John, and Thomas were written circa 180-200 CE. But there were exceptions to the inclusion of the earliest materials. For example, the excluded 1 Clement was written circa 96 CE while the included 2 Peter was written circa 130 CE.[3] Parts of the gospel of Thomas and the gospel of Peter may have been written earlier than the four canonical gospels.[4]

The gospels of Thomas and Peter were widely read. Thomas, quoted in chapter 12, is a collection of sayings attributed to Jesus, and it was accepted as scripture by some Christians.[5] The gospel of Peter was also in use among some early churches.[6] It contains a passion narrative, and it is noteworthy because the cross of the crucifixion actually speaks! In front of a gathered crowd, Jesus emerges from the tomb, supported by two angels, and followed by the cross. A voice from the sky asks, "Have you preached to those who are asleep?" and the cross says, "Yes" (Lines 41-42).[7]

Irenaeus, writing about 180 CE, made an early attempt to settle the gospel canon. He argued that there should be four gospels, not more or fewer, because "there are four zones of the world in which we live, and four principal winds."[8] To be fair, this was not his only or even primary reason. But it is a risible one, and it should be cause for concern that someone positing such views was among the shapers of the religion. The fact that Irenaeus felt the need to resort to such an argument and to do so as late as he did reveals the extent and nature of canon debate.

Other writings were also accepted as scripture by some churches. The earliest compilations of sacred Christian writings included the Apocalypse of Peter, 1 and 2 Clement, the Epistle of Barnabas, the Shepherd of Hermas, and the Didache.[9] None of these was ultimately included in the New Testament.

On the other hand, some books that were included in the New Testament appear to have been accepted by mistake; they are either anonymous, misattributed, or forged.

Texts written in someone else's name are often called by scholars pseudonymous, and they were common in the ancient world.[10] Whether written with fraudulent intentions or in a sincere effort to extend the teachings of a deceased leader, the writer's goal was to invest a document with an authority that it would otherwise lack. The word "forged" rather than "pseudonymous" is used here because it reflects the modern sensibility that it is misleading to claim something was written by someone who didn't write it.

Of the fourteen letters traditionally attributed to Paul, only seven are accepted as genuine by most modern biblical scholars.[11] These are: 1 Thessalonians, Galatians, Philippians, Philemon, 1 and 2 Corinthians, and Romans. Of the other seven, Hebrews was written anonymously, and the other six—2 Thessalonians, Colossians, Ephesians, Titus, 1 and 2 Timothy—were written by other people in Paul's name, i.e., forged.

See appendix 5 for brief comments on why these letters and the others mentioned below are not considered authentic by many scholars today.

The books 1 and 2 Peter were forged in the name of the apostle Peter.[12] The authors of the books of James and Jude were believed, mistakenly, to have been the brothers of Jesus, and their books were included in the canon for that reason.[13] The books 1, 2, and 3 John are anonymous.[14] Church leaders mistakenly attributed them to the apostle John and included them accordingly.

Tradition holds that there was a consistent approach to the selection of books to be included in the canon. First, there had to be a belief that the author enjoyed a link to Jesus's circle (apostolicity); second, there had to be relevance for all Christians (catholicity); third, the teachings had to conform to accepted doctrine (orthodoxy); fourth, there had to be longstanding use of the book among Christians (usage).[15]

This list of criteria is striking in several respects. First, it was not really followed very closely. Some excluded books, such as the Shepherd of Hermas, 1 Clement, and the Epistle of Barnabas, met the four criteria at least as well as some which were included.[16] Second, it is, at least in part, circular. Scripture is clearly a source of Christian doctrine, yet according to this list, doctrine determined the selection of scripture. Third, it omits historical accuracy. This omission indicates that the standards of factuality and evidence we take for granted today were not foremost during this process, a major deficiency for a religion that claims to be grounded in historical reality. Finally, the list omits divine inspiration. Given the prominence of this last criterion in the popular imagination, a bit more discussion is warranted.

"All scripture is God-breathed" (2 Timothy 3:16). By this, the author meant that scripture is inspired by god and therefore truthful. But there are several problems with this claim. First, the author did not specify what he meant by scripture. The Rig Veda is sacred scripture for Hindus. Did the author of 2 Timothy intend to include the Rig Veda? More generally, anyone can write anything and assert that it is scripture. So 2 Timothy's claim, even if true, is unhelpful. Second, there is no reason to believe that 2 Timothy's claim is true. To argue that it must be true because it is scripture would be circular: there is no reason to believe that scripture is true unless 2 Timothy is true, but there is no reason to believe 2 Timothy is true unless it is scripture.

Leaving aside these difficulties, how exactly would "god-breathed" scripture come about? Some hold to a divine dictation model in which a human being writes exactly what a god tells him. This is the manner in which the Koran was purportedly written. A more subtle alternative is that the god implants ideas into a human being's mind, after which that human being uses his own words to communicate what he understands. The result is a co-creation that is correct on religious matters but may contain inconsequential inaccuracies.

These alternative models share several defects. First, if a god wanted to communicate with human beings, why would he need other human beings to help? He could have caused to appear everywhere on earth indestructible and unalterable scrolls that conveyed his exact words and intended meaning in the language of any person holding them. Or if literacy were an obstacle, he could have instructed each person's guardian angel to recite and interpret relevant verses as needed. Creating or co-creating a document through the human pen would make sense only if one of his objectives were to inject into the process doubts about its authenticity.

Second, had the writer been aware of a god's participation in the process? If he had, then he would have been excited and honored, if not duty-bound, to disclose that fact to his readers. On the other hand, if he had not been aware, then how could anyone else be? Of the twenty-seven books in the New Testament, only one, Revelation, claims to have been inspired (1:10). Since none of the other twenty-six books makes this claim, it appears that their authors did not believe that they were. So why should we? From a modern standpoint, this should be fairly obvious.

A traditional response is that those who chose the books for inclusion in the canon were inspired during the selection process. But this merely pushes the inquiry back one step: did they say this, and would we have any good reasons for believing them if they had? Ultimately, a belief that the canon was inspired is simply an article of faith, one which is at variance with the manifestly human process by which it was cobbled together.

The book of Revelation (circa 90-100 CE) was the most contested book of the New Testament and the last added. It was one among many Christian writings (called apocalypses if translated directly from the original Greek or revelations if translated via Latin) that purported to offer glimpses of coming cosmic events. The controversy over its status extended through the first half of the fourth century, when Eusebius, reflecting this irresolution, listed it as both "accepted" and "illegitimate."[17]

It was written by someone known to history only as John of Patmos. The pious claim that it was written by Jesus's apostle John was little more than an attempt by some Christians to lend the book legitimacy in the eyes of other Christians (see appendix 5). In 363 CE, the Synod of Laodicea listed as scripture twenty-six of the twenty-seven books in the present-day New Testament, excluding Revelation. But in 367 CE, the politically savvy Bishop Athanasius added the book to his own listing. He saw that its description of a dramatic victory of good over evil could usefully be interpreted to fit many circumstances.

Originally intended to prefigure Christianity's defeat of a persecuting Rome, Revelation needed to be reinterpreted when Christianity and Rome became partners. Under Athanasius, the text was used as a weapon against those Christian minorities who held views at odds with the church hierarchy. Indeed, Athanasius declared all other books of revelation, including some that lent support to these minority views, to be heretical and ordered them destroyed.[18] Athanasius's list, including John's Revelation, was first recognized as canonical at the Synod of Hippo in 393 CE; and that recognition, though not binding, became the norm throughout most of the church.[19]

In summary, of the twenty-seven books in the New Testament, scholars are confident of the identity of the authors of only eight: Seven letters were written by Paul, and Revelation was written by John of Patmos. The four gospels, Acts, and Hebrews are anonymous. James and Jude were misattributed to Jesus's brothers, and the three letters of John were misattributed to the apostle John. The remaining eight were forged in the names of Paul or Peter. In other words, 22 percent of the books of the New Testament are anonymous, 19 percent were misattributed, and 30 percent were forged.

25

GOSPEL COMPOSITION

The word "gospel" comes from the old English "godspell," which was a translation from the Greek, ευαγγελιον, meaning "good news." Before it came to refer to the unique literary genre of Jesus biographies, the term meant simply a message of good news.

What kind of writings are the gospels? This question brings us to the heart of the nature of evidence. The gospels do not read like histories, at least not by any modern standard. Real historians do two things the gospel writers uniformly fail to do: they identify their sources and they evaluate conflicting evidence.[1]

The gospel writers do not identify any of their sources—not a single one. They don't even identify themselves. In this regard, what we see in the gospels appears consistent with the capture on paper of oral tradition that circulated widely among people who simply heard it from other people, with none able to verify its origins. Nor do the gospel writers address conflicting evidence. Because data is often limited and sources contradictory, real historians must make critical judgments about which versions of events are more likely true. They do this in plain view of the readers so that we can share in their conclusions or at least understand the reasons if we disagree.

Although the four canonical gospels share the above shortcomings as histories, highlighted for each below is a different difficulty: literary features in Mark, outlandish tales in Matthew, errors in Luke, and unabashed theology in John.

Mark

Mark was the first gospel, written circa 60-75 CE, about a decade after Paul's letters were written. The shortest and simplest of the four gospels, Mark appears to have been assembled from anecdotes. But its author imposed a dramatic structure on them, giving the final product many literary characteristics: omniscient narrator, structural repetition, symbolism, wordplay, and parallelism with scripture.

Like a novelist, the author knows what characters are thinking and what they do when no one else is around. For example, he knows what Jesus felt (1:41, 3:5) or what the hemorrhaging woman thought (5:25-28) or what Pilate thought (15:10). He knows what Jesus said in his prayer when he was alone in Gethsemane (14:35-36).

The author constructed the text artfully and with symbolism, juxtaposing story elements to help the reader reach correct conclusions. For example, at one point, Jesus is hungry, but there are no figs growing on the fig tree because it is out of season. In anger, he curses the tree (11:13-14). If the story is taken literally, Jesus behaved like a petulant child, a character flaw, Bertrand Russell noted, never exhibited by the likes of Socrates or Buddha.[2] But this story brackets another story. After cursing the tree, Jesus clears the temple. The next morning, Peter points out the tree to Jesus. "Rabbi, look! The fig tree you cursed has withered" (11:21). Symbolically, the tree is the temple. The old teachings are insufficient, even corrupted, and their foundations must be replaced. So what the author of Mark was really saying was not that Jesus cursed a tree but that he anticipated a radical change in religious practice.

The disciples do not understand how Jesus could feed a second multitude of hungry followers (8:2-9), even though they had recently helped him feed a first (6:37-44). Jesus chides them, "Do you still not understand?" Immediately afterward, he cures a man of blindness. But he needs two tries to cure him fully (8:21-25). Surely, the all-powerful creator of the cosmos could have cured the man's blindness, or all blindness for that matter, with one try. But by juxtaposing the two feedings with the two-step blindness cure, the author emphasized that the gospel is so different from conventional expectation that it can only gradually be seen or understood.

The author also used wordplay. Pilate offers the mob a choice between pardoning Jesus and pardoning a convict named Barabbas. The crowd chooses Barabbas, thereby sending Jesus to his death. There is no record that any such pardoning tradition existed, so it is logical to ask what purpose the episode serves within the story.[3] Significantly, in Aramaic *bar* means "son of" and *abba* means "father." So Barabbas means "son of the father." Jesus, the reader knows, is the son of his father, the god Yahweh. So symbolically, the Jews chose the wrong son. (In some manuscripts of Matthew, the comparison is made even more explicit because Barabbas is given a first name: Jesus.)[4]

Another example of wordplay appears to be the burial of Jesus by a man named Joseph of Arimethea. This is a new character appearing out of nowhere. The town of Arimethea does not exist. It never did. It does not appear on any real map, ancient or modern. Nor is there is any mention of its existence outside of the gospels. Strong's Concordance asserts, without any explanation, that Arimethea is another name for Ramah.[5] While that is possible, there is no particular reason to believe it. Where else might the name have come from?

The historian Richard Carrier has suggested that Arimethea can be broken down as follows: *ari*—means "best"; *mathai*—means "disciple"; and *a* means "place" or "town." Therefore, Arimethea can be rendered as "best disciple town."[6] In contrast to Jesus's closest followers, nowhere to be seen, "Joseph from the best disciple town" bravely asks Pilate for the body and dutifully entombs it. At the same time, his first name, Joseph, is an implicit reproach to Jesus's "father," Joseph, who, like the others, is nowhere to be seen.

The author of Mark created parallelism with scripture by borrowing Old Testament story elements. For example, Mark's description of the crucifixion borrows heavily from Psalm 22.

Psalm 22	Mark 15
They divide my garments among them and cast lots for my clothing.	Dividing up his clothes, they cast lots to see what each would get.
All who see me mock me; they hurl insults, shaking their heads: "He trusts in the Lord; let the Lord rescue him."	Those who passed by hurled insults at him, shaking their heads and saying, "So! You who are going to destroy the temple and build it in three days, come down from the cross and save yourself!"
"My God, my God, why have you forsaken me?"	"My God, my God, why have you forsaken me?"

The practice of borrowing from earlier writings was not unusual. The New Testament contains over 1,300 passages and phrases from the Old Testament, including seventy in the gospel of Mark alone.[7] Some readers draw the wrong conclusions from these parallels. They believe that Mark reports historical fact, from which starting point they convince themselves that the events in Mark 15 were actually fulfillments of prophecies made in Psalm 22.

Literary borrowing is a simpler and more plausible explanation. Both the author of Mark and his protagonist were intimately familiar with scripture. Jesus's cry of forsakenness, for example, was a well-known quotation from Psalm 22. The fact that someone else said something previously does not make repeating it a prophetic fulfillment. If someone quotes, say, *The Iliad* on his deathbed, that does not mean that Homer prophesied his death.

The author of Mark fashioned a literary narrative by combining fragments of oral tradition with themes, and even text, from the Old Testament. Does this constitute lying? Well, he was communicating meaning through a story. But if the first gospel is a literary creation, then so too must be substantial parts of Matthew and Luke, both of which drew heavily upon it.

Matthew

Matthew was written circa 80-90 CE. Its author's dishonesty (see chapter 27) and his penchant for the fabulistic require us to read with caution. Consider the following Matthean howlers.

Matthew 2:16-18 claims that, out of fear of a newly born challenger, Herod ordered the slaughter of all boys under the age of two in Bethlehem and environs. Such a slaughter is not mentioned in any of the other three gospels. Nor is it mentioned in any historical chronicle outside the Bible. This would have been a sensational atrocity, and it would have garnered wide attention, if not triggered an uprising. Not even the Jewish historian Josephus, who criticized Herod extensively, mentions such an occurrence. On the other hand, a tyrant preempting an infant challenger is an element of the hero archetype, figuring in the stories of Romulus and Perseus (previously discussed) as well as those of Horus, Oedipus, Jason, and Cyrus the Great.[8] Closer to home, the author was probably evoking parallels with the Pharaoh's effort to kill the infant Moses (Exodus 1:15-2:10).

Matthew 2:1-12 claims that a star led a group of wise men to the infant Jesus. Such a star is not mentioned in any of the other three gospels. Nor is it mentioned in any of the secular history or science of the time, such as Seneca's *Natural Questions* (circa 65 CE) or Pliny the Elder's *Natural History* (circa 80 CE). It is, moreover, implausible on its face: only a star emitting a single precision beam could lead people to an exact location on earth. If such a celestial marvel occurred, wouldn't the entire countryside have followed the beam to discover whatever it was pointing to? How then could Jesus have grown up in obscurity? And wouldn't it have been easier for Herod's soldiers to follow that same star rather than kill every boy under the age of two?

Matthew 27:52-53 states that after Jesus's resurrection, a pack of reanimated corpses wandered the streets of Jerusalem. "The bodies of many holy people who had died were raised to life. They came out of the tombs, and after Jesus's resurrection went into the holy city and appeared to many people." This is not mentioned in any of the other three gospels. No other writer, in the Bible or out, including Philo or Josephus, mentions such a carnivalesque event. One would think that what happened next would be of wide interest. Did they ascend to heaven? Did they retire to their graves? We are never told, perhaps because even the inventive author of Matthew realized he was in over his head.

Luke-Acts

Luke-Acts was written circa 80-90 CE. Of the gospel writers, only this one claims to have made investigations (Luke 1:1-4). But that may be a charitable interpretation. Richard Carrier points out that what Luke actually says is that eyewitnesses handed down information "to us," Christians of his time, not to the author of Luke personally. In other words, he was collecting the commonly held beliefs of Christians. His contribution was to write them down in an orderly manner. He did not indicate that he had personally interviewed any witnesses, much less evaluated conflicting claims and assessed their credibility.[9]

He based significant portions of his text on that of Mark.[10] He does not identify any eyewitnesses, and he leaves the reader with the impression that the stories he received were consistent. But there were conflicting claims among believers, and if he were really acting as a historian, he would have addressed them.

For example, Mark says that Jesus walked on water (Mark 6:45-52), but Matthew says of the same episode that both Jesus and Peter walked on water (Matthew 14:25-31). Instead of exploring this discrepancy, Luke omits the episode altogether. Why? The author of Luke-Acts wrote independently of Matthew, but if he had really investigated, then he would have come across Matthew's sources and version of the story. Given his silence, it is difficult to avoid the conclusion that he found both Mark and Matthew to be wrong. A competent historian would have mentioned the previous errors and explained how he knew that they were, in fact, errors.

Some argue that the author of Luke-Acts was an accurate historian because many of the things he wrote can be verified. For example, Acts includes the correct location of cities, the correct titles for certain officials, and the best route to sail given certain wind conditions. The author is therefore trustworthy, they claim, with respect to things he wrote that cannot be verified.

There is a fatal problem with this reasoning. The presence of true details does not make a story true. After all, most works of fiction have historical settings. *The Adventures of Huckleberry Finn* includes the correct names of cities along the Mississippi River, reliable descriptions of the water currents, and accurate observations on the institution of slavery. Does that mean that Huck Finn really existed? A story intended to convince people of something untrue would almost certainly include verifiable or recognizable elements. Furthermore, the author of Luke-Acts does, in fact, make errors. The following are a half-dozen examples, three of historical misconstruction and three of internal consistency:

In Luke, Mary became pregnant with Jesus "in the time of Herod king of Judea" (1:5). But Jesus was born during a census that "took place while Quirinius was governor of Syria" (2:2). Both statements cannot be correct because Herod died in 4 BCE, and Quirinius's census took place ten years later, in 6-7 CE.[11] So either Luke is garbled or Mary's sainthood is well-deserved, for enduring the world's only decade-long pregnancy.

In Acts 5:35-37, Gamaliel says that Theudas led a revolt before Judas the Galilean did. But this chronology is backward. Judas the Galilean's revolt was in 6-7 CE, and Theudas's revolt was in 45-46 CE, about thirty years later. In fact, at the time Gamaliel is depicted as speaking, circa 36 CE, Theudas's revolt had not yet occurred.[12]

The account of Paul's activities in Acts contradicts Paul's own. According to Acts, the first thing Paul did upon leaving Damascus was go to Jerusalem (Acts 9:22-26). In contrast, Paul wrote, "My immediate response was not to consult any human being. I did not go up to Jerusalem to see those who were apostles before I was, but I went into Arabia. Later, I returned to Damascus" (Galatians 1:16-17).

In Mark (15:15) and Matthew (27:26), Jesus is flogged before being crucified. In Luke, Jesus is not flogged. Did the author of Luke conclude that Mark and Matthew were wrong about that fact too? Probably not: Luke's Jesus predicted that he would be flogged (Luke 18:31-33). It appears that the author intended to include a flogging in his story but then forgot to do so.

The book of Acts provides two discrepant accounts of Paul's celebrated conversion on the road to Damascus. Acts 9:7 states that the other people travelling with Paul heard a voice but saw no one, whereas Acts 22:9 says that the others did not hear a voice but saw a light.

The author contradicted himself regarding the timing of Jesus's ascension. In Luke 24:13-53, it appears that Jesus ascended at the end of the day on which he was resurrected or at most one or two days afterward. Acts 1:3-9, on the other hand, states that Jesus ascended forty days later.

An ascension is portrayed only in Luke-Acts. The other gospels are strangely silent about Jesus's departure, which suggests that, having resurrected him, their authors were unsure of what to do with him or how ultimately to dispose of him. Luke states that Jesus "was taken up into heaven" (24:51). Acts adds the detail that eventually "a cloud hid him from their sight" (1:9). This is a description of a literal ascension in which Jesus floated bodily into the air, gradually gained elevation, and receded from view. It corresponds poorly with our modern knowledge of the skies, as no human bodies have been found orbiting the planet or elsewhere in space. On the other hand, it fits perfectly the three-storied cosmology of the ancient Middle East, in which an underworld is physically located below, and heaven up above, a flat earth. The author of Luke-Acts, in other words, was either fabricating a tale of Jesus's departure based on the cosmological misconceptions of his day or repeating someone else's.

John

The gospel of John was the last of the four canonical gospels to be written, most likely 90-100 CE, and is the most theologically self-conscious. John presents Jesus as the eternal creator of the world. "In the beginning was the Word, and the Word was with God, and the Word was God. He was with God in the beginning. Through him all things were made" (John 1:1-3).

How would the author of John know any of this? He did not even pretend to be writing history. He was writing theology. And he was frank about his objective, disclosing to the reader that his story was "written that you may believe" (20:31).

John's famous opening lines refer to Jesus as "the Word." But John was written in Greek, and the term actually used was λογος, written in English as "logos." While "word" is one common translation, "logos" has a broader meaning and an older history.

Centuries earlier, the Greek philosopher Heraclitus (circa 500 BCE) had used the term "logos" to refer to the underlying rationality of the universe. Although the material world is in constant flux, it is nevertheless governed consistently by a logos.[13] Building on Heraclitus, the Stoic philosophers had thought of the logos as the creative energy that flows through otherwise inert matter.[14] For example, Cleanthes (circa 250 BCE) wrote, addressing Zeus, "You direct the logos which permeates everything."[15]

Philo of Alexandria (circa 40 CE) synthesized Greek philosophy and Judaism. He borrowed the concept of the logos from the Stoics and associated it with the Jewish idea of "God's Word" in Psalm 119 and "Wisdom" in Proverbs 1-9.[16] He also borrowed from Plato the notion that our world is an imperfect copy of an ideal world.[17] Combining these ideas, he wrote that the logos is a copy of god's mind, occupying an intermediate position between god and the universe. The universe was created through the logos and continues to be governed by it.[18] At one point, he even referred to the logos as god's "first born son."[19]

It appears that, consciously or not, the author of the gospel of John drew upon this philosophical tradition. He personified the logos, identifying it specifically with Jesus. This connected Jewish expectations of a messiah with philosophical ideas in circulation among non-Jews. The notion of an underlying rationality to the universe was a concept with a long pedigree in pagan thinking. Characterized as the logos, Jesus was positioned to be consistent with Greek philosophy, if not its very culmination.

26

GOSPEL PRESERVATION

Not only were the gospels written anonymously, in the third person, and long after the purported events, but we do not have the original documents. Despite scholarly and religious desires to "go back to the originals," none of them exist. Direct linkage cannot be established. As the gospels are foundational to Christianity, this is a shattering blow to the religion's claims to be grounded in historical fact.

For their first fourteen centuries, the New Testament writings were reproduced by hand. What we possess today are copies of copies of copies, many of them incomplete, and—with the exception of palm-sized fragments—no two completely alike.[1]

Among the earliest manuscripts in existence, there are many variations in the text. According to New Testament scholar Barton Ehrman, upon whose work much of this chapter is based, there are more differences between these manuscripts than there are words in the New Testament.[2] In many cases, it is possible to reconstruct which variant of the text is older (and presumably more accurate); but in other cases, it is not.

Moreover, scholars possess no New Testament manuscripts, or even fragments, dating from the first century CE. As a result, it is impossible to trace changes made to the very earliest manuscripts. These changes are completely undetectable. The earliest surviving New Testament document dates from circa 125 CE, a playing-card-size fragment of the gospel of John containing only a few lines. The earliest manuscripts of complete individual books date from circa 350 CE.[3] A gap of several hundred years therefore exists between the original writings and our earliest copies of them. And among the copies we have, there are thousands of variations in the text.

How did all these changes arise? Some were unintentional, caused by fatigue, distraction, carelessness, poor handwriting, or poor eyesight. These problems were especially prevalent in the work of the earliest copiers, who were usually not professional scribes but simply the most literate people available.

But copiers also made intentional changes. Sometimes they thought, correctly or not, that a previous copier had made a mistake, and they wanted to fix it. Sometimes they sought to harmonize accounts of events that seemed to them to disagree in two or more gospels. Sometimes they wanted to eliminate text that could be interpreted in a doctrinally troublesome manner.

Altered texts were a source of frustration for early church leaders. The Christian writer Origen (circa 250 CE) complained: "The differences among the manuscripts have become great, either through the negligence of some copyists or through the perverse audacity of others; they either neglect to check over what they have transcribed, or, in the process of checking, they make additions or deletions as they please."[4] Jerome (circa 400 CE), esteemed for his influential Latin translation of the Bible known as the Vulgate, complained of copyists who "write down not what they find but what they think is the meaning; and while they attempt to rectify the errors of others, they merely expose their own."[5]

There are about 5,700 Greek manuscripts, or fragments thereof, in existence. Some people point to this large number and think it is evidence of the text's accuracy. But a moment's reflection reveals this not to be the case. Suppose I hand copied a document, introducing into it some changes (intentional or unintentional). Suppose further that the original document, from which I had copied, was lost or destroyed. Someone could make a thousand copies of my copy, but that would not make it any more accurate. In fact, that would make it less accurate because each of those one thousand would also be hand copied. Each would contain its own copier's changes (intentional or unintentional) in addition to mine.

And so changes increase exponentially over time. It is better to have one very early copy than thousands of late ones. Of the Greek manuscripts in existence, the vast majority was produced after 400 CE.[6] They have, for that reason, limited value in determining original content. And it is original content that Christian theologians consider the word of god.

While most variations in the texts are inconsequential, some have significant doctrinal implications. The following are three examples:

The last twelve verses of Mark (16:9-20), in which Jesus appears after his resurrection, were late additions. They are not present in the oldest manuscripts.[7] The original version of Mark ends with the empty tomb. The discrepancy between the older manuscripts without the final verses and the more recent ones with them cannot be explained as a case of losing and then finding the original ending. Scholars have a high level of confidence that verses 9-20 were not written by the same person who wrote the rest of Mark.[8] The final verses, containing the story of Jesus's postmortem appearances, were most likely added years later in order to harmonize Mark with the other gospels.

Another doctrinally motivated change was the insertion of 1 John 5:7-8, which reads, "For there are three that bear record in heaven, the Father, the Word, and the Holy Ghost: and these three are one." This quotation is from the King James translation.

The New International Version includes the line as a footnote, acknowledging that it was a late insertion into the manuscript chain. 1 John 5:7-8 is important because it is the only place in the Bible where the doctrine of the trinity is stated. There are other places where the three persons are mentioned, but this is the only assertion that the three are one. While this sentence is present in most of the later manuscripts, it does not appear in any Greek manuscript before the 16th century![9] Not only is the church-made doctrine of the trinity illogical, as shown in chapter 11, but with the exception of a single fabricated, post hoc verse, it has no foundation in the Bible.

Some changes were made because of debates within the early church. Factions arose because church doctrine had not yet been established, and the text of some writings was changed to support one position or the other. One of the better-known controversies that marked the maturation of Christian doctrine was adoptionism, the understanding that Jesus was born a man like any other but that, at some point in his life, he was chosen by god and adopted as his son.

In Luke 3:22, a voice from heaven speaks to the recently baptized Jesus. In some manuscripts, the earlier ones, the voice says, "You are my Son; today I have begotten you." In other manuscripts, the later ones that came to predominate, the voice says, "You are my Son, whom I love; with you I am well pleased." The earlier version suggests that Jesus was not a god before that day, a reading which supports adoptionism. The later version of the text eliminated this troublesome interpretation.[10]

In summary, we possess a text that has been changed in many places and rendered unreliable by exponential copyist errors. In some cases, even when scholars know there has been a change, it is not possible to determine which version of the text is truer to the original. In other cases, we cannot even be aware that a change has been made because the earliest surviving manuscripts were produced long after the originals. There is a profound missing link to the original content.

All of these textual problems raise a big question: If a god didn't bother to preserve accurate copies, on what basis do we assume he communicated originals? If an omnipotent deity had taken the trouble to give sacred writings to human beings, he would have preserved them so they were available not just for the initial recipients, but also for their entire intended audience. Given the New Testament's glaring textual inconsistencies, it is obvious that no deity has bothered to preserve its words over the past two thousand years. It is correspondingly unlikely that a deity ever gave these words to human beings in the first place.

By virtue of gaps in the chain of transmission, textual alterations both intentional and unintentional, and the absence of supernatural safeguards against all of the above, the authority of scripture, even if it had existed to begin with, is fatally undermined.

27

MISREPRESENTATION

Before the New Testament existed, the Old Testament was the scripture recognized by Jesus and his followers. All of the New Testament writers were familiar with the older scripture. Some of them, it seems, misrepresented it in order to give the appearance of legitimacy to their innovative views. The following are a half-dozen examples:

1. *Paul and Deuteronomy*

As discussed in chapter 22, Paul advanced the argument that Israel's god had given it the law not as a permanent gift but as an interim curse, a burden preparatory for Jesus.

In order to support his argument that faith was the only path to righteousness, Paul excerpted from the Old Testament selectively. In his letter to the Romans, he quotes a passage from Deuteronomy in which Moses gave the Israelites Yahweh's instructions. Compare Paul's version with the original:

Deuteronomy 30:11-14	Romans 10:8
"Now what I am commanding you today is not too difficult for you or beyond your reach . . . the word is very near you; it is in your mouth and in your heart so you may obey it."	"The word is near you; it is in your mouth and in your heart, that is, the message concerning faith that we proclaim."

According to the original passage, the law is intended to be obeyed and humans are capable of obeying it. But Paul omitted the words at the beginning and the end which make those points clear. That may have enabled him to fool gentiles who were unfamiliar with the Old Testament, but it was unlikely to fool many educated Jews.

2. Paul and Isaiah

One of the primary themes of the Old Testament is the need for the Israelites to repent of wrongdoing in order to stand in proper relation to their god. Referring to the Israelites as "those in Jacob," the prophet Isaiah had promised that Yahweh would accept those who repent. In other words, individuals can and must take action for themselves. In Romans, Paul pretended to quote Isaiah, but he made a critical change:

Isaiah 59:20	Romans 11:26
"The redeemer will come to Zion, to those in Jacob who repent of their sins."	"The deliverer will come from Zion; he will turn godlessness away from Jacob."

Notice that in Romans, the people are passive, and it is the deliverer who saves them. This is another misrepresentation intended to convince people that their own actions, such as following the law, are futile and that only faith in Jesus will bring salvation.

3. Matthew and virginity

The author of Matthew was determined to portray Jesus as the fulfillment of Old Testament messiah prophecies. In his eagerness, he even claimed fulfillment of a prophecy that did not exist, namely, that the messiah would be born of a virgin. Of Jesus's birth, he wrote, "All this took place to fulfill what the Lord had said through the prophet: 'The virgin will conceive and give birth to a son, and they will call him Immanuel' (which means 'God with us')" (Matthew 1:22-23).

Matthew here refers to Isaiah 7:1-16. Check the source: King Ahaz and his people feared attack by Aram and Ephraim. The prophet Isaiah reassured them that Yahweh would destroy their enemies soon. He said of an unnamed woman that she will "give birth to a son and . . . before the boy knows enough to reject the wrong and choose the right, the land of the two kings you dread will be laid waste." In other words, their god would destroy their enemies by the time this young boy reached the age of reason.

Where is the virgin? Isaiah refers to the woman as an עלמה. This Hebrew word is written in English as *almah*, and it means "young woman."[1] So Isaiah says that a young woman will have a baby. But the author of Matthew misrepresents almah as "virgin" and asserts that this is a prophecy of a virgin birth.

No such prophecy exists. If Isaiah had wanted to say that this woman was a virgin, he would have done so. He would have used the word בתולה. This Hebrew word, written in English as *betulah*, unambiguously means "virgin." Isaiah was familiar with the word betulah because he used it five times elsewhere (23:4, 23:12, 37:22, 47:1, 62:5). Its absence here was intentional.

The root cause of the confusion may be traced further back in time. The author of Matthew may have utilized the Septuagint (the Greek translation of the Hebrew Bible, discussed in chapter 24). In it, the word used is παρθενος (written in English as *parthenos*) which means "virgin." If that is the case, a poor translation of Isaiah into Greek lies at the heart of the muddle. The important point here, however, is that the author of Matthew contrived a momentous theological claim from a few crucial words, words he appears not to have researched very carefully. Even if he did not know how to read Hebrew, he could have verified the original meaning of the text by consulting someone who did.

4. *Matthew and genealogy*

In another questionable effort to link Jesus to prophecy, the author of Matthew presented a genealogy in order to demonstrate that Jesus was descended from King David. He wrote portentously that there were fourteen generations from Abraham to David, fourteen from David to the exile, and fourteen from the exile to Jesus. (The number 14 is associated, in Jewish numerology, with David and hence kingship.)

Unfortunately, however, the author of Matthew had to massage the data in order to generate three groups of fourteen. Compare his genealogy with the one provided in 1 Chronicles. The author of Matthew had the effrontery to delete names from the list in order to alter the count. Here is the middle group of fourteen, from Solomon to Josiah:

1 Chronicles 3:10-17	Matthew 1:6-11
Solomon	Solomon
Rehoboam	Rehoboam
Abijah	Abijah

Asa	Asa
Jehoshaphat	Jehoshaphat
Jehoram	Jehoram
Ahaziah	
Joash	
Amaziah	
Azariah (Uzziah)	Uzziah
Jotham	Jotham
Ahaz	Ahaz
Hezekiah	Hezekiah
Manasseh	Manasseh
Amon	Amon
Josiah	Josiah

The author of Matthew deleted Ahaziah, Joash, and Amaziah from the list. In fact, he was so committed to discarding names that he ended up with only thirteen instead of the advertised fourteen.

5. Luke and blindness

According to the New Testament's gospel of Luke, Jesus appeared in the synagogue in Nazareth and read from the Old Testament book of Isaiah. The comments he made after he completed the reading caused a riot, but what is of interest here is Luke's representation of the passage itself. The passage read by Jesus does not match that found in Isaiah; it has been changed.

In the original, Isaiah had made a general statement, but the changed version included a new and very concrete promise, namely, that the speaker will heal the blind:

Isaiah 61:1	Luke 4:18
"The spirit of the Sovereign Lord is on me, because the Lord has anointed me to proclaim good news to the poor. He has sent me to bind up the broken hearted, to proclaim freedom for the captives and release from darkness for the prisoners."	"The spirit of the Lord is on me, because he has anointed me to proclaim good news to the poor. He has sent me to proclaim freedom for the prisoners and recovery of sight for the blind, to set the oppressed free."

Why would the author of Luke insert such a promise into scripture? One obvious explanation is that he could then proceed to recount how this promise has been fulfilled. And sure enough, in Luke 7:21 and 18:42, Jesus heals the blind.

6. Hebrews and sacrifice

The author of Hebrews depicted Jesus citing Psalm 40:6. There, the psalmist says that what Yahweh really wants is not sacrifice but for people to follow his teachings, that is, to keep the law. Notice the change made by the author of Hebrews:

Psalm 40:6	Hebrews 10:5-6
"Sacrifice and offering you did not desire, but my ears you have opened; burnt offerings and sin offerings you did not require."	"Sacrifice and offering you did not desire, but a body you prepared for me; with burnt offerings and sin offerings you were not pleased."

The changed version turns the psalmist's meaning upside down. In fact, it does so by contradicting itself: the god did not desire a sacrifice, but he prepared a body to be sacrificed. The author of Hebrews tampered with the Old Testament text here in order to give the false impression that it contained a prophecy of Jesus.

What kind of person tampers with scripture to add new meanings? How much credence can be given to anything written in this manner? To those who believe it, scripture is sacred and foundational. Because it is written, it can be checked. If these writers took this many liberties with sacred, written scripture, how many more liberties would they be willing to take with a sketchy oral legend about previously undocumented events, one or two generations removed, in the life of Jesus?

28

CONTRADICTION

The New Testament contradicts itself. Readers often overlook these contradictions because they read the books sequentially, rather than side by side, and devotionally, rather than critically. But problems arise as soon as one applies to these writings the same critical thought customarily applied to other important documents. The following are a half-dozen examples:

1. *What was Paul's view on the role of women in the church?*

According to Paul, women could pray and prophesy in church (1 Corinthians 11). He writes approvingly of women missionaries and women deacons, for example, "our sister Phoebe" (Romans 16:1), and he praises a woman by the name of Junia, who was "outstanding among the apostles" (Romans 16:7).

But then in 1 Corinthians 14:34, the opposite view is expressed: "Women should remain silent in the churches . . . If they want to inquire about something, they should ask their own husbands at home; for it is disgraceful for a woman to speak in the church."

How did these contradictory statements come about? The most plausible explanation is that the gender-discriminatory language was interpolated by someone else long after Paul had written. This textual alteration may reflect changing worship patterns. It is likely that as Christian practice became institutionalized and worship shifted from homes to public meeting places, power shifted away from women. Written near the end of the first century, 1 Timothy stipulated, "A woman should learn in quietness and full submission. I do not permit a woman to teach or to have authority over a man; she must be quiet" (2:11-12).

2. When did Jesus die?

According to the synoptic gospels—Mark, Matthew, and Luke—Jesus was crucified on Friday, the day after the Passover meal. According to the gospel of John, Jesus was crucified on Thursday, the day before the Passover meal.

"On the day when it was customary to sacrifice the Passover lamb, the disciples asked Jesus, 'Where do you want us to go and make preparations for you to eat the Passover?'" (Mark 14:12). That night, they eat the Passover meal, and then Jesus is arrested (Mark 15:1). The next morning, Friday, he is brought before Pilate and crucified (Mark 15:25).

Contrast this timetable with John's. Jesus is crucified on "the day of preparation for the Passover" (John 19:14-16). This is before the Passover meal, on Thursday.

In the synoptics, Jesus dies on Friday. In John, he dies on Thursday, precisely when the Passover lambs are being slaughtered. An obvious parallel is being drawn between Jesus and the lambs, and it is no coincidence that John is the only gospel in which Jesus is called the "Lamb of God" (John 1:29, 36). The author of John modified the crucifixion timeline in order to engineer theological symbolism.

3. What was Jesus's genealogy?

According to the Old Testament, the messiah is supposed to come from the line of King David. Matthew 1:1-16 and Luke 3:23-38 both provide genealogies of Mary's husband, Joseph, to demonstrate that Jesus was, in fact, descended from David and therefore eligible to be the messiah.

There are, however, two problems with these genealogies. First, they are wildly contradictory. For example, between King David and King Shealtiel, Luke provides a total of twenty names while Matthew provides a total of fourteen names. Not only is the count different, but of all those names, not a single name between David and Shealtiel is on both lists. See below. Second, if Jesus were, as Christianity claims, a divine offspring, then he would have lacked a human father, and Joseph's genealogy could not have linked him to David anyway.

Matthew 1:6-12	Luke 3:27-31
David	David
Solomon	Nathan
Rehoboam	Mattatha
Abijah	Menna
Asa	Melea
Jehoshaphat	Eliakim (Jehoiakim)
Jehoram	Jonam
Uzziah	Joseph
Jotham	Judah
Ahaz	Simeon
Hezekiah	Levi
Manasseh	Matthat
Amon	Jorim

Josiah	Eliezer
Jeconiah	Joshua
Shealtiel (Salathiel)	Er
	Elmadam
	Cosam
	Addi
	Melki
	Neri
	Shealtiel (Salathiel)

Apologists have responded with their customary ingenuity. Some argue that while Matthew provides a genealogy of Joseph, Luke provides a genealogy of Mary. This retreat has two problems of its own. First, Luke begins the genealogy with "Joseph, the son of Heli," not with "Mary, the daughter of Heli." In fact, Mary is mentioned nowhere in the entire chapter. Second, according to Jewish law (Numbers 1:1-18), family identity is determined exclusively by the father's, not the mother's, bloodline, so Mary's lineage is irrelevant.

Incidentally, even if we ignore all these problems, the genealogies still fail. Here's why: Matthew lists Jeconiah as a descendant. But Jeconiah was cursed, and none of his descendants can inherit the throne (Jeremiah 22:28-30). Luke's genealogy runs through David's son Nathan rather than through Solomon. But only descendants of Solomon can inherit the throne (2 Samuel 7:12-13). So Matthew's genealogy fails because it runs through the cursed Jeconiah, and Luke's genealogy fails because it runs through the wrong son of David. Therefore, if either one of the two genealogies were accurate, it would decisively disqualify Jesus as an heir to David's throne.

4. How did Judas die?

In Matthew, Judas was full of remorse, so he returned the silver to those who had bribed him, and then he hanged himself (27:5). In Acts, Judas used the silver to buy some land, but he fell there, and his body burst open (1:18). So there are two contradictions: what Judas did with the money and how he died.

Apologists have, of course, attempted to harmonize these contradictory accounts. They claim that Judas returned the money to those who had bribed him and that those individuals bought the land with it. Then Judas hanged himself on that land, and while he was hanging, the noose broke, causing him to fall, whereupon his body burst open, killing him at last.

This is a bit of a strain. If that is what happened, then why doesn't either Matthew or Acts say so? To conflate the two stories in this manner is to write one's own, fifth gospel. If this fifth gospel is true, then both the authors of Matthew and Acts were unpardonably careless.

Apologists justify the conflation on the grounds that Matthew does not explicitly state that the hanging killed Judas, merely that he "hanged himself." But intellectual honesty requires consistency. Acts does not explicitly state that the body burst killed Judas either. To be consistent, one would have to conclude that Judas survived both events and lived to a ripe old age.

5. Who were the twelve apostles?

The terms "disciple" and "apostle" are imprecise. Adopted here is the most common usage in which "disciple" refers to someone who followed Jesus during his lifetime, with "apostle" reserved for the closest twelve plus, later, Paul (even though Paul referred to Andronicus and Junia in Romans 16:7 as "apostles" also).

The number 12 is of course symbolic of the twelve tribes of Israel. Jesus may have chosen twelve apostles for this reason.

In fact, Matthew's Jesus promised them that they would sit upon twelve thrones and judge the twelve tribes. In any case, as discussed in chapter 29, the apostles were empowered to perform miracles every bit as spectacular as those performed by Jesus. Each of them would have made a significant impact on world history. Their identity is therefore no small matter.

Both Mark (3:16-19) and Matthew (10:2-4) list Thaddeus as an apostle. By contrast, Luke (6:13-16) lists Judas of James and does not list Thaddeus. Other than error, is there any explanation for this contradiction? Perhaps one apostle had two very different names, or two men were both apostles, but one replaced the other chronologically.

But if the author of Luke, the odd man out here, had really conducted research as the apologists want us to believe, then he would have explored and explained this contradiction. If the two names refer to the same person, then he was a poor historian for injecting this confusion into the record. On the other hand, if Thaddeus had left the circle of the twelve and Judas of James had come off the bench to replace him, an even more interesting story cries out to be told.

6. *Who saw what at the resurrection?*

In Mark, the two Marys and Salome go to the tomb and find the stone already rolled away. The gospel never explains why they went in the first place if they expected to find the stone, too big for a man to move, still in position. They enter and see a young man dressed in white. He tells them that Jesus will be seen in Galilee. The story ends with the women leaving, frightened, telling no one. As noted in chapter 26, there are no postmortem appearances in the original version of Mark, which ends at verse 16:8.

In Matthew, the two Marys go to the tomb without Salome. Whereas in Mark, the stone was already rolled away, here the stone is still in place. The tomb is also guarded, a feature absent in the other three gospels. At this point, there is an earthquake. An angel paralyzes the guards, rolls the stone away, and says Jesus will be seen in Galilee. As the women leave, they meet Jesus, who repeats what the angel said and allows them to touch his feet. Later, the apostles go to a mountain in Galilee and see Jesus.

In Luke, the two Marys, along with Joanna and other women, find the tomb with the stone already rolled away. They enter, and suddenly, there appear two men (or two angels). Jesus does not appear to the women at all. Later, two of the disciples converse with Jesus, although they don't recognize him at the time, on the road to Emmaus. After Jesus reveals who he is, the two return to Jerusalem and tell the rest of the disciples. As they are talking, Jesus appears again. He commands them to touch him, eats a fish, explains some of the scriptures, and ascends.

In John, Mary Magdalene goes to the tomb alone. The stone has already been removed, but she does not go inside at all, running to tell the disciples instead. They enter and see that it is empty. After they leave, Mary stands outside, crying. Two angels appear to her, then she turns around and sees Jesus, who tells her to instruct the disciples that he is returning to his father. Then the elaborate Doubting Thomas cycle begins: Jesus appears to some of the disciples through a locked door. Thomas, who is not present, disbelieves them when they tell him about this. A week later, the same thing happens, and Thomas is present. Jesus commands Thomas to put his hand in his wound. Later, Jesus reappears, helps the disciples fish, and gives instructions to Peter.

These four accounts are difficult to reconcile without doing violence to the texts. Who went to the tomb? Was the stone already rolled away or not? Who was there—a man, an angel, two angels? Did Jesus appear to the women or not? In Mark, the women leave, telling no one. This raises an interesting question. If they told no one, then how do we know any of this? Finally, it is difficult to believe that some witnesses but not others felt an earthquake and watched a commando angel subdue the guards.

The car accident analogy

In summary, the New Testament contains contradictions, many of them on salient facts. Bear in mind that people are asked to change their lives on the basis of these writings. If the stories do not match one another, why should we assume that any one of them matches actual events?

Apologists argue that eyewitness reports of, say, car accidents, are seldom identical and, furthermore, that it would be suspicious if they were. That argument is a good one. Notice, however, that it concedes that the documents were written by fallible human beings. If an omnipotent god had wanted humans to have perfectly consistent stories, he could have arranged for that to have happened.

Given that the stories were written by fallible humans, can the examples cited here really be explained away by differences in perspective as suggested by the car accident analogy? The first example, concerning the role of women, is about church policy, not an event, so the argument is inapplicable. The second example is about what day Jesus died. One can imagine discrepancies arising here if the witnesses were asked to recall the date long afterward. This may help explain the discrepancy, but it does so at the expense of the stories' credibility generally.

The third example, Jesus's genealogy, is about accurately presenting a historical record, one which was, and remains, accessible to anyone who can read. So the argument is inapplicable. The fourth example, Judas's death, is not about two versions of one event but rather about two completely different stories.

The fifth example, the identity of the twelve apostles, does not concern a single event. On the contrary, the twelve had accompanied their rabbi for an extended period. The sixth example involves the multiple alleged appearances that occurred over a period of days, and the writings have discrepancies not easily explained by differences in perspective. For example, Luke and John each include entire episodes completely alien to the others, the Emmaus encounter and the Doubting Thomas cycle, respectively.

While the car accident analogy is applicable in many circumstances, it is largely unhelpful to the apologist here. To go one step further, observe that some of these differences are significant. If the apologist wants to say that differences of this magnitude can be explained by the unreliability of the sources, then he impeaches the credibility of everything in the gospels.

29

CORROBORATION

The stories about Jesus and his apostles lack corroboration from non-Christian sources. Many people assume that the historical Jesus is extensively documented. After all, the individual at the center of Western civilization's most important religion would have been the subject of intense historical and scientific interest for writers of his day.

It is remarkable, therefore, that the extraordinary events described in the gospels are not corroborated by any other documents from their time. Outside of the Bible, there are no sources written during Jesus's life that even mention him. Nor are there any other sources that mention Jesus for sixty years after his death. The first appear to be Josephus's *Antiquities of the Jews*, circa 94 CE, and the epistle 1 Clement, circa 96 CE.

The case grows even more mysterious when we inquire into the twelve apostles. They had been given the power to perform miracles and instructed to use it to spread the gospel. Jesus gave them his authority to drive out demons and cure illnesses (Matthew 10:1-4) telling them that they would perform even greater miracles than he had (John 14:12). And yet, outside of the Bible, there are no sources that mention any of the twelve for sixty years after Jesus's death.

Jesus

Recall these Bible stories: Out of fear of a newborn challenger, King Herod ordered the slaughter of all male children under the age of two in Bethlehem (Matthew 2:16-18). Jesus fed five thousand people with five loaves of bread and two fish (Mark 6:30-44). "News about him spread all over Syria . . . Large crowds from Galilee, the Decapolis, Jerusalem, Judea and the region across the Jordan followed him" (Matthew 4:24-25). A crowd watched Jesus raise a boy from the dead, and the "news about Jesus spread throughout Judea and the surrounding country" (Luke 7:11-17).

It is difficult to explain how, if they really happened, events so spectacular and widely witnessed would have escaped the notice of contemporary writers. The silence cannot be explained by a lack of interested parties. There were many historians and scientists (called at that time "natural philosophers"), both Roman and Jewish, active during this period. The Roman historian Livy (circa 10 CE) wrote near the time of Herod's alleged slaughter, but he mentioned it nowhere. The Roman philosopher Seneca (circa 65 CE) was alive during Jesus's ministry, but he failed to mention Jesus. The Roman naturalist and philosopher Pliny the Elder (circa 80 CE) was also alive during Jesus's ministry, but he too neglected to mention it. The Jewish philosopher Philo (circa 40 CE) wrote extensively about both religion and Pontius Pilate, yet he never mentioned Jesus. The Jewish historian Justus of Tiberius (circa 80 CE) was even a native of Galilee. He wrote a history of the Jews from Moses to Agrippa II but never mentioned Jesus.[1]

Jesus's immediate followers appear to have been simple, uneducated people. One might therefore argue that it is unsurprising that we have little written record of his career. But as pointed out above, there were many others who would have been curious and capable. How can we have confidence in the historicity of events so thinly attested? Beyond the echo chamber of the early Christian community, where is the evidence for the religion's claims?

After three generations, more writings appeared, most of them by Christians. Non-Christians had barely begun to take notice.

Christian writings by Clement, Ignatius, Polycarp, and Quadratus of Athens repeat beliefs commonly held by the faithful. These authors wrote with religious devotion, and there is no indication that they drew upon sources independent of oral tradition. From Papias, we possess only fragments. He does, however, claim to have spoken to people who had spoken to some of the apostles. This is the closest the historical record comes to eyewitness corroboration. On the other hand, his reliability is questionable. Regarding the traitor Judas, Papias reported, "His flesh was so bloated that he could not pass where a wagon could easily pass through, not even the mass of his head."[2] This description must arouse discomfort among even the most credulous of readers.

The earliest non-Christian writings that deal with these issues fall into two categories. The first category includes Epictetus, Pliny, and Suetonius. Their writings simply document the existence of Christians, something no one disputes. The second category includes Josephus, Tacitus, and the Talmud. These writings may have more useful information. Josephus and Tacitus mention the execution of Jesus (though the authenticity of the passages in Josephus is contested). The Talmud has several passages that may refer to the Jesus of Christianity, but this is not clear. If these passages do indeed refer to him, then they contradict as much as corroborate the gospels.

These sources, along with others sometimes cited on this topic, are discussed in appendix 6.

The gaps in the historical record have persuaded many that Jesus did not exist at all, that he was for instance simply a solar deity who was anthropomorphized into the god-man Jesus, a view known as mythicism. While that is possible, it may go too far. The mythicist position is that the man Jesus was invented gradually. The position taken here, by contrast, is that the man Jesus was real but that his divinity was invented gradually.

The apostles

The names of the twelve apostles are not listed in any early non-Christian sources. But if this group really existed, its members would be among history's most important figures. Whereas Jesus's ministry lasted only one to three years, the apostles would have preached for decades. And even excluding the latecomers James and Paul, there were a dozen of them. (Judas was replaced by Matthias according to Acts 1:23-26.) If they had really existed and performed the signs they were empowered to perform, we would have inherited armfuls of attestation of their deeds.

As mentioned above, Jesus promised that they would perform even greater miracles than he. Why do we not read of these? It might be logical to expect that where Jesus turned water into wine, the apostles could have turned desert into farmland; where Jesus cured blind people, the apostles could have eradicated blindness; where Jesus rose from the dead, the apostles could have refrained from dying at all. The world would be a different place had such things happened, and people would have noticed.

Perhaps Jesus simply meant that the apostles would perform similar miracles, but more of them. Let's explore the implications of that. According to Mark, Jesus had a one-year ministry. If 12 apostles had ministries lasting on average, 30 years, then they would have ministered 360 times as much as Jesus had. If that is true, then we should find a miracle scale factor (MSF) of 360 to 1.

In Mark, Jesus exorcised demons out of at least 9 people.* Given an MSF of 360:1, the apostles should have performed 3,240 exorcisms. Even the New Testament contains nothing on this scale. And outside of the New Testament, there is very little documentation of the apostles' existences, much less their miracles.

Consider the best-known of the twelve, Peter. If the life of any of the apostles were well-documented, it would be his. According to Tertullian and Origen, writing over a century later, Peter was executed in Rome somewhere between 62 and 67 CE. If that is correct, then about thirty-five years had elapsed between Jesus's death and Peter's. What was he doing all that time? The book of Acts describes him spreading the gospel and employing his supernatural powers to heal the sick, resurrect the dead, and demonstrate the truth of his message with signs and wonders.

If he really did these things, why is there no extrabiblical account of them? His deeds would have made electrifying news. And if he had continued to perform miracles year in and year out for over three decades, there would have been ample time for word to spread and for sober observers to verify and catalogue the events. As confirmation of his supernatural abilities became known, people from all over the empire would have taken notice.

The healing temples of Asclepius would have emptied. People would have flocked to Peter from great distances to be healed. But there are no records of any such pilgrimages. Roman statesmen and foreign princes would have invited him to their courts. But there are no records of any such invitations or audiences.

---

* Mark 1:23-27 one; 1:32-34 "many" say three; 1:39 "demons" say two; 5:1-18 one; 7:25-30 one; 9:17-29 one.

Scientists and historians would have sought him out to pose questions and witness his wondrous deeds. But there are no records of any such investigations.

There is little historical record of the careers of the other eleven either. A few Christian writers, such as Clement of Alexandria (circa 200 CE) and Eusebius (circa 320 CE), mention tidbits, but they do not appear to be citing reliable sources. For example, describing the missions of some of the more prominent apostles, Eusebius wrote, "Thomas, *tradition tells us*, was chosen for Parthia, Andrew for Scythia, John for Asia . . . Peter *seems to have* preached in Pontus, Galatia . . ." (italics added).[3]

So the inexplicable omissions in the life of Peter must be multiplied by twelve. This leaves an immense gap in the historical record. Apologists provide two possible explanations for this gap: first, the apostles were self-effacing, emphasizing Jesus and the gospel, not themselves; second, the destruction of Jerusalem by the Romans in 70 CE destroyed records of the apostles' activities. Neither of these arguments is persuasive. Wonder workers would not have needed to promote themselves; others would have done it for them. And the destruction of Jerusalem is irrelevant because the apostles are said to have fanned out far beyond Jerusalem to spread the word. The most plausible explanation for the gap in the historical record is that nothing worth recording actually happened.

It was not until long after they lived that popular legendary stories about the lives of the apostles began to appear in writing. For example, the Acts of Peter (circa 180 CE), the Acts of John (150-200 CE), and the Acts of Thomas (after 200 CE) tell entertaining and inspiring stories about their namesake heroes.[4] These may be among the earliest forms of historical novels, and they led to a long line of hagiographic literature in the centuries that followed.

In one of these noncanonical works, the Acts of Peter, the apostle not only cures the sick and resurrects the dead, but he even makes a dog speak and resurrects a smoked tuna! In a duel of miracles, he defeats his archrival, the wicked sorcerer Simon Magus, in front of a big crowd. He is so successful in preaching chastity that the mistresses, and even the wives, of some of Rome's civic leaders refuse to sleep with their men. Consequently, he is arrested and sentenced to death. He requests to be crucified upside down, during which procedure he delivers an unintelligible speech explaining the symbolism behind the manner of his death.[5]

Some apologists argue that the willingness of the apostles to die for their beliefs is evidence of the truth of those beliefs. There are, however, serious problems with this argument. First, being willing to die for a belief is no indication that the belief is true. Suicide bombers die for questionable beliefs every day. Second, there is no more historical evidence for the apostles' deaths than there is for their lives. The New Testament mentions the execution of only one of the twelve, James, the brother of John (Acts 12:2). The death of Stephen is also mentioned (Acts 7:58-59), but he was not one of the twelve. As stated above, Peter's death was discussed by Tertullian and Origen. About the others, there is little reliable information.

Early Christian writers would have been eager to fill the historical gaps, either for inspirational or apologetic reasons. Tales of the apostles' courage in the face of persecution could inspire later generations of Christians facing their own difficulties. And so, unsurprisingly, stories that met this demand arose over time.

In summary, Jesus's life and death appear to have been little noticed outside of the Bible. No document even mentions him until sixty years after his death, and the same silence exists for the apostles. The lack of contemporaneous historical documentation for what would have been spectacular and widely witnessed events, the understandable desire of Christians of later generations to romanticize the courage and faith of their predecessors—especially during times of persecution—and the late appearance of popular legends to meet this demand reveal a very human process of invention and backfill.

30

RESURRECTION

The resurrection of Jesus is the central historical claim of Christianity. As with the religion's other historical claims, much of the evidence for it is found in the gospels. But in the case of the resurrection, we must address also the existence of the Jesus movement itself. The early church could only have arisen, so goes a common argument, in response to a resurrection.

Most inquiries into the historicity of the resurrection are based on gospel details, but as we have seen, they are unreliable. The reasons are worth recapitulating here. Before being committed to paper, the stories circulated for years among unlettered, prescientific people. Differing versions of the stories were then composed by anonymous authors who never claimed to have been eyewitnesses. These authors imposed literary features and their own theological views on the material, even to the point of misrepresenting the Old Testament when it suited their purposes. In addition, the original texts were repeatedly altered by scribes, and because no first-century manuscripts exist, the earliest alterations are undetectable. Finally, the writings we have inherited contradict one another on salient facts and lack corroboration from non-Christian sources.

Taken together, or even singly, these shortcomings render the gospels untrustworthy. Accordingly, this discussion does not dwell upon them but instead contemplates the likely origins of an initial, primitive belief. The clear historical fact is that in the minds of some of his followers, Jesus rose from the dead. The question then is: how did this belief come about? One possible explanation is that Jesus did, in fact, rise from the dead. But there are many possible naturalistic explanations as well. Rather than catalogue these alternatives, presented below for simplicity is a discussion of only one.

The argument here is that a belief in a resurrection did not require an actual resurrection. The conditions were right for the belief to arise. That belief provided the basis for the early movement. As the movement gathered strength, the initial belief was embellished in understandable ways.

An alternative explanation

Assume a historical core: a charismatic rabbi and faith healer named Jesus gathered a following, made some powerful enemies, and was executed. Four factors contributed to a resurrection belief among his followers. (The first of these is common to all the gospel miracle stories; the others are particular to the resurrection.)

First, the vast majority of the people of that time and place were unschooled and superstitious. For example, they thought demon possession was the cause of illness. Mark, the shortest gospel, mentions demon possession twelve times.* Ancient Middle Easterners freely assumed that gods appeared in the form of human beings. For example, people thought Paul had healed a cripple, from which fact they concluded that he and Barnabas were the gods Hermes and Zeus (Acts 14:8-12). As discussed in

---

* Mark 1:23-27, 1:32-34, 1:39, 3:11, 3:15, 3:22-30, 5:1-18, 6:7, 6:12, 7:25-30, 9:17-29, 9:38-41.

chapter 23, the literacy rate in Roman Palestine was at the low end of the 3 to 15 percent range, with higher rates concentrated in the cities rather than in backwaters, such as Galilee.[1]

By contrast, in the United States today, the literacy rate is about 99 percent.[2] People use airplanes and microwaves. Some even understand how they work. Most are familiar with the concepts of investigation, experimentation, and corroboration and recognize that these are tools to guard against error, fraud, and delusion. And yet many hold fantastic beliefs. A substantial fraction of Americans, 29 percent, report that they have felt the presence of someone who has died.[3] If people can come to hold such beliefs in the U.S. today, imagine how much more prevalent they would have been in the ancient world.

Second, Jews of first-century Palestine were members of a culture in which resurrection and ascension were widely discussed and even expected. The ascensions of Enoch (Genesis 5:24) and Elijah (2 Kings 2:10-12) were well known. The martyrs of the Maccabean Revolt were believed by some to have been rewarded with resurrection and ascension.[4] King Herod's reaction upon first hearing about Jesus was, "This is John the Baptist; he has risen from the dead!" (Matthew 14:2).

There was a wide diversity of beliefs within Judaism, but most people believed in some type of general resurrection—one of large numbers of people. Some believed that all the dead of Israel would be raised; others believed that only the righteous would be.[5] The Sadducees appear to have been one of the few groups that did not believe in a resurrection, but their disbelief was a well-known exception that provoked debate (Mark 12:18-27).

Because Jesus was an apocalypticist, his followers, more so than most, were anticipating the end of time. They "thought that the kingdom of God was going to appear at once" (Luke 19:11). They, more so than most, were expecting the general resurrection that would accompany the apocalypse. It would have been consistent with this perspective to believe that Jesus had been resurrected and that others would soon follow. In fact, this is exactly how Paul described it, writing that Jesus was the "first fruit" (1 Corinthians 15:20). His word choice refers to an ancient tradition of dedicating the first pickings of the harvest to a god. He was saying that just as the first fruit immediately precedes the rest of the harvest, Jesus's resurrection precedes those of his followers.

Jesus's circle, it must be acknowledged, consisted of unsophisticated people in a prescientific setting who were expecting a general resurrection to begin at any moment.

Third, human beings, particularly when distraught, can imagine things. After the crucifixion, Jesus's followers were overcome with grief, stunned that their leader had been ignominiously killed, suffering from the guilt of having abandoned him, and still afraid that they might be arrested next. Such people do not make reliable witnesses.

Even in the gospels, no one actually saw Jesus rise from the dead. He was reported to have appeared only after death. Bereaved people commonly report feeling the presence of recently deceased loved ones. This feeling is sometimes accompanied by the departed's visual image, voice, and even touch, a phenomenon referred to in the psychology of bereavement as a "sense of presence."[6]

The grief of Jesus's followers would have been compounded, at least for some of them, with guilt at having abandoned him at his arrest. This powerful combination of emotions may have made them especially susceptible to experiencing a sense of presence.[7] It may also explain the otherwise suspicious tradition that Jesus appeared exclusively to friends, not enemies, to Mary and the twelve, not Pilate, Herod, or the Sanhedrin. "He was not seen by all the people, but by witnesses whom God had already chosen—by us who ate and drank with him after he rose from the dead" (Acts 10:41).

Fourth, Jesus's followers would have wanted to believe. Such people are less reliable than impartial observers. They had abandoned their livelihoods and families to follow this charismatic rabbi and await the imminent apocalypse. "We have left everything to follow you" (Mark 10:28). If Jesus had died like any other man, then their most cherished beliefs would have been disconfirmed. They would have been embarrassed that their messiah had died, his great work unfinished.

Resurrection, by contrast, would have meant vindication. It would have confirmed their beliefs, justified their actions, renewed their hopes, and restored their reputations. It is common for people to seek meaning in tragedy, and Jesus's story had ended too abruptly. Just as the classical prophets had reinterpreted the Jews' defeats by the Assyrians and the Babylonians (see appendix 3), Jesus's followers would have been eager to reinterpret his death.

Given these four social and psychological factors, it is not difficult to imagine one or more of Jesus's followers having dreams or visions of him. The germ of a resurrection rumor could have been a sense of presence by one or more followers.

We can go further. Given the culture's lack of education, superstition, and widespread expectations of an imminent apocalypse, one might venture to say that if there had not been a rumor of Jesus's resurrection, then there would have been a rumor of someone else's resurrection.

A rumor can be created in minutes and spread in hours. False rumors, if they're exciting, can be difficult to dispel. Once the exciting rumor had been born among Jesus's followers, people outside his circle accepted the story without requiring much, if any, evidence. The earliest Christians were not data-driven: according to Acts 2:41, the first time the disciples preached, three thousand people converted. No one demanded to see and no one offered to provide any evidence.

Objections

Those who believe that Jesus actually rose from the dead will of course object to any naturalistic explanation for the rumor. Three of the most common objections are discussed below.

The first objection is that the resurrection stories must be true because otherwise eyewitnesses alive at the time the stories circulated would have corrected them.

This objection withers quickly. There are no eyewitnesses to an event that never occurred. To the extent eyewitnesses were consulted, they would certainly have disagreed with false stories, but they had no power to prevent others from telling them. Anyone raising this objection would be forced to acknowledge that it could be employed to justify any number of miracle claims. Recall the Buddha's miracles from chapter 18. In front of large crowds, his disciple restored a man's amputated hands and feet, and the Buddha multiplied himself and levitated into the sky. By the apologist's logic, these events must really have occurred because otherwise eyewitnesses would have corrected the stories.

It is worth adding that the majority of the prospective witness pool did, in fact, disagree with stories of Jesus's resurrection. Most people of that time and place did not become followers of Jesus. Christianity grew primarily among gentiles and Diaspora Jews living far away from Palestine. Those closest to the alleged events and the alleged witnesses did not find the stories convincing. As mentioned in chapter 14, this was, and remains, an embarrassment for Christianity.

Some apologists, eager to deflect attention from this embarrassment, exaggerate the number of early converts or the depth of their conversions. "Five weeks after he's crucified, over ten thousand Jews are following him and claiming that he is the initiator of a new religion. And get this: they're willing to give up or alter all five of the social institutions that they have been taught since childhood have such importance . . ."[8]

Of course, none of that is accurate. According to Acts 1:15, there were only 120 followers at the time of Jesus's ascension, 40 days after his resurrection. This is a far cry from 10,000. Moreover, the emergence of a distinct new religion was a gradual process. It is clear from Paul's letters, written a quarter century after Jesus's death, that most members of the Jesus movement were still Jews and that debates were ongoing regarding the role of the Jewish law in the life of a Christian. In arguing that the law was no longer necessary, Paul was fighting for an equal place for the minority gentiles entering the movement. His position triumphed in the end because the weight of gentile numbers eventually overwhelmed the movement's original Jewish composition.

A second objection is that Paul and James believed in the resurrection and even became leaders in the Jesus movement, yet they were not "grief stricken followers who wanted to believe." Quite the contrary, they were initially hostile to Jesus and his message.

This objection misses the point. The naturalistic explanation for the resurrection belief is that the original rumor came from grief-stricken followers, not that everyone who joined the movement afterward fell into that category. Paul and James both came to the movement later. And both had, or came to have, self-interest at stake in its perpetuation. Paul believed that he had been chosen as a leader of the fledgling movement, and as such, he would have had an incentive to exaggerate his own experience: *"What? You didn't see Jesus?" "Of course I saw Jesus!"* Paul's visions were his credentials as an apostle, a sensitive topic about which he was quite defensive. See, for example, 2 Corinthians 11:5 and Galatians 2:6-9. The politics of succession were even more important for James. He is portrayed as Jesus's brother, and apparently, some believed that this elevated him to leadership after the latter's death (Acts 15:13-21, 21:18-26). His own prestige and power were therefore positively correlated to the esteem in which his brother was held.

What evidence did Paul and James have for believing in the resurrection? Paul saw visions. Therefore, his writings do not support claims of a bodily resurrection. As for James, the only claim that he saw the risen Jesus is Paul's statement in 1

Corinthians 15:7-8, a statement uncorroborated by the gospels or even the epistle of James.

A third objection is that if Jesus had not risen from the dead, skeptics would have dug up his corpse to prove it.

This objection has at least two major flaws. First, so much time would have passed between the death and an inquiry that identification of a body would have been impossible. According to John 11:17 and 11:39, Lazarus, in a private tomb and therefore uncontaminated by proximity to other bodies, had begun to decompose and stink after only four days. In fact, Jewish law at the time stated that a corpse could only be legally identified within three days of death.[9] But according to Acts 2:1-41, the disciples did not proclaim Jesus's resurrection publicly until the Feast of the Pentecost, about fifty days after his crucifixion.

Second, this objection presupposes that Christianity was important enough to the authorities, Jewish or Roman, to warrant an exhumation. Only the authorities could have exhumed a body because an individual would have been charged with grave robbery. People today, knowing that Christianity is a major world religion, assume it was newsworthy from the outset. But first-century Palestine was a religious hothouse, teeming with Jewish sects espousing many different beliefs. Richard Carrier identifies between ten and thirty, depending on the degree of overlap.[10] Some are well known, the Pharisees and Sadducees, for example. Others are less well known: the Ossaeans, the Bana'im, the Masbotheans, and the Maghariya. The Mandeans, who venerate John the Baptist and believe Jesus was a false prophet, still exist to this day.

There would have been little reason for the authorities to become alarmed over yet another sect, and it would be understandable if they did not take the earliest resurrection claims seriously. Perhaps they anticipated that even if they had produced a partially decomposed corpse, Jesus's followers would have scoffed and denied the body was Jesus's. They would probably have construed it as a test of their faith.

In summary, these three objections do little to weaken the naturalistic explanation for the resurrection belief. Of course, speculation could be endless. But is that not itself a reason to be skeptical?

A competent deity wishing to demonstrate that he had been resurrected could have arranged events in order to reanimate himself in front of a large crowd instead of alone in a dark corner; he could have appeared posthumously to outsiders and enemies, not just erstwhile followers; he could have remained on the scene indefinitely so that nonpartisan observers could investigate, rather than conveniently ascending prior to any public proclamations, and so on. A competent deity who wished others to know that he had been resurrected could have done so in a manner that was not open to endless speculation but rather one which was convincing for all humankind for all time.

Rumor

A rumor born of someone's sense of presence might naturally be expected to produce some divergent reports or confusion, and that is precisely what we find. While the naturalistic explanation advanced here is not based on the gospels, it is not entirely inconsistent with them either, as they preserve what might be termed a "confusion tradition." Put aside Mark (as discussed in chapter 26, Mark's original ending at verse 16:8 lacked postmortem appearances) and consider the other three.

In addition to the fact that the three gospels provide post-resurrection accounts that are very different from one another (see chapter 28), each account preserves its own confusion episode. In Matthew 28:16-17, Jesus gave his valedictory speech to the disciples, "but some doubted." In Luke 24:13-32, Jesus talked at length with two followers on the road to

Emmaus, but "they were kept from recognizing him" until they sat down to eat. In John 20:14-16, Mary wept outside the tomb and talked with Jesus, "thinking he was the gardener," a case of mistaken identity offering not a little comedic potential.

A sense of presence experience by one or more followers and the rumor these reports would have ignited can explain not only the Jesus movement but the gospel confusion tradition as well.

Let's resume tracing the path of the resurrection belief once the rumor had begun. Claims that Jesus appeared to multiple individuals simultaneously were probably added to the rumor later. They are precisely the sorts of embellishment one might expect as an oral tradition evolves. The earliest written record of such a report comes twenty-five years after Jesus's death, when Paul wrote that Jesus appeared to five hundred people, a claim discussed at length in the next chapter.

Stories about an "empty tomb" were probably added later still. Even Paul never mentions one. It seems unlikely that he would have travelled to Jerusalem and not visited the site of the religion's foundational miracle or, having done so, that he would fail to mention it. An empty tomb probably never existed. But the idea of one served the purpose of shoring up the credibility of post-resurrection appearance stories, particularly since these stories originated among Jesus's followers who were, as everyone would have recognized, biased.

In closing, the launch of Christianity did not require a resurrection; it only required a belief in a resurrection. The germinal rumor that Jesus rose from the dead has at least one satisfactory naturalistic explanation. It emerged from the garbled retellings of what were the subjective experiences of a few superstitious and grief-stricken followers. It was then seized upon uncritically by those attracted to the promise offered by the faith—the exciting promise that they too could be resurrected, that there is, after all, a cure for death.

31

LEGEND

Given the vindication that a rumored resurrection provided to the previously demoralized and publicly humiliated disciples, and the promise it offered to all, it is not difficult to imagine Jesus's followers undertaking a reinterpretation of events. It is also not difficult to imagine stories becoming more elaborate with subsequent retellings. Humans make mistakes, exaggerate, and embellish. (At least we know that about the stories *other people* believe.) So the rumors took on a life and grew into legends. Years later, versions of the legends were fashioned into written narratives.

Below are two examples of this process. The first is an oft-cited passage from Paul in which the risen Jesus allegedly appeared to five hundred people simultaneously. It is difficult to accept this claim as factual. The second is a comparison of how different gospels appear to understand the inception of Jesus's divinity. A clear progression is visible as Jesus's stature grows over time.

Paul's five hundred

In 1 Corinthians 15:3-5, Paul states that Jesus was crucified and resurrected and that he then appeared to Peter and the twelve. As mentioned in chapter 22, scholars believe these verses were originally a hymn. But there is debate about where the original hymn ends and Paul's addition begins. Paul probably added verses 6-8, which continue the list: Jesus appeared to more than five hundred people at the same time, then to James, then to all the apostles, then finally to Paul himself.[1]

These verses raise a number of problems for anyone interested in historical accuracy. First, the hymn neglects to mention Mary and the other women who, according to the gospels of Matthew and John, were the first to see the risen Jesus. Second, neither the gospels nor the epistles of James or Peter mention an appearance to James.

Third and most relevant here, neither the gospels nor the epistles of James or Peter mention an appearance to five hundred people. An omission of this significance would be a problem in even one of these writings, let alone all six.

Some apologists try to argue that there is, in fact, a possible reference to this appearance in one of the gospels. In Matthew 28, Jesus appears to the apostles on a mountain. These apologists argue that there may have been other people there too. That is possible. But it is without foundation in the text. One could, with equal justification, assert that Jesus appeared in the form of the elephant-headed Hindu god Ganesh. That at least would explain why, as the others worshipped him, "some doubted" (28:17).

The lack of corroboration is only a foretaste of the difficulties presented by this claim. The text states: "After that, he appeared to more than five hundred of the brothers and sisters at the same time, most of whom are still living, though some have fallen asleep" (1 Corinthians 15:6). Upon a first reading, one might be tempted to say, as the apologists wish us to do, *"This is strong evidence for the resurrection. How could five hundred people be wrong? It's not possible for five hundred people to have the same hallucination!"* But the correct question to ask is: did five hundred people make this claim, or did one person make this claim about them?

Notice that Paul does not provide statements from any of these people. Nor does he provide their names. In other words, we do not have the testimony of five hundred people. We simply have the statement of one man. There are reasons to be skeptical of it.

First, none of these five hundred left any evidence of what is claimed on his behalf. None left any writing—either in his own hand or dictated to another—describing in the first person what he saw. No other source, inside the Bible or out, makes the claim Paul makes about them.

Second, if the 500 really existed, then most of them did not witness anything life-changing. According to Acts 1:15, Jesus had only 120 followers after his post-resurrection appearances and ascension. What happened to the other 380? Either the appearance to 500 never occurred or the majority was unimpressed by what it had seen.

Finally, how would Paul have known about the five hundred? If he had heard about them from Peter and James, then why do no other New Testament writings mention them? If he had interviewed the five hundred personally, he could not have done so for seventeen years after his conversion, twenty years after the death of Jesus. (According to Galatians 1:22-2:1, during the time he was persecuting the Jesus sect, he was "unknown to the churches of Judea," and during his first visit to Jerusalem, three years after his conversion, he met with Peter and James only. It was then another fourteen years before he returned.)

Apologists argue that Paul must have been telling the truth because anyone could have tested his claim by talking with some of the five hundred. But could the recipients of Paul's letter, the Christians in Corinth, really have done this? It is unlikely that anyone skeptical enough to require corroboration would have tried to do so. Such journeys even today are generally the province of those who are already true believers. And travel in that day was expensive, time-consuming, and dangerous. Paul did not even say where the five hundred were. Jerusalem? Galilee? Of course it is possible that someone could have travelled hundreds of miles from Corinth to Palestine—by sail, by foot, or on the back of a beast—and then gone house to house in the most likely towns, looking for witnesses to an event that occurred twenty years prior. Not surprisingly, there is no record of anyone doing this.

Suppose someone actually did. He survived the journey from Corinth and began to canvass the most likely locations of the event. At the time of Paul's writing, the mid-fifties, there were Christians active in Palestine. It is unlikely they would have let our investigator return home disappointed. And even if he had, would his colleagues back in Corinth have accepted his failure? More likely, after his long and fruitless absence, they would have sided with Paul. *"He never had faith to begin with!" "He was jealous of Paul from the beginning. That's why he went . . . or did he really?"*

The appearance to five hundred is uncorroborated by any other source, including any other source in the Bible, despite numerous passages where it would have been appropriate to mention it (for example, Matthew 28:16, Luke 24:50, or John 20:30). That alone is reason to doubt its historical authenticity.

We cannot know if Paul imagined the five hundred and then, in his zeal, convinced himself that it was true or if he simply passed on, uncritically, something someone else had told him. But he is the sole source for this story, and its reliability is highly suspect. He is a man who lurched between extreme beliefs, from persecutor to zealot, who claimed to have received serial revelations from a god, and who misrepresented the scripture he pretended to hold sacred in order to invent doctrines antithetical to its traditional meaning. The appearance to five hundred is just another story, without details and without corroboration, told by one man, not five hundred, and a man not very reliable at that.

Jesus's divinity

As discussed in chapter 22, Paul appears to have been uninterested in Jesus's biography, save his death and resurrection. What was important was that Jesus had died as an atonement sacrifice and his resurrection promised eternal life. Jesus started out, for Paul, as a divine being; his incarnation as a man was in service of this salvific mission.

But those who wanted to tell the story of the Nazarean's life and ministry seem to have had a different perspective. For some of them, Jesus started out as an ordinary man, not a divine being. Ultimately, Paul's viewpoint would prevail and these others would be declared heretical. But we can see evidence for the other viewpoints fossilized in the scriptures. We can see that the story was progressively revised until it came to exhibit a christology every bit as exalted as Paul's. In Mark, Jesus becomes divine only at the time of his baptism; in Matthew and Luke, at the time of his birth or conception; and in John, Jesus is eternally divine.

In Mark, there is no genealogy, nativity story, or virgin birth. Jesus first appears as a grown man at the time of his baptism, and there is no discussion of his past. This suggests that nothing out of the ordinary had previously occurred.

At his baptism, "as Jesus was coming up out of the water, he saw heaven being torn open and the Spirit descending on him like a dove. And a voice came from heaven: 'You are my Son, whom I love; with you I am well pleased'" (1:10-11). The phrase "Spirit descending on him" suggests that the spirit was absent previously, i.e., that Jesus is being adopted by god at this time and not before.

This is adoptionism, mentioned in chapter 26, the belief that Jesus was born a man but that at some point he was chosen by god and adopted as his son, becoming divine then only. An adoptionistic understanding is further supported by the fact that Jesus went to be baptized in the first place. After all, baptism is a washing away of sins. If Jesus were already divine, why would he have sins that needed to be washed away?

Later, while Jesus taught, those around him thought he was "out of his mind" (3:21). Such a reaction would make no sense if Jesus had been born in the crosshairs of a miraculous navigational star beam or spent 3 days as a youngster precociously schooling the temple priests—story elements that would later be added by the authors of Matthew and Luke—or if Jesus had previously displayed any other superhuman attributes. The reaction of those around him suggests that Mark's Jesus was a normal man until the time of his baptism.

As discussed in chapter 23, Matthew and Luke were written after Mark. They are the earliest writings to claim that Jesus was born of a virgin. In Matthew, Jesus is divine from birth, and by implication, from conception. An angel explains to Joseph that supernatural forces are afoot, so he marries the pregnant Mary anyway. As in Mark, Jesus launches his career by being baptized. Here, however, John the Baptist objects that it is senseless and proceeds only after Jesus insists (3:15).

In Luke, Jesus is divine from conception. This point is made explicit when John the Baptist jumps in his mother's womb at the moment that Jesus, still in his mother's womb, comes near (1:41). Unlike Matthew's angel, who appears to Joseph, Luke's angel appears to Mary. Jesus's baptism is further de-emphasized. The narrative states matter-of-factly that Jesus and his followers were baptized. But the descent of the holy spirit is relocated. It is not until after the baptism, while Jesus is praying, that the holy spirit descends (3:21-22). In this way, the author of Luke was able to retain the Marcan plot element but rearrange the story so that John the Baptist's act was not the catalyst for Jesus's divinity.

Throughout the synoptic gospels, there is no indication that Jesus existed prior to his birth or conception. That final development awaited the fourth evangelist. In John, Jesus is eternal, the preexisting logos (see chapter 25) who created the world. John's Jesus abstains from plot elements that are beneath the dignity of a deity: he is not baptized at all, nor does he go into the desert to be tested by temptation, as he does in the three earlier gospels.

There is another piece to this puzzle, one which precedes the gospels. In Romans, Paul repeated an early Christian creed or hymn that reveals something interesting about the oldest stratum of the Jesus tradition. He wrote that Jesus "was appointed the Son of God in power by his resurrection" (Romans 1:3-4). It would appear, according to this hymn, that Jesus was adopted by god at the time of his resurrection.[2]

In the teachings of Jesus's biographers, a progression is plain to see. The inception of his divinity has been steadily pushed further back in time. The pre-Pauline hymn in Romans shows that the earliest Christians probably believed that Jesus was a man like any other until adopted by god *at his resurrection.* Mark reflects the view that he was a man like any other until adopted *at his baptism,* Matthew and Luke that he was divine *from birth or conception,* and, finally, John *for all eternity.* Instead of the biography driving the theology, the theology drove the biography. With the fourth gospel, Jesus was well on the way to Nicaea.

32

GROWTH

Christianity is the world's largest religion, claiming about 32 percent of the population. Some Christians assert that their religion's success is evidence of supernatural favor. Is that true? This chapter presents the case that Christianity's expansion, like its origin, has completely naturalistic explanations.

Christianity's rise was impressive, but other religions have enjoyed steep growth curves as well. Its growth rate of about 3 1/2 percent per year within the Roman Empire has been matched, for example, by that of Mormonism in the United States.[1] Scholars have identified many factors behind Christianity's success, but the following sketch seems more than adequate to render supernatural explanations unnecessary:

First, Christianity promised what people want—blissful immortality. At the same time, for those who found the promise insufficiently alluring, it threatened eternal torment. The latter could be avoided and the former secured by the simple step of accepting baptism. Unlike the competing monotheism of Judaism, Christianity required no initiatory ordeals, such as circumcision. Later, Christianity would add more elaborate sacraments, but these were never onerous.

The specificity of Jesus's promises, however, created an early crisis. As discussed in chapters 20 and 23, Jesus had stated that some listening to him would still be alive at a second coming (Mark 9:1 and Matthew 16:28), and as the earliest generation of followers began to die, this was beginning to look doubtful. The crisis of confidence occasioned by Jesus's failure may explain the prominence of martyr stories, which served the purpose, at least temporarily, of shoring up faltering confidence.[2] Eventually, with the dissemination of the gospel of John, the problem was addressed through doctrinal sleight of hand. Its author subtly revised the expectation. Instead of a future kingdom of god on earth, the spotlight was shifted to an ongoing kingdom of god in heaven.[3]

Christianity's promise of blissful immortality and threat of eternal torment were a carrot and stick that anyone could understand. Unlike the competing philosophy of Stoicism, Christianity did not favor a reflective temperament or require acceptance of death's permanence. And while a monotheistic god might have seemed remote, the story that his son lived and suffered as a human enabled people to relate to him emotionally. These emotional attachments would later be deepened, as reverence for Mary became organized and the saints absorbed the functions of local pagan patron gods.

Second, Christianity was open to anyone, and it encouraged proselytization. Judaism was attractive to many pagans because of its antiquity and monotheism, but the Jews did not proselytize energetically. For the most part, they thought of themselves ethnically as a people chosen by god. Christianity, on the other hand, had wider horizons, and part of its message was to spread the message.

Christians recruited from all classes, including the large slave population, and sought out women. The pagan philosopher Celsus mocked this indiscriminate proselytization, "Let no one educated, no one wise, no one sensible draw near. For these abilities are thought by us to be evils. But as for anyone ignorant, anyone stupid, anyone uneducated, anyone who is a child, let him come boldly. By the fact that they themselves admit that these people are worthy of their god, they show that they want and are able to convince only the foolish, dishonorable and stupid, and only slaves, women, and little children."[4]

Indiscriminate though it may have been, Christian missionary zeal paid dividends in the long run. Reaching out to women was especially effective if the prize included the next generation. By contrast, the competing mystery religion of Mithraism, discussed in chapter 21, accepted only men as initiates, a policy fatal to its longevity.

Third, Christian worship required exclusivity. While other gods were less jealous, the Christian god would not tolerate continued belief in others. This exclusivity had two effects: it increased the likelihood of persecution, and it created an asymmetric conversion dynamic.

Why were Christians persecuted? In addition to the fact that they proselytized and ruffled feathers in the process, their exclusive worship was sometimes deemed a threat to the community. Most people in the ancient world had a collective rather than individualistic view of humankind's relationship with the divine. If some failed to pay proper respect to a god, that god might vent his anger on the city as a whole, not just the offending individuals. It was therefore important for everyone to participate. For polytheists, this was not a problem because the worship of one god did not preclude the worship of others.

But for Jews and Christians, this would have been blasphemy. As a result, they refused to worship the civic deities. Some pagans feared grave consequences for the entire community if such "atheism" were allowed to continue. And while Judaism was generally respected as an exception of long standing, Christianity was new and spreading.

Emperor Nero began the persecutions in 64 CE, and, though enforcement was sporadic, Christianity remained outlawed until

Constantine. Official persecutions generally targeted leaders.[5] More common were mob-led persecutions that could be less discriminating. Did this violence deter conversions to Christianity? Perhaps, but in other cases, a victim's courage might inspire even more conversions. In this regard, Tertullian boasted, "the blood of Christians is seed."[6]

Christian exclusivity also changed the arithmetic of conversion. When a polytheist converted to worshipping another polytheistic god, he did not necessarily forfeit his loyalties to others; he simply added one more to the list. But when he converted to Christianity, he was required to deny the existence of the rest. Over time, this asymmetry worked powerfully in favor of Christian numbers and stability.

Fourth, Christians, like Jews, often modeled a morality that was attractive. Perhaps because of its origins on the margins of society, Christianity developed an organization that enabled it to deliver social services to its adherents. This became crucial in an era when official systems were increasingly breaking down through corruption, plague, and strife. Even the pagan Emperor Julian remarked upon the unusual effectiveness of Christian welfare networks.[7]

During the second and third centuries, the Roman Empire experienced at least two plagues, each of which killed up to a quarter of the population. During such crises, many deaths were caused by secondary factors, such as breakdowns in food and water supply for a populace already weakened by sickness. Christian organizations were resilient.[8] A direct result was a higher survival rate among Christians; an indirect result may have been the interpretation by outsiders of this higher survival rate as divine endorsement, which in turn may have fueled further conversions.

Moreover, Christianity put into practice beliefs that had the effect of increasing its birthrate relative to that of its pagan competitors. It inherited from Judaism the injunction to "be fruitful and increase in number" (Genesis 1:28), along with ongoing Jewish prohibitions of abortion and infanticide.[9]

Fifth, Christianity won a prize convert in Emperor Constantine in 312 CE. Although its survival was by this time secure, Christianity's dominance of the empire was made possible only through imperial favor. After Constantine, with the brief exception of Julian (ruled 361-363 CE), all Roman emperors were Christians. Government support came in two forms: first, Christianity was privileged; second, paganism was suppressed.

The Edict of Milan in 313 CE decreed toleration of all religions, but Constantine gradually favored Christianity. He endowed it with land, building materials, and money, and he exempted church properties from taxation. He made grain allowances to church charity networks, and he relieved church officials from burdensome civic responsibilities. Much of this government largesse was funded by confiscation of valuables from pagan temples.[10] Newfound church wealth supported an expansion of social services, which in turn may have accelerated the conversion of the poor, who were probably less interested in theology than in tangible benefits (and the assumption that divine favor must lie with those able to provide them).

The weight of the empire was also brought to bear against paganism. Many edicts applied only to specific provinces, and many were unevenly enforced. Nevertheless, their cumulative effect over a century was the complete destruction of the pagan competition. In 341 CE, Constantius banned temple sacrifices.[11] Theodosius I actively encouraged the demolition of temples. Accordingly, mobs led by Christian monks or detachments of soldiers ransacked them.[12] Many were razed while others were conveyed to the Christian church or commandeered for civic use. To prevent backsliding, Theodosius also decreed that any Christian who left the faith would be stripped of his property. In some cases, pagans were ordered to convert to Christianity or be exiled or executed.[13]

The evolution of Christianity from persecuted cult to state religion has a robust set of naturalistic historical causes. After Rome's fall, it remained the dominant belief system of nearly all of the former empire, though it lost ground on the periphery to a rising Islam. At the dawn of the early-modern era, around 1400, and accelerating thereafter, Europe's economic growth and corresponding military power began to outpace that of its nearest civilizational competitors, China and the Islamic caliphate. The colonial conquests that followed took Christianity to new lands and peoples.

But some of the same forces that propelled Europe to military-industrial preeminence began to erode faith. The scientific method demythologized the natural world. The rise of printing and literacy enabled people to read scripture for themselves and to think critically about its difficulties. Exposure to other cultures had the subversive effect of encouraging people to recognize in their own beliefs the same type of unfounded assumptions that were plain to see in the beliefs of others. A question to which we must turn in concluding is no longer how Christianity grew, but how it survives.

CONCLUSION

Religious beliefs have important consequences and, for that reason, should be subject to the same scrutiny that we apply to other important issues and areas of our lives. Part 1 of this essay made the case that Christianity's beliefs are incoherent and part 2, that its evidence is unreliable. In concluding, we can combine elements from these two dimensions to summarize Christianity's defects under five headings: it is arbitrary; it has been disconfirmed; it is human-made, illogical, and immoral. The following are brief samplings:

Christianity is arbitrary because it puts faith in unproven beliefs at the heart of its value system. These beliefs originated in Middle Eastern miracle stories whose meanings were then mediated through the politics of revelation. Faith is arbitrary because without reason or evidence, a person could have faith in any one of an infinite number of beliefs, each of which, again without reason or evidence, would be just as valid as any other. What is more, because different groups of people will have different faiths, which are by definition irreconcilable on the basis of shared reason or evidence, faith is unavoidably divisive. "I have faith" too often means "I believe without reasons." This alarming attitude toward knowledge, whether exhibited by a Christian, a Muslim, or anyone else, is an affront to truth and an obstacle to peace and progress.

Christianity has been disconfirmed by the empirically verifiable failures first, of its god to make himself known to billions of sincere seekers; second, of prayer to perform as advertised;

and third, of a second coming to materialize by the prophesied deadline. Jesus was a failed apocalyptic prophet, erroneously promising that a kingdom of god would vanquish evil and suffering on earth within the lifetime of some of his listeners. The illusionist who authored the gospel of John drew the audience's gaze away from Jesus's failure, the nonexistent kingdom of god on earth, and fixated it upon the unverifiable promise of a kingdom of god in heaven. Two thousand years later, with no sign of the truant deity, suffering continues unabated. In the meantime, more non-Christians are born and die every year, swelling the ranks of the hell-bound so that suffering on earth can be followed by even greater suffering in hell by even greater numbers of people.

Christianity is human-made, as opposed to divinely given, because we can see the development of many of its component beliefs over time. The most interesting of these stem from its mixed parentage. Jewish apocalypticists replaced the older concept of Sheol with Zoroastrian ideas about resurrection, judgment, and a two-tiered afterlife. Jesus's followers retained the idea of a resurrection but eventually interpreted it in terms of a mystery religion, teaching that those properly initiated might somehow participate in the god's triumph. Paul persuaded non-Jews to believe that his god's blessings, previously available only to those meeting the demands of the Jewish law, were now on offer at the easy access price of faith. Later church leaders and writers combined oral tradition and appropriated elements of pagan religion, such as the virgin birth, to craft what eventually became the authorized versions of Jesus's life.

The most prominent of Christianity's illogicalities are dressed up as mysteries beyond human understanding. Christian pretensions to monotheism, for example, derive from the Jews' longstanding pride that their national champion, Yahweh, was in fact the world's one true god. Those first construing Jesus as divine were impaled on the horns of a dilemma—if Jesus were a god like his father, then there must have been two gods—until the laws of arithmetic were overruled in the guise of the trinity. This illogicality masquerading as profundity is the reason one of the world's most popular religions does not know how many gods it has.

Christianity's marquee immorality is a judgment-based afterlife that rewards embrace of a belief rather than the merits of a person's conduct. Eternal torture for those who fail the faith-in-Jesus test is a doctrine of cruelty that only humans could invent, inconsistent with either the love of a benevolent creator or his purported resourcefulness. The root of this evil is vicarious sacrifice, the doctrine that a god accepts the suffering of the innocent as payment for the crimes of the guilty. The face-saving reinterpretation of Jesus's humiliating death as a victory for his followers could only be purchased at the price of promulgating this monstrous doctrine.

For reasons such as these, Christianity is no longer the first recourse of most educated people in understanding the world and their place in it. It has long sought the status of a coherent, historically based system, and talented thinkers—from Anselm to Schweitzer—have attempted to provide the necessary grounding and harmonize it with the world we observe. But it cannot stand without taking refuge in debunked categories such as faith and mystery, and the project of reconciling it with modernity has largely been abandoned. At the intellectual level, Christianity is a spent force. At the popular level, however, it remains formidable. What sustains it?

One factor is social influence. The painful reality behind generational consistency in religious belief is the systematic indoctrination of the young. Children adopt the attitudes and beliefs of the authority figures around them. Most Christians, convinced that Hinduism, for instance, is wrong, have never actually studied it, much less been exposed to it throughout their formative years.

Related to childhood indoctrination is conformity. The only way a modern person would assent to claims such as those made by Christianity would be if most people around him do too. The old cliché rings true: if only one person believed in an invisible overseer who listened and answered, it would be considered insanity; but because millions believe it, it is respected as religion.

Finally, a weekly assembly of worshippers meets the nonreligious need to be a part of a community. This community shares the experiences of its members' life transitions, such as births, marriages, and funerals through the lens of its religious teachings. Reinforcement of a worldview at weekly intervals can help make strange things sound normal.

A second factor is Christianity's own malleability. The extraordinary profusion of denominations is a monument to the fecundity of a free market in ideas unleashed by the absence of a central authority. The resulting diversity provides choice for the consumer at the institutional level.

Further choice exists at the individual level. Many Christians privately concede that they don't actually believe some of their church's teachings. For example, some do not believe in bodily resurrection or hell or a virgin birth. In order to justify to themselves and others this selective disavowal of their religion, they interpret some of its teachings metaphorically.

While it is a caricature, those practicing selective disavowal can be classified as one of two types. The more skeptical type sees the church's teachings and the Bible almost completely symbolically. A process of winnowing the reasonable from the unreasonable leaves them with little more than a deistic prime mover who may have created the universe but plays no discernible role in governing it. The second type is less skeptical, rejecting some teachings but replacing them with others. Many are really New Agers in the sense that they believe all religions have something to offer and that there are multiple paths to some greater power. Typically retaining the notion of a soul, they cherry-pick appealing ideas from diverse religious and psychological traditions to confect their own articles of faith.

These two types stand in opposition to a third, the literal-minded, which accepts a church's teachings at face value.

The world's largest and most enduring religions, Christianity included, have a capacity to house both the literal-minded and the metaphorically minded under one roof. All listen to the same sermon but hear different things. Their continued participation in the same church, however, lends one another moral and financial support as well as legitimacy in the eyes of outsiders.

A third factor is more basic. When we strip away the cultural forms, we come to psychological bedrock. Some of the most profound needs that religions seek to meet find little satisfaction elsewhere. This brings us full circle to the problems of suffering and death with which this essay began.

Suffering and death constitute a unique challenge for humans—call it the human predicament. The powerful human mind endows us with a terrifying insight: the body will die. Here, the sense of duality between mind and body, discussed in chapter 6, is felt most acutely. Our minds can take us out of animality and into a sphere of immutable abstractions, such as beauty, goodness, and justice. But our bodies, with their insistent and degrading requirements to kill and eat, to defecate, to bleed, and ultimately to die and be consumed, keep pulling us back. Our consciousness is tethered maddeningly to these ridiculous and doomed bodies.

Within Christianity, the dual aspect of humankind is symbolized by the incarnation of Jesus, in which he is simultaneously fully human and fully divine, 200 percent of a person. What is logically impossible becomes psychologically understandable. Jesus's divine aspect from his father, Yahweh, represents pure consciousness. His human aspect from his mother, Mary, represents pure animal nature. In terms of more explicit mythologies, Yahweh is the sky god, and Mary is the earth goddess. Jesus successfully unified these two aspects and then defeated death. His resurrection and ascension out of the womb of the earth and into the sky symbolize the birth of pure consciousness or of a purely spiritual being. The appeal of imitating or participating in Jesus's triumph is obvious.

The human predicament impels people to prove to themselves that they matter, in part by distinguishing themselves from others, but at the same time, given their animal weakness, to seek reassurance as part of a larger system.[1] In religious terms, these impulses can be described as needs for meaning (or purpose) and spirituality (a sense of connection to something larger than the self). Religions gratify these impulses by embedding the individual in a system of which the visible world is only one part and then giving him a role to play in that system.

For example, Christian rituals enable even the most unenterprising among us to participate in a cosmic drama. The sacrament of the eucharist, in which the follower consumes the flesh and blood of Jesus, nourishes spiritual rather than animal life. The central requirement of animal life, killing and eating, is transmuted into a promise that consciousness can escape the animal nature in which it is mired and, like Jesus, join the father.

A major challenge for the secular community and modern society is to help people address the human predicament without these time-worn and imaginary crutches. Meaning, as discussed in chapter 15, requires that an individual pursue something of value, even if temporary, that can be contributed to the world. From this comes an authentic connection to something larger than the self.

Instead of deferring our hopes for betterment to a supernatural world imagined by Bronze-Age people and populated by projections of their best and worst impulses, we can protect and improve the one in which we live. Instead of perceiving ourselves almost schizophrenically as either undeserving wretches or as the objects of a divine plan, or both, we can find meaning on a human scale by recognizing our ability to shape our own lives and impact those of others. We can put our talents into the service of that which we love rather than waiting for this to be done for us in a hypothetical afterlife. In summary, because it is up to us, we can take full responsibility for making life better here and now.

APPENDICES

APPENDIX 1

CHRISTIANITY'S JEWISH ROOTS

According to the gospels, Jesus and his immediate followers were all Jews (Matthew 10:5-6, John 1:45, 4:9, 4:22) living in Roman-occupied Judea two thousand years ago. Jesus was circumcised (Luke 2:21) and observed other Jewish religious practices (Luke 2:22-24, 2:41-42, 22:13-15).

The earliest Christians were products of Jewish presuppositions. For example, they took for granted the Jewish worldview known as ethical monotheism, the belief that a personal, transcendent god is active in human history and is the source of moral authority. They retained the Jewish Bible as part of their scripture, renaming it the Old Testament to distinguish it from the documents written circa 50-130 CE that eventually became known collectively as the New Testament.

Christianity teaches that Jesus was the fulfillment of the Jewish Bible (Matthew 5:17, Luke 24:44, John 4:25-26, 5:39, Romans 10:4) and that prophecies of the Jewish messiah were fulfilled by him, that he was descended from the Jews' King David, for example.

The cosmic drama at the center of Christian doctrine begins with the Jewish story of Adam and Eve and concludes with

Jesus's death, explained in terms of a Jewish atonement sacrifice (Romans 8:3, 1 Corinthians 15:3, Hebrews 10:10). Through Jesus, the covenantal promises that Israel's god made to the Jewish people have now been transferred to Christians (Luke 22:20, 1 Corinthians 11:25, Hebrews 8:7-13).

Jesus preached in synagogues and the temple (Mark 1:21, Matthew 4:23, Luke 4:15-16, 21:37, John 18:20), and his followers called him rabbi (Mark 9:5, 10:51, Matthew 26:25, John 1:38, 3:2). Jesus quoted the Jewish Bible extensively. For example, in Mark 12:29-31, he was asked what the most important commandment was. He replied, "Love the Lord your God with all your heart and with all your soul and with all your mind and with all your strength. The second is this: Love your neighbor as yourself." These are nearly word-for-word quotations from Deuteronomy 6:5 and Leviticus 19:18 in the Jewish Bible/Old Testament.*

Christianity's break from its mother religion would be an acrimonious one. Pious Jews deemed proclamations of Jesus's divinity to be blasphemous. Jesus's followers countered that their former coreligionists were blind or stubborn in the face of the miraculous truth. The rupture between the two groups would have lasting and tragic consequences, further discussed in chapter 14.

---

* Other examples of Jesus quoting the Jewish Bible include the following: in Matthew 4:4 and Luke 4:4, he quotes Deuteronomy 8:3; in Matthew 4:6 and Luke 4:10, he quotes Psalm 91:11-12; in Matthew 4:7 and Luke 4:12, he quotes Deuteronomy 6:16; in Mark 7:6-7 and Matthew 15:8-9, he quotes Isaiah 29:13; in Matthew 23:39, he quotes Psalm 118:26; in Matthew 26:31, he quotes Zechariah 13:7; in Luke 20:41-43, he quotes Psalm 110:1.

APPENDIX 2

HISTORICAL OUTLINE OF ANCIENT ISRAEL

The ancient Israelites considered themselves chosen by their god and promised by him a homeland along the southeastern coast of the Mediterranean. After the golden age of David and his son, Solomon, their kingdom split into two. The Northern Kingdom, called Israel, was home to ten of the twelve tribes. The smaller Southern Kingdom, called Judea (origin of the term "Jew"), was home to the other two.

In 722 BCE, the Assyrians invaded and obliterated the Northern Kingdom. Its population was absorbed into that of the surrounding peoples, and its Jewish culture disappeared. The Northern Kingdom's former inhabitants are sometimes known as the lost tribes of Israel.

The Southern Kingdom endured for another century but was conquered by the Babylonians in 587 BCE. The victors deported the Judean elite to Babylon as slaves, an event known as the Babylonian Exile (or Captivity). Over time, some of these enslaved Jews assimilated into Babylonian society. Others, however, became even more zealous of their ancestral customs, their national identity, and their god, Yahweh.

In 539 BCE, the expanding Persian empire under Cyrus the Great conquered Babylon. Cyrus emancipated groups that had been enslaved by the Babylonians, including the Judahites. The exiles that chose to return home reinvigorated exclusive worship of Yahweh and began rebuilding the temple (the second temple) in Jerusalem. Judea remained a Persian client state from 539 BCE until its conquest by Alexander the Great in 332 BCE.

During the Hellenistic period, Palestine was ruled by Alexander's successors, first those based in Egypt (the Ptolemies) and later those based in Syria (the Seleucids). One Seleucid ruler, Antiochus IV, tried to impose Greek ways on his subjects, a misjudgment that fueled a Jewish uprising known as the Maccabean Revolt beginning around 167 BCE. After decades of intermittent fighting, the Maccabees prevailed, and Palestine experienced a brief period of autonomy under their descendants known as the Hasmonaeans.

The Hasmonaeans had initially enjoyed Roman support, but in 63 BCE, Pompey occupied Judea, turning it into a Roman province. About a century later, religiopolitical grievances triggered the first Jewish-Roman War, 66-70 CE, at the climax of which the Romans brutally destroyed Jerusalem, including the second temple, slaughtering much of its population and enslaving much of the rest. Finally, the Jews launched the Bar Kochba Revolt, 132-135 CE. This too was bloodily suppressed, and it was followed by Hadrian's order that no Jew be permitted in Jerusalem. These conflicts left Palestine with few Jews. Most now lived in the Diaspora, minority communities dotting the Mediterranean, created by successive waves of deportation, expulsion, and escape.

APPENDIX 3

THE SUFFERING SERVANT OF ISAIAH 53

Of the many purported Jesus prophecies in the Old Testament, one of the most popular is that of the "suffering servant" of Isaiah 53. That chapter describes a servant who suffered for the wrongdoings of others but who will be exalted in the future. While it is certainly possible to read Jesus into the text, it is not necessary. And as will be shown, there is at least one other interpretation that appears more plausible.

Who is the suffering servant? Isaiah's poetic language admits of several possible meanings, but there are three traditional non-Christian interpretations. First, it could be the Jewish nation as a whole. This is the most common non-Christian interpretation, and it is attested as early as 250 CE by the Christian writer Origen.[1] Second, it could be an individual—a king, priest, or prophet. Some rabbinic commentary toyed with the idea that the servant could be a messiah.[2] But this was generally a secondary interpretation.[3] Third, it could be a righteous minority (or remnant) within the Jewish nation.[4]

The discussion that follows compares a righteous minority interpretation with Christianity's Jesus interpretation.

In the Jesus interpretation, the suffering servant is an individual, the messiah, who is taken by Christians to be Jesus. His undeserved suffering and death constituted a sacrifice that atoned for the wrongdoing of humankind. In the end, Jesus is resurrected and exalted, much to the dismay of those who condemned or scoffed at him.

In the righteous minority interpretation, the suffering servant is a subset of the Jewish people. The servant died when this subset was deported to Babylon and separated from the promised land and temple. Their undeserved suffering constituted a sacrifice that atoned for the wrongdoing of those who were not righteous, "the many," within the nation. In the end, a surviving remnant is restored to life upon its return to Jerusalem, much to the astonishment of the many.

These two interpretations share many features, but one deserves special attention: the morally problematic concept of vicarious sacrifice. According to this doctrine, a god accepts the suffering of the innocent as payment for the transgressions of the guilty. In the Jesus interpretation, Jesus did not need atonement for himself, but he suffered to atone for his fellow humans (he possessed a fully human nature). In the righteous minority interpretation, the righteous minority did not need atonement for itself because it had remained steadfast toward Yahweh, but it suffered to atone for its fellow Jews.

To understand these competing alternatives and to weigh their merits, following is: one, background on Israel's prophetic tradition and the Book of Isaiah; two, broad observations on the applicability of the text to Jesus or the righteous minority; and three, a line-by-line analysis.

One: background

At critical times throughout Israel's history, a prophet would arise, claiming to bring instruction, warning, or encouragement from the nation's god. Many of the Old Testament's prophetic writings follow a pattern, a cycle of transgression, punishment, and finally redemption. Israel has misbehaved and is now being punished for it (or has been or will be soon). The transgression that triggers this "prophecy cycle" is sometimes social injustice but is typically interpreted as insufficient fidelity toward Yahweh. The Jews were his chosen people. "The Lord your God has chosen you out of all the peoples on the face of the earth to be his people, his treasured possession" (Deuteronomy 7:6). But the covenant had strict terms. God's people were obligated to follow the law and worship him exclusively.

The Assyrian and Babylonian defeats induced crises of confidence among Jewish thinkers. Many concluded that Yahweh had given up on them or that he was not as powerful as the gods of their conquerors. But a minority developed a radical reinterpretation of events. To them, Israel's defeats were not signs of Yahweh's weakness but rather of his strength. Israel's conquerors were, in actuality, Yahweh's unwitting instruments: he was using the Assyrians and the Babylonians to punish Israel. But for that to be true, then Yahweh must control the Assyrians and the Babylonians. Extending this reasoning, these thinkers concluded that Yahweh was not merely the most powerful god but that he was the only god. The god of Abraham, Isaac, and Jacob was the world's one true god—an explicit monotheism.

Because the Jews came to see their god as the god of all history, they came to see themselves as playing a special role in that history. Just as Moses and the prophets had brought the nation to god, so the nation would bring the rest of the world. The Jews found justification for this viewpoint in their scripture. "All peoples on earth will be blessed through you" and "through your offspring all nations on earth will be blessed" (Genesis 12:3 and 22:18). "You will be for me a kingdom of priests and a holy nation" (Exodus 19:5-6).

The Book of Isaiah, probably the most influential of the prophetic writings, is the longest; but most scholars agree that it was written by at least two and probably three different individuals. First Isaiah, writing at the time of the Assyrian conquest of the Northern Kingdom, composed chapters 1-39. Second Isaiah, writing at the end of the Babylonian exile, composed chapters 40-53 or 55. Third Isaiah, writing immediately after Second Isaiah, composed chapters 54 or 56-66. There is also a geographic seam in the writing of the later chapters. Most likely, chapters 40 through 49 were written in Babylon and 49 through 66 in Jerusalem.[5]

Two: broad observations

In its mission to bring the rest of the world to its god, Israel is sometimes described as god's servant. "Do not be afraid, Jacob my servant; do not be dismayed, Israel" (Jeremiah 30:10 and 46:27-28). Such passages demonstrate that the Old Testament writers were comfortable referring to groups in the singular by using collective nouns and that Israel was frequently referred to in this way.

Second Isaiah continues this practice and clearly names Israel as god's servant frequently: "Israel, my servant . . . you are my servant" (41:8-9). "Listen, Jacob, my servant, Israel, whom I have chosen" (44:1). "Remember these things, Jacob, for you, Israel, are my servant. I have made you, you are my servant; Israel, I will not forget you" (44:21-22). "For the sake of Jacob my servant, of Israel my chosen" (45:4). "You are my servant, Israel, in whom I will display my splendor" (49:3).

The interpretation becomes more complicated, however, in 49:5-6. Here, another servant appears, one with a mission to Israel. He refers to god as, "he who formed me in the womb to be his servant to bring Jacob back to him and gather Israel to himself."

Who is this second servant? And which servant is the one who suffers in chapter 53? Before reviewing the text line by line, there are general reasons for believing the righteous minority interpretation is more plausible than the Jesus interpretation. The following are a half-dozen:

One: Isaiah was not able to predict the future. Writing at the end of the Babylonian Exile, circa 539 BCE, he captured the excitement of emancipation and encouraged his countrymen who may have been daunted by the task of rebuilding. Part of this encouragement was the promise that their work would never again be undone. He wrote, "Jerusalem, the holy city. The uncircumcised and defiled will not enter you again" (52:1). "Whoever attacks you will surrender to you" (54:15).

He could not have been more wrong. The Romans laid waste to Jerusalem in 70 CE. And after the Bar Kochba revolt in 135, Emperor Hadrian banished all Jews from the city. As it turns out, it was the circumcised, not the uncircumcised, who were forbidden to enter Jerusalem. Hadrian's ban lasted over two hundred years until repealed by Julian. Jerusalem was conquered by Sassanid Persians in 614. Then it was reconquered by Byzantine Christians in 629. The Christians surrendered the city to the ascendant Arab Muslims in 636. They, in turn, surrendered the city to the Seljuk Turks in 1073. It was reconquered by European Christian crusaders in 1099. Then it was reconquered by Ayyubid Muslims in 1187. It was conquered by Khwarezmian Tartars in 1244 and then Mamluk Turks in 1263. It was sacked by Armenian-led Mongols in 1299, but they lost interest and control reverted to the Mamluks. Then it was conquered by the Ottomans in 1517. It was conquered by an Albanian-led Egyptian army in 1831 but then reoccupied by the Ottomans in 1840. Then it was conquered by the British in 1917.[6]

Jerusalem was conquered, brutally so, on multiple occasions. Whatever else one might say about Second Isaiah, he was not able to predict the future. He lived through the exiles' enslavement and the eventual return of a remnant. Consequently, he could write about a righteous minority, its undeserved suffering, and what all of it might mean. But the career of Jesus was over five hundred years in the future. He could not have written about Jesus without the ability to predict the future, an ability he plainly lacked.

Two: If Isaiah's text were about Jesus, it could have been written at any time. The fact that it was written at the end of the Babylonian exile suggests it was addressed to the people's needs then. As such, it fits the traditional prophecy cycle perfectly.

This leads to a broader point about the prophets. If their purpose had been to foretell the New Testament, then there would be no particular pattern to their appearance throughout Israel's history. Instead, they cluster around national crises. All of the major prophets and half the minor prophets wrote around the times of the Assyrian or Babylonian conquests. This suggests that they were writing to interpret events for their contemporaries, not future generations. To think that these prophets, living through times of nation-shattering upheaval, would be encoding messages for modern readers would be self-centered of us.

Three: There is scant prophecy of suffering in Isaiah 53. The suffering of the servant is in the past tense, not the future tense. He "was pierced"; he "was crushed"; the Lord "laid on him the iniquity of us all"; he "was oppressed"; he "was cut off from the land of the living"; he "was assigned a grave." By contrast, there is a prophecy of exaltation, and it is in the future tense. He "will see his offspring and prolong his days"; he "will see the light of life"; his god "will give him a portion"; and he "will divide the spoils."

Suffering in the past tense cannot apply to Jesus because he will not appear until the future. In the righteous minority interpretation, however, the distinction between past suffering and future exaltation fits perfectly. The destruction and captivity of the nation are now in the past. The prophet is offering encouragement to the returning exiles that their nation will regain and even surpass its former glory.

Four: Isaiah 53 does not contain the word "messiah" at all. If the Jesus interpretation were correct, that word would likely be prominent.

The only time Second Isaiah used the word "messiah" was in an earlier chapter when he described the Persian King, Cyrus the Great: "This is what the Lord says to his anointed, to Cyrus . . ." (45:1). The Hebrew word for anointed is "messiah" (משיח), and that is the word the text uses for Cyrus here.

If Second Isaiah had been prophesying Jesus, he would likely have reserved the term "messiah" for him. Moreover, if Cyrus was worthy of mention by name, why was Jesus not? Either Isaiah thought Cyrus was more important than his suffering servant or his suffering servant was not an actual individual.

Five: The chapters that follow Isaiah 53 make more sense if that chapter refers to a group of Jews than if it refers to Jesus.

In chapter 54, their god assures the people that not only will they repopulate Jerusalem, but they will also multiply to such an extent that their "descendants will dispossess nations and settle in their desolate cities" (54:3). This builds upon the promise in 53:10 that the servant will "see his offspring."

In chapter 55, the god says, "'Give ear and come to me; listen, that you may live. I will make an everlasting covenant with you, my faithful love promised to David . . . Surely you will summon nations you know not, and nations that do not know you will come running to you'" (55:3-5). This cannot apply to Jesus because according to Christian doctrine, Jesus does not have to "listen, that you may live." The god is addressing the nation here. He is transferring to it the mission he had formerly bestowed upon David. Just as David led Israel, now Israel would lead the world.

Six: To the extent that details in Isaiah are found in the gospel stories, it is likely that the gospel writers tailored their stories to match Isaiah. Paul had utilized Isaiah's theology of vicarious sacrifice, so it may have been natural for the gospel writers to borrow narrative details from him too.

The author of Mark could have read Isaiah's "with the rich" and accordingly added the story element that Jesus was buried in the tomb of a rich man. He could have read Isaiah's "numbered with the transgressors" and accordingly located Jesus's cross between those of two common criminals. The authors of Matthew, Luke, and John indisputably wrote with Isaiah 53 in mind because they cite it. "This was to fulfill what was spoken through the prophet Isaiah" (Matthew 8:17). "It is written: 'And he was numbered with the transgressors,' and I tell you that this must be fulfilled in me" (Luke 22:37). "This was to fulfill the word of Isaiah the prophet" (John 12:38).

Three: line-by-line analysis

The discussion below cites the most important verses, including those prior to chapter 53, which are relevant to the comparison.

> And now the Lord says—he who formed me in the womb to be his servant to bring Jacob back to him and gather Israel to himself, for I am honored in the eyes of the Lord and my God has been my strength—he says: "It is too small a thing for you to be my servant to restore the tribes of Jacob and bring back those of Israel I have kept. I will also make you a light for the gentiles, that my salvation may reach to the ends of the earth." (49:5-6)

As noted above, this is the first clear reference to a second servant. In the Jesus interpretation, the speaker is Jesus, communicating supernaturally through the prophet. He here adumbrates his mission to save humankind.

In the righteous minority interpretation, the speaker is the prophet writing in the first person on behalf of the righteous minority. The righteous minority will restore Israel, which will then fulfill its mission to lead the world to the one true god.

> The sovereign Lord has given me a well-instructed tongue . . . the sovereign Lord has opened my ears, I have not been rebellious; I have not turned away. I offered my back to those who beat me, my cheeks to those who pulled out my beard; I did not hide my face from mocking and spitting. (50:4-6)

In the Jesus interpretation, this is Jesus speaking again. But it seems strange for him to say that god has opened his ears, as if the eternal second person of the trinity could not hear beforehand.

In the righteous minority interpretation, this is the prophet Isaiah speaking again. In the tradition of the prophets, he is humble, attributing his prescience to the divine rather than to himself. As one of the exiled slaves in Babylon, he would have been subjected to scorn and probably physical abuse. He typifies the suffering servant in that he accepted the abuse as if it were deserved punishment.

> He will be raised and lifted up and highly exalted . . .
> his appearance was so disfigured beyond that of any human being and his form marred beyond human likeness. (52:13-14)

The speaker here is Israel's god. Some Christians believe "raised and lifted up" refers to Jesus being nailed to a cross and hoisted aloft for crucifixion. But it seems simpler to read these words as synonyms for "exalted," with the idea repeated for emphasis.

Could the servant's disfigurement refer to Jesus's flogging and crucifixion? Perhaps, but Jesus was never "beyond human likeness." His corpse was nowhere mistaken for that of another species or some unidentifiable protoplasm.

On the other hand, Isaiah's words fit the righteous of Israel in the sense that they were, as enslaved exiles, unrecognizable as god's people—they were a nation without a country, a people without a land.

> Who has believed our message and to whom has the arm of the Lord been revealed? He grew up before him like a tender shoot, and like a root out of dry ground. (53:1-2)

The speakers here (53:1-10) are onlookers who are astonished by the servant's vindication. In the Jesus interpretation, these are the early Christians; they are telling the world the gospel. In the righteous minority interpretation, they are the first of Israel's many to have realized that the minority had been correct all along; they are sharing that realization with their countrymen.

The text likens the servant to a tree in inhospitable soil. It could be a prophecy that Jesus would come from humble beginnings or that his own society would reject him. First Isaiah described the messiah with a plant metaphor, "A shoot will come up from the stump of Jesse" (Isaiah 11:1), so it is possible that Second Isaiah was alluding to this. Elsewhere too, the messiah is compared to a branch (Isaiah 4:2, Jeremiah 23:5).

But the imagery of a displaced plant is also applied to the nation of Israel. "Now it is planted in the desert, in a dry and thirsty land" (Ezekiel 19:13). Yahweh said, "I will plant Israel in their own land, never again to be uprooted from the land I have given them" (Amos 9:15). Indeed, many of the remnant who will return to Jerusalem are second generation exiles who have never set foot in the promised land. They were born and grew up in the "dry ground" of Babylon.

> He had no beauty or majesty to attract us to him . . .
> he was despised and rejected by mankind. (53:2-3)

The Bible provides no physical description of Jesus. Whether intentional or not, this omission serves the theological aim of universality; he represents "every man." The messiah, on the other hand, is described by First Isaiah as beautiful: "The Branch of the Lord will be beautiful and glorious" (Isaiah 4:2). Therefore, Second Isaiah's phrase "he had no beauty" does not fit a messiah well.

Nor does "despised and rejected" fit Jesus because according to the gospels, he was admired. He "grew in wisdom and stature, and in favor with God and man" (Luke 2:52). He was thronged wherever he went and made a triumphal entry into Jerusalem, hailed by large crowds (Matthew 21:8-11, John 12:12). Of course, the gospels describe Jesus as scorned during his execution, but Isaiah's text suggests a general description, not one specific to the servant's death.

The text applies well to the righteous minority in that they were enslaved along with the many. As captives, they were despised by the Babylonians. What is more, their beliefs were rejected by their own countrymen who had concluded from Judah's defeat and enslavement that faith in Yahweh was futile.

> Surely he took up our pain and bore our suffering, yet
> we considered him punished by God, stricken by him
> and afflicted. (53:4)

The first clause could apply to Jesus in the capacity of an atoner. But as pointed out in chapter 5, his execution failed to meet the requirements for an atonement sacrifice.

This passage applies well to the righteous minority. "The many" had mocked those still trusting in Yahweh. Their initial interpretation of Israel's defeat was that Yahweh was either weak or no longer cared, that the righteous minority had been rejected despite its piety. Now that emancipation is at hand, they are astonished that the minority has been vindicated.

> But he was pierced for our transgressions; he was crushed for our iniquities. (53:5)

In a crucifixion, the victim's wrist bones and sometimes feet were nailed to a cross. Additionally, in one gospel, John, a centurion pokes Jesus with a spear to see if he is dead. So "pierced" could apply to Jesus very well. But it is difficult to see how "crushed" would apply to him other than in the general sense of being killed.

Conversely, it is difficult to see how "pierced" applies to Israel other than in the general sense of being killed. But the description "crushed" applies to Israel very well because that term was, and remains, a common way to describe defeated nations. God told Israel, "I will crush you" (Amos 2:13) and elsewhere the Israelites lamented, "You crushed us" (Psalm 44:19). Jeremiah wrote, "Israel is a scattered flock that lions have chased away. The first to devour them was the king of Assyria; the last to crush their bones was Nebuchadnezzar king of Babylon" (Jeremiah 50:17).

> The punishment that brought us peace was upon him, and by his wounds we are healed. (53:5)

This passage is at the heart of the idea of vicarious sacrifice. The speaker states that the servant's suffering has healed them.

Christians interpret "healed" here as "atoned with god through Jesus's sacrifice." But there are two problems with applying this passage to Jesus. First, Christian doctrine states that it was by Jesus's death, not his wounds, that humankind was atoned. But Isaiah's text here refers only to wounds. Second, even if we were to relax this distinction, there is no evidence that Jesus's death ever atoned for anyone. That is the theological interpretation that Christians place upon his otherwise humiliating execution. So the argument is circular: the text does not support the Christian interpretation unless one already believes that Jesus's death atones, that is, unless one is already a Christian.

On the other hand, the passage fits the righteous minority interpretation in a verifiable manner. The speakers are "the many" of Israel who had shown insufficient faith in Yahweh. They are "healed" in the sense that the nation's restoration gives them and their descendants another opportunity to live in the promised land. Yahweh has accepted the undeserved suffering of the righteous minority as payment for the whole people. Unlike the unverifiable, faith-based assertion that Jesus's suffering atones for his followers, it is a historical fact that many exiles returned to Jerusalem.

> He was oppressed and afflicted, yet he did not open his mouth; he was led like a lamb to the slaughter, and as a sheep before her shearers is silent, so he did not open his mouth. (53:7)

If understood literally, this passage does not fit either interpretation. It cannot apply to Jesus because Jesus was not silent. In all four gospels, Jesus spoke during his arrest, during his trial, and during his crucifixion.*

In the sense that the servant accepted the punishment willingly, however, the adjective "silent" could apply to Jesus. But the passage's ovine similes fit him poorly because he was generally described as a shepherd rather than a member of the flock. The lone exception is in the gospel of John, where Jesus is called the

---

* Mark 14:48, 14:62, 15:34; Matthew 26:50-56, 26:64, 27:46; Luke 22:48-53, 22:68-70 and 23:3, 23:34, 43, 46; John 18:4-11, 18:20-23, 34-37, 19:26-30.

lamb of god. But as explained in chapter 28, the author of John was rearranging the synoptics' timetable so that Jesus's crucifixion coincided with the slaughter of the Passover lambs.

The willing acceptance of punishment could also apply to the righteous minority. They fought against the Babylonians, but once defeated, they did not blame their god. On the contrary, they developed a radical reinterpretation of events and concluded that their god was using the Babylonians to punish the nation for its impiety. Although the minority did not deserve this punishment, it accepted it.

This acceptance is described in vocabulary that fits the righteous minority well and even echoes Second Isaiah's earlier description of Israel, where he wrote that god, "tends his flock like a shepherd: He gathers the lambs in his arms" (40:11). The comparison of the Jews to sheep had a long tradition: "You gave us up to be devoured like sheep . . . we are considered as sheep to be slaughtered" (Psalm 44:11, 22). God says, "I myself will search for my sheep and look after them" (Ezekiel 34:11).

> He was cut off from the land of the living . . . He was assigned a grave with the wicked, and with the rich in his death. (53:8-9)

The text does not support the Jesus interpretation. According to the gospels, Jesus was put in an unoccupied tomb alone.

The text applies well to the righteous minority interpretation. They died when they were separated from their land and when their temple, where god's presence dwells, was destroyed. They are in the grave of exile with "the wicked" (the unrighteous many of their countrymen) and "the rich" (their Babylonian masters). The phrase "land of the living" creates the double meanings of death and separation from the promised land.

Does the literal death of Jesus fit the passage better than the figurative death of the righteous minority? On the contrary, in

53:9, the correct translation of *bemotov* (במתיו) is not "in his death" but the plural "in his deaths."[7] Many of Israel's righteous died in the conquest and deportation or in servitude in Babylon. So there were many deaths among the righteous minority. Jesus, by contrast, died only once. The plural "deaths" better fits a collective servant than an individual one.

It is possible to apply the plural "deaths" to Jesus in the sense that pluralization was a poetic way to describe an extremely violent death, such as crucifixion.[8] But the figurative death of several generations of people (many of whom died literal deaths in the process) appears to fit the text at least as well, if not better, than the literal death of a single individual.

> Though he had done no violence, nor was any deceit in his mouth. (53:9)

Note that the text does not say the servant was sinless. It says the servant was without violence or deceit, but there are many other things considered sinful, such as lust, greed, or idolatry. It fits Jesus poorly because he was not free of violence as the following three examples show:

Jesus made and then used a whip to chase the money changers from the temple (John 2:13-16). Why were they there? Pursuant to their god's instructions in Deuteronomy 14:24-26 and Exodus 30:11-16, Jews travelling from afar needed to acquire animals for temple sacrifice, and all Jews needed to pay an annual temple tax. Many coins bore the images of deified Roman rulers, images deemed by Jews to be idolatrous and hence not permitted in the temple. The money changers provided the service of exchanging the unacceptable coins for acceptable ones.[9] Either Jesus did not understand the service being provided or he didn't like the exchange rates. Either way, he could have taken grown-up action instead of creating a melee. And to go one step further, even if his violence could be justified, it was still violence.

Second, if the story of the fig tree (Mark 11:13-14) is taken literally, Jesus cursed a tree to death because, through no fault of its own, figs were out of season. A god, even a minor demigod, could just as easily have blessed the tree to produce fruit year-round. Jesus could have chosen life and bounty, but instead, he chose death and sterility.

Third, Jesus exorcised a bevy of demons out of Legion (Mark 5:1-13). Well, who can blame him for manhandling demons? But then without regard for the animals or for the people whose livelihoods depended on them, he dispatched the demons into a herd of pigs, which dashed into the water and drowned. If it had been his intent to drown the demons, why burden the pigs with them, causing their deaths and economic hardship for their owners?

Jesus was not free of deceit either. He promised within a generation an apocalypse that never materialized (Mark 9:1, Matthew 16:28). He said falsely that prayer could accomplish anything (Mark 11:24, Matthew 21:22). He told Caiaphas, "I said nothing in secret" (John 18:20), but he told his disciples, "The secret of the kingdom of God has been given to you. But to those on the outside everything is said in parables so that, 'they may be ever seeing but never perceiving, and ever hearing but never understanding'" (Mark 4:11-12).

A lack of violence and deceit does not apply to the nation of Israel as a whole, but it applies well to a righteous minority. In fact, the "remnant"—that subset of Israel that survives and returns to Jerusalem (Isaiah 10:20, Jeremiah 23:2-3)—was traditionally described in precisely these terms. "The remnant of Israel will trust in the name of the Lord. They will do no wrong; they will tell no lies. A deceitful tongue will not be found in their mouths" (Zephaniah 3:12-13).

> He will see his offspring and prolong his days. (53:10)

Jesus was unmarried and had no children, so the text does not fit him well. It could apply to him figuratively in the sense that Christians are his spiritual descendants. But this appears unlikely because the Hebrew word Isaiah used is *zera* (זרע) meaning "seed" or "offspring," which typically refers to physical descendants. When the Old Testament writers meant spiritual descendants, they typically used the word *banim* (בנים), which means "sons" or "children."[10]

The remnant can prosper and multiply, so this fits the righteous minority interpretation well. At the same time, it is consistent with the promises in chapters 54 and 55 of a restored and populous nation.

A prolongation of days could refer Jesus's resurrection. But does that really work? As the second person of the trinity, he was already eternal, so he would have no need of prolongation. Of course, this terminology could work if applied to Jesus's human part only rather than to his full self.

A prolongation of days could also apply to the restoration of Israel. The same idea is depicted in Ezekiel's vision of a valley of dry bones brought back to life by Yahweh: "Breath entered them; they came to life and stood up on their feet—a vast army. Then he said to me: 'Son of man, these bones are the people of Israel'" (Ezekiel 37:10-11).

> By his knowledge my righteous servant will justify many and he will bear their iniquities. (53:11)

In 53:11-12 the god of Israel is speaking again, this time summarizing what has come before. There are several interesting points here. First, the servant is called "righteous"; and second, the text reads, "will justify" and "will bear," using the future tense.

Within Judaism, righteousness is attainable by mere humans provided they follow the law and sincerely ask for forgiveness when they falter. So Isaiah could have been referring to a human or a group of humans. But Jesus, according to Christianity, was much more than simply righteous; he was sinless. If Isaiah had intended to communicate such an extraordinary status, stronger words would have suggested themselves. This is the second time (53:9 was the first) that Isaiah could have said the servant was sinless, and that is precisely what he did not say. Therefore, the wording fits the righteous minority better than it fits Jesus.

This is the only time the future tense is used to describe the efforts of the servant, and the passage could therefore conceivably apply to the future life of Jesus. Equally, it could mean that the suffering of the righteous minority had restored the Judahites to proper standing with their god and that, consequently, future generations would be able to atone for their transgressions in the manner prescribed by the law (Jeremiah 33:17-18, Ezekiel 40:38-43 and 43:18-27).

> Therefore I will give him a portion among the great, and he will divide the spoils with the strong, because he poured out his life unto death, and was numbered with the transgressors. For he bore the sin of many and made intercession for the transgressors. (53:12)

It is unclear why Jesus would be rewarded by god for doing god's will since he is himself that god. Similarly, with whom could Jesus intercede, if not himself, because "the Father judges no one, but has entrusted all judgment to the Son" (John 5:22).

"Numbered with the transgressors" could apply to Jesus because he was crucified, so the story goes, between two common criminals. But it could equally apply to Israel's righteous minority, which suffered in captivity alongside the unrighteous many.

"Spoils," taken literally, refers to booty taken in wartime, something for which Jesus would have no use. If "spoils" is intended figuratively, as in, say "converts to Christianity," then it is not clear why Jesus would have to share with anyone.

On the other hand, "divide the spoils with the strong" applies well to the righteous minority because the reconstituted Israel has ambitions to assume preeminence among nations. This interpretation becomes more persuasive when one sees that First Isaiah used the exact same metaphor to describe the jubilation of exiles returning to the promised land: "They rejoice before you . . . as warriors rejoice when dividing the plunder" (Isaiah 9:3).

In closing

Given the ambiguities of poetic language, either interpretation is tenable. But if a divinely inspired author intended the Jesus interpretation, then we must ask why he communicated it in a manner so open to misunderstanding and which so closely followed the time-worn prophecy cycle of the Israelites. Perhaps both interpretations were intended. But that seems plausible only on the presumption that the inspiring deity did not mind engendering centuries of confusion.

The righteous minority interpretation is at least as compelling, if not more so, than the Jesus interpretation. Most tellingly, unlike the latter, it does not require the assumption that Second Isaiah possessed the supernatural ability to predict the future. The only truly novel aspect of Isaiah 53 is the immoral doctrine of vicarious sacrifice. This theological Trojan Horse, not a prophecy of a suffering messiah, was Second Isaiah's gift to Christianity.

APPENDIX 4

DESCENTS AND RESURRECTIONS

Osiris

The Egyptian gods Geb the earth and Nut the sky gave birth to Osiris; his younger brother, Set; and two sisters, Isis and Nephthys. Osiris, as oldest, ruled the world. Set, jealous, killed him and scattered his body parts all over Egypt. After long searching, his sister and consort, Isis, found the parts, reassembled them and, in the form of a bird, fanned the breath of life into him. He was resurrected and impregnated her. Osiris became ruler of the afterlife and the judge of the dead. Isis gave birth to Horus. To protect the infant from Set, Isis put Horus into a reed basket and floated him down the Nile, where he was guarded by magical animals. He ultimately defeated Set in battle and reclaimed his father's throne as ruler of the world. All pharaohs were worshipped as the incarnation of Horus. So Osiris was resurrected once for all time, and Horus was reincarnated with each new pharaoh.[1]

Baal

Baal was a Canaanite fertility and storm god. He was the son of either Dagon, the god of grain, or El, the sky god. The god of the sea (called either Yam or Lotan) approached the council of the gods and demanded they turn Baal over to him. Fearful, they agreed. But Baal defeated Lotan in battle, and the other gods proclaimed him a hero. Baal built a palace to commemorate his newfound status and announced that he would no longer pay tribute to death. He foolishly accepted a challenge from the god of death, Mot, to meet him in the underworld. Baal descended and was devoured by Mot. In the wake of his death, there was drought and sterility on earth. Baal's consort, Anat, descended to the underworld and defeated Mot, thereby bringing Baal back to life and ending the drought. Seven years later, Mot challenged Baal again. This time, the sun god Shapash joined with Baal, and together they defeated Mot.[2]

Tammuz

Ishtar/Inanna was the Akkadian/Sumerian goddess of sex and fertility. She had many lovers, but her favorite was Tammuz/Dumuzid. He was originally a human shepherd or king or both, but he became divine through his association with her. Ishtar became Queen of Heaven by tricking Enki/Ea into giving her his powers. She then desired unwisely to add to her domain the underworld, where her sister, Ereshkigal, ruled. As she descended, she had to surrender one power every time she passed a gate. When Ishtar finally arrived, Ereshkigal ordered her attacked by Disease, which killed her. As a result, the earth became sterile. Eventually, Ea sent an envoy to retrieve her. As a result of Ea's intercession, Ereshkigal sprinkled water of life on Ishtar, and she was resurrected. But someone needed to take Ishtar's place in the underworld, so she selected Tammuz. Tammuz's sister

(Geshtinanna/Belili) pleaded that he be able to spend part of each year in the land of the living, and her wish was granted. Every year, when Tammuz returns, so does the earth's fertility. So Ishtar was resurrected once, and Tammuz was resurrected annually.[3]

Dionysus

Zeus/Jupiter, head of the Greek/Roman pantheon, came to Persephone/Proserpine (one of his daughters) in the form of a snake and impregnated her. The offspring was Dionysus/Bacchus (also called Zagreus). The jealous Hera/Juno enlisted the titans to kill the infant. They attacked him as he was gazing at himself in a mirror, and he dodged them by morphing into the shapes of various animals. Finally, in the form of a bull, he was cut to pieces. Another daughter, Athena/Minerva, retrieved the heart and Zeus ate it. He later impregnated the human princess Semele with the reconstituted Dionysus. Infuriated again, Hera put into Semele's mind the desire to see Zeus in all his glory. He granted her wish, but it killed her. Zeus grabbed the unborn Dionysus, sewed the fetus into his thigh, and carried it there to term. He then entrusted the infant to Hermes/Mercury to raise in safety. As Dionysus matured, he longed to meet the mother he had never known. He descended into Hades to retrieve her and brought her to Olympus, where she was accepted to live among the gods. As an adult, Dionysus journeyed the world, teaching viniculture to humankind and establishing his mystery religion.[4]

Persephone

Persephone/Proserpine (also called Kore) was the daughter of Zeus and Demeter/Ceres, the goddess of wheat. Hades/Pluto, the god of the underworld, kidnapped her for a bride. Demeter left Olympus and wandered the earth disguised as a human, searching for her daughter. Distraught, she rendered the earth barren, inducing a famine among humans. Zeus sent Hermes to negotiate Persephone's release. But she had eaten a pomegranate seed while in the underworld, which meant she could never leave completely. Zeus brokered a compromise. Persephone would spend one-third of each year in Hades and the other two-thirds in Olympus with her mother. At this, Demeter ended the famine. She later returned to the town of Eleusis, where she had searched for Persephone, taught humankind how to grow wheat, and established her mystery religion known as the Eleusinian mysteries.[5]

Asclepius

Asclepius was the son of Apollo and the human virgin Coronis. While she was pregnant, Apollo became jealous of her and killed her with an arrow. Remorseful, he seized the unborn infant and charged the centaur Chiron with its upbringing. Chiron taught his ward medicine and Asclepius, fulfilling a prophecy by Chiron's daughter, became a great healer. He was compassionate toward humankind, even raising many from the dead. He resurrected so many, it seems, that Hades complained of a slow-down. Irked, Zeus killed Asclepius with a thunderbolt, but later, either out of sympathy for humankind or as a favor to Apollo, he brought the healing god back to life. Asclepius ascended to resume his career and his presence dwelled thereafter in his healing temples.[6]

APPENDIX 5

CANON

Old Testament

Christianity's three main branches disagree about which books to include in the Old Testament. The table on the next page lists their respective canons. Protestants generally refer to the books they exclude as apocryphal (meaning hidden or obscure), while Catholics and the Orthodox refer to them as deuterocanonical (of the secondary canon).

In addition to disagreements over which books are included, there are also disagreements about the text of some of them. In Daniel, Psalms, and Esther, the Catholic and Orthodox Bibles include Septuagint materials that were later removed from the Protestant Bible. These include the following: in Daniel, the Prayer of Azariah, the Song of the Three Holy Children, Susanna, and Bel and the Dragon; in Psalms, Psalm 151; in Esther, Mordecai's Dream.

All three Christian canons, unlike the Jewish, are organized by genre, with histories followed by wisdom literature and the prophets. This arrangement has the advantage of concluding the Old Testament with a view to the future.

Canons of the Jewish Bible/Old Testament

Jewish	Catholic	Orthodox	Protestant
Genesis	Genesis	Genesis	Genesis
Exodus	Exodus	Exodus	Exodus
Leviticus	Leviticus	Leviticus	Leviticus
Numbers	Numbers	Numbers	Numbers
Deuteronomy	Deuteronomy	Deuteronomy	Deuteronomy
Joshua	Joshua	Joshua	Joshua
Judges	Judges	Judges	Judges
1 Samuel	Ruth	Ruth	Ruth
2 Samuel	1 Samuel	1 Samuel	1 Samuel
1 Kings	2 Samuel	2 Samuel	2 Samuel
2 Kings	1 Kings	1 Kings	1 Kings
Isaiah	2 Kings	2 Kings	2 Kings
Jeremiah	1 Chronicles	1 Chronicles	1 Chronicles
Ezekiel	2 Chronicles	2 Chronicles	2 Chronicles
Hosea	Ezra	1 Esdras	Ezra
Joel	Nehemiah	Ezra (2 Esdras)	Nehemiah
Amos	Tobit	Nehemiah	Esther
Obadiah	Judith	Tobit	Job
Jonah	Esther	Judith	Psalms
Micah	1 Maccabees	Esther	Proverbs
Nahum	2 Maccabees	1 Maccabees	Ecclesiastes
Habakkuk	Job	2 Maccabees	Song of Songs
Zephaniah	Psalms	3 Maccabees	Isaiah
Haggai	Proverbs	Psalms	Jeremiah
Zechariah	Ecclesiastes	Job	Lamentations
Malachi	Song of Songs	Proverbs	Ezekiel
Psalms	Wisdom of Solomon	Ecclesiastes	Daniel
Proverbs	Sirach (Ecclesiasticus)	Song of Songs	Hosea
Job	Isaiah	Wisdom of Solomon	Joel
Song of Songs	Jeremiah	Sirach (Ecclesiasticus)	Amos
Ruth	Lamentations	Hosea	Obadiah
Lamentations	Baruch	Amos	Jonah
Ecclesiastes	Ezekiel	Micah	Micah
Esther	Daniel	Joel	Nahum
Daniel	Hosea	Obadiah	Habakkuk
Ezra	Joel	Jonah	Zephaniah
Nehemiah	Amos	Nahum	Haggai
1 Chronicles	Obadiah	Habakkuk	Zechariah
2 Chronicles	Jonah	Zephaniah	Malachi
	Micah	Haggai	
	Nahum	Zechariah	
	Habakkuk	Malachi	
	Zephaniah	Isaiah	
	Haggai	Jeremiah	
	Zechariah	Baruch	
	Malachi	Lamentations	
		Epistle of Jeremiah	
		Ezekiel	
		Daniel	

New Testament

Determining the authorship of ancient documents is a complex affair, typically involving historical and linguistic analysis, best left to scholars, such as Barton Ehrman and Raymond E. Brown. Below is a brief indication of why modern scholars suspect the traditional attributions of authorship for the listed documents.

Hebrews

Hebrews was included in the canon because church leaders thought it had been written by Paul.[1] But Paul identified himself in his writings, while the author of Hebrews did not. More tellingly, the author of Hebrews wrote, "This salvation, which was first announced by the Lord, was confirmed to us by those who heard him" (2:3). That means the author had never met Jesus nor had received personal revelation. But Paul tells us repeatedly that he had received precisely this type of revelation.

Colossians and Ephesians

About 60 percent of critical scholarship believes that Colossians was not written by Paul and about 80 percent believe so of Ephesians.[2] Since these letters begin by saying they are from Paul, they are most likely forged. They differ from letters actually written by Paul on at least one substantive issue. Paul taught that Jesus's followers will be raised when Jesus returns and not before. "In Christ all will be made alive. But each in his own turn: Christ, the first-fruits; then, when he comes, those who belong to him" (1 Corinthians 15:22-23). By contrast, Ephesians reads, "God raised us up with Christ and seated us with him in the heavenly realms" (Ephesians 2:6). Colossians reads, "In him you were also circumcised . . . having been buried with him in baptism, in which you were also raised with him through your faith" (Colossians 2:11-12). In summary, both Colossians and Ephesians suggest, unlike Paul, that Jesus's followers have already been raised in some manner.[3]

The Pastorals (1 and 2 Timothy and Titus)

1 Timothy, 2 Timothy, and Titus were all forged, most likely by the same person, in Paul's name.[4] These letters are known as the pastoral letters (*pastor* is Latin for "shepherd," so pastoral concerns are those of a priesthood or ministry), and their focus is church organization. But Paul, like Jesus, believed that the kingdom of god was going to appear at any moment. See chapter 22. Consequently, he showed little interest in building enduring institutions. To the extent organization was required, he believed that the holy spirit would provide it (1 Corinthians 12-14).[5]

2 Thessalonians

Most scholars believe 2 Thessalonians is forged.[6] In 1 Thessalonians, Paul is clear that the end is imminent, that it will come unannounced, and that he will probably still be alive when it occurs. The author of 2 Thessalonians, on the other hand, is certain that the end is not near because other things have to occur first. "For that day will not come until the rebellion occurs and the man of lawlessness is revealed, the man doomed to destruction. He will oppose and will exalt himself over everything that is called God or is worshipped, so that he sets himself up in God's temple, proclaiming himself to be God" (2:3-4).

James and Jude

The books of James and Jude were included because church leaders mistakenly thought they had been written by the brothers of Jesus with those names.[7] But the books do not make this claim; they do not claim to be written by any particular James or Jude. Moreover, Jesus's brothers would likely have been illiterate.[8] The James who is believed to have been Jesus's brother was renowned for keeping the law, including all of its dietary restrictions and so on. But the book of James does not emphasize these things. Instead, it argues that people must conduct themselves morally and treat the poor justly.

The author of Jude claims to be "a brother of James" (1), but he does not say which James, and it was a common name. If he were a brother of the James who was the brother of Jesus, then he would have been a brother of Jesus too. But he did not say this. He wrote, "Remember what the apostles of our Lord Jesus Christ foretold" (17), which suggests he wrote at a later date than that of Jesus's generation.[9]

1, 2, and 3 John

1, 2, and 3 John are anonymous, but they were included in the canon because it was believed that their author was the apostle John, presumed author of the gospel of John.[10] The author of 1 John did not identify himself at all, and the author of 2 and 3 John identified himself only as "the elder," which indicates that he was writing to a specific audience who knew him.[11] These letters were not written by the same individual who wrote the gospel of John. Whereas the gospel of John typically depicts the Jews as adversaries, 1 John does not.

More tellingly, the author of the gospel of John and the author of 1 John have different understandings of the identity of the "paraclete." This is supposed to be humankind's advocate or counselor. The author of the gospel of John considered the paraclete to be the holy spirit (John 14:15-17 and 15:26-27), but the author of 1 John considered the paraclete to be Jesus (1 John 2:1). In John 14:15-17, the paraclete is an "advocate to help you and be with you forever—the Spirit of truth." Whereas in 1 John 2:1, the paraclete is an "advocate with the Father—Jesus Christ." But the Greek word is the same Παρακλητον in both verses.

1 and 2 Peter

1 Peter was probably not written by the apostle Peter, and 2 Peter was definitely not.[12] There is an initial improbability arising from the description of Peter as illiterate (Acts 4:13). In addition, 1 Peter addresses gentiles, not Jews (2:10, 4:3-4), but gentiles were not Peter's primary audience; they were Paul's. Also, the author of 1 Peter sends greetings from Babylon, which became a codename for Rome after the latter's destruction of Jerusalem in 70 CE. If Peter had died somewhere between 62 and 67 CE, he would not likely have referred to Rome in that manner.[13] In addition, 2 Peter attempts to address the embarrassment that Jesus did not return within a generation as promised in Mark 9:1 and Matthew 16:28. This problem, which became known as the "delayed parousia," did not become a widespread concern until after Peter's death.

Revelation

Revelation's first chapter tells us that it was written by John on the island of Patmos. But John was a common name, and the true identity of the author has long been bound up with church politics. Because Revelation could be taken as an endorsement of preaching "in the spirit" (1:10), its enthusiastic proponents upset the fledgling church hierarchy. Some of those in positions of authority dismissed it as nonsensical, and others denounced it as heretical. By contrast, Justin Martyr (circa 160 CE) and Irenaeus (circa 180 CE) respected Revelation because they believed that Rome's persecution of Christians in their own day had been foretold in its pages. To defend the book from attacks by others in the church, they asserted, though without offering any evidence, that it had been authored by the apostle John, who they presumed had written the gospel of John.[14]

For both linguistic and doctrinal reasons, however, most modern scholars do not believe that Revelation was written by the same person who wrote the fourth gospel. The linguistic dissimilarities were highlighted as early as circa 250 CE by a bishop named Dionysius of Alexandria. In simplest terms, while the author of John wrote Greek well, the author of Revelation did not. The doctrinal difficulty is that John and Revelation have very different views of the end times. The author of Revelation, like Jesus and Paul before him, was an apocalypticist who believed that god's kingdom would be established on earth at any moment. Jesus tells him, "I am coming soon" (22:20). By contrast, the author of John reorients the Christian expectation toward a different eschatology: an ongoing kingdom in heaven rather than a future kingdom on earth.[15]

APPENDIX 6

CORROBORATION

Christian non-Bible Sources

Clement (circa 96 CE)

Clement was the fourth bishop of Rome and the presumed author of 1 Clement, a letter primarily concerned with conflicts inside the church in Corinth. Clement quotes Paul but does not indicate an awareness of the gospels, so his information probably came from the oral tradition. Like Paul, Clement makes no mention of healings, parables, or an empty tomb. And when he wants to remind his readers of the promise of resurrection, he does not write about evidence but instead compares Jesus's resurrection to the rebirth of the mythical bird, the phoenix. "Do we then deem it any great and wonderful thing for the Maker of all things to raise up again those that have piously served Him in the assurance of a good faith, when even by a bird He shows us the mightiness of His power to fulfill His promise?"[1] This excerpt suggests a paucity of real historical evidence for the resurrection and, at the same time, throws into bright light the prescientific worldview of the most esteemed leaders of the early church and their willingness to accept the mythological at face value.

Ignatius (circa 110 CE)

Ignatius was a bishop in Antioch. He wrote seven letters while travelling to Rome to be executed during a persecution of Christians. In them, he warns against false teachers and insists Jesus existed bodily, apparently in a polemic against gnostics and others who believed Jesus was a god only and that his human nature was illusory. There is no indication that he had read any of the gospels, so it is possible that he possessed knowledge of Jesus directly from those who had known him. On the other hand, he does not make this claim, so he could have been simply repeating elements of the oral tradition.[2]

Polycarp (circa 115 CE)

Polycarp was bishop of Smyrna who died a martyr's death. He wrote to the church in Philippi a cover letter atop a set of Ignatius's letters. It is full of praise for those who have faith, and it exhorts Christians to behave morally. The letter mentions in particular a case of someone absconding with the local church's money. He did not write with the intention of providing evidence for the historical claims of Christianity, and he provided none. On the contrary, because much of his letter is a concatenation of excerpts from other Christian writings (e.g., 1 Timothy 6:10, 1 Peter 2:11, 1 John 4:2-3, Ephesians 4:26), it is clearly not an independent source.

Papias (circa 120 CE)

The writings of Papias survive only in fragments. He is the earliest source for the gospel authorship tradition discussed in chapter 23. While he quotes the gospels and so clearly derives some information from them, he also claims to have spoken to people who had spoken to some of the apostles. Any information he derived from them is therefore only secondhand. He wrote, "Whenever someone arrived who had been a companion of one of the elders, I would carefully inquire after their words, what Andrew or Peter had said, or what Philip or what Thomas had said, or James or John or Matthew or any of the other disciples of the Lord . . . For I did not suppose that what came out of books would benefit me as much as that which came from a living and abiding voice."[3] Partly because we possess fragments only and partly because Papias seems to have been less than fully coherent himself (see chapter 29), it is difficult to draw trustworthy conclusions from his writings.

Quadratus of Athens (circa 130 CE)

According to Eusebius, Quadratus of Athens wrote to Emperor Hadrian defending Christianity. The extant fragment reads, "But our Savior's works were permanent, for they were real. Those who had been cured or rose from the dead did not just appear to be cured or risen but were ever present, not only during the Savior's stay on earth but also after his departure. They remained for a considerable period, so that some of them even reached our times."[4] He is contrasting the miracles claimed on behalf of Jesus with those claimed on behalf of other healers. Unfortunately, he did not share with the reader how he knew these things. He did not indicate, for example, that he knew them personally. Nor did he express skepticism that some of those healed were still living, nearly a hundred years later.

Barnabas (circa 130 CE)

The letter of Barnabas was traditionally ascribed to the travelling companion of Paul by that name (Acts 13-14), but most scholars agree that it was actually written much later. Popular and even deemed scripture by some early churches, the letter focuses on the Jews' loss and the Christians' inheritance of Yahweh's covenant.[5] The author excerpted from the Old Testament selectively to support his argument. For example, he wrote, "Moses . . . received the covenant from the Lord, even tablets of stone written with the finger of the hand of the Lord. But they lost it by turning unto idols . . . Moses understood, and threw the two tables from his hands; and their covenant was broken in pieces, that the covenant of the beloved Jesus might be sealed unto our hearts in the hope which springeth from faith in Him" (4:7-8).[6] This letter repeats Christian beliefs, and its primary historical value is its representation of early Christian anti-Jewish polemics (touched upon in chapter 14). There is nothing in it that could not have come from a reading of Mark and Paul or from ideas circulating within the Christian community at the time of its writing.

Basilides (circa 130 CE)

Basilides was a gnostic and branded a heretic. Although he claimed his information came from either an interpreter of Peter or from Matthias, he quotes Romans and the gospels of Mark and Luke. Very little of his writings survive, and he is known primarily because Irenaeus, Clement of Alexandria, and others criticized him. Surviving excerpts include a sophomoric discussion of suffering and virtue. It is difficult to consider his writings documentation of the early Jesus movement given the late date of their composition and the fact that Christianity itself rejects them.

Jewish Sources

Josephus (circa 94 CE)

The only first-century references to Jesus that are not by Christians come from the Jewish historian Flavius Josephus in his book *The Antiquities of the Jews*. This is the most common source cited for the historical authenticity of Jesus. It has two possible references to him. The first is known as the "Testimonium Flavianum" (18.3.3) and the second is known as the "James passage" (20.9.1).

Few scholars believe the Testimonium Flavianum to be entirely authentic, but many believe it to be partially so. The passage is shown below, with the phrases in brackets widely acknowledged to be later interpolations:

> At this time there appeared Jesus, a wise man [if indeed one should call him a man]. For he was a doer of startling deeds, a teacher of people who receive the truth with pleasure. And he gained a following both among many Jews and among many of Greek origin. [He was the Messiah.] And when Pilate, because of an accusation made by the leading men among us, condemned him to the cross, those who had loved him previously did not cease to do so. [For he appeared to them on the third day, living again, just as the divine prophets had spoken of these and countless other wondrous things about him.] And up until this very day the tribe of Christians, named after him, has not died out.[7]

The bracketed phrases are clearly partisan, and Josephus, who lived and died a Jew, would never have referred to Jesus as the messiah. These must be forged interpolations. But what about the rest of the passage? This is hotly debated. There are two key arguments against authenticity.

First, early church leaders, such as Irenaeus, Origen, and Tertullian, quoted *The Antiquities of the Jews* often, but they never mentioned this paragraph.[8] Suspiciously, it does not appear to have been mentioned prior to the writings of Eusebius in the early fourth century.

Second, the paragraph sticks out of Josephus's narrative flow. The paragraph immediately before the Testimonium describes a water project initiated by Pilate and his violent suppression of opposition to it. The passage immediately following the Testimonium begins, "About the same time also another sad calamity put the Jews into disorder . . ." and describes events in Rome in which both Jews and followers of Isis were temporarily banned from the city. It seems unlikely that the author of the Testimonium would characterize Jesus's career as a "sad calamity." This description better fits the previous paragraph's water project protest. The chapter flows more logically and more smoothly without the Testimonium.

On the other hand, just because a paragraph is not quoted does not mean it didn't exist. And Josephus's writing includes other instances where he digresses from one topic to another.

The second passage, known as the James passage, tells of the high priest Ananus, who "assembled the Sanhedrim of the judges, and brought before them the brother of Jesus, who was called Christ, whose name was James, and some others and when he had formed an accusation against them as breakers of the law, he delivered them to be stoned."[9]

This passage seems less problematic. Those who doubt its authenticity question the phrase "who was called Christ." They hypothesize that this phrase was originally a note made by a scribe in the margin of one manuscript and then mistakenly incorporated into the body of the text by another scribe making a copy. That is possible, but it is also possible that the passage is genuine.

The Talmud (between 200-600 CE)

This huge collection of writings includes the Jewish oral law (Mishnah) and rabbinic commentary on it (Gemara). The Mishnah was written down circa 200 CE, and the Gemara was added between 200 and 600 CE. These writings have several passages that may refer to the Jesus of Christianity. But there are problems with accepting them as historical documentation.

Jesus was a popular name. Josephus mentions twenty different individuals named Jesus.[10] More importantly, while it is based on older oral tradition, the Talmud was written after the four canonical gospels. Any references to the Jesus of Christianity, therefore, could be either repetition of, or responses to, Christian claims. The following is a brief discussion of three possible strands of reference:

First strand—Ben Stada or Ben Pandera:

In one passage, a man named either Ben Stada or Ben Pandera was reputed to practice sorcery and was the illegitimate son of a woman named Miriam (Babylonian Talmud, Seder Mo'ed, Tractate Shabbath, Folio 104b).

Another passage describes how blasphemers are dealt with, a procedure followed in the town of Lydda for Ben Stada, who was hanged on the eve of Passover (Babylonian Talmud, Seder Nezikin, Tractate Sanhedrin, Folio 67a).

There is little to suggest that either passage refers to Jesus except for a possible play on words in the name. *Ben* means "son of" in Hebrew, and "Panthera" could be a garbled rendering of *parthenos*, the Greek word for "virgin." Claims that Jesus was born of a virgin were popularized circa 80-90 CE, when Matthew and Luke were written. So if this does indeed refer to the Jesus of Christianity, it is relatively late and does not line up well with the gospels.

Second strand—Jesus or Yeshu or Yeshu the Nasarean:

In one passage, Yeshu lived during the reign of Alexander Jannaeus (104-78 BCE), and he was a sorcerer who bowed down to a brick and worshipped it (Babylonian Talmud, Seder Nezikin, Tractate Sanhedrin, Folio 107b). This passage does not work because of the timing, one hundred years before the Jesus of Christianity.

In another passage, Yeshu is stoned and hanged on Passover eve for the crimes of sorcery and leading the people astray. For forty days prior to his execution, heralds unsuccessfully sought witnesses in his favor. He had five disciples who were also executed (Babylonian Talmud, Seder Nezikin, Tractate Sanhedrin, Folio 43a). The passage reads:

> On the eve of the Passover Yeshu was hanged. For forty days before the execution took place, a herald went forth and cried, "He is going forth to be stoned because he has practiced sorcery and enticed Israel to apostasy. Anyone who can say anything in his favor let him come forward and plead on his behalf." But since nothing was brought forward in his favor he was hanged on the eve of the Passover!—Ulla retorted: "Do you suppose that he was one for whom a defense could be made? Was he not an enticer, concerning whom Scripture says, neither shalt thou spare, neither shalt thou conceal him? With Yeshu however it was different, for he was connected with the government (or royalty, i.e., influential)." . . . Yeshu had five disciples, Matthai, Nakai, Nezer, Buni and Todah.[11]

The passage goes on to say that Yeshu's five disciples were put to death. While it could refer to the Jesus of Christianity, the stated facts are quite different from those in the gospels. In the gospels, the trial was hasty and in the middle of the night; here, the inquiry consumes over forty days. In the gospels, the execution was by crucifixion; here, it is by stoning (the means of execution) and hanging (the subsequent public display). In the gospels, there were twelve apostles, and they were not executed. Here, there are five, and they are executed. Intriguingly, the Yeshu in this passage is associated with the government in some way. That certainly conflicts with the gospels—unless one interprets it to refer to Jesus's alleged Davidic ancestry.

Third strand—combining the Ben Pandera and the Jeshu strands in the Tosefta:

The Tosefta, written 200-300 CE, is a supplement to the Mishnah. In one of its passages, a student offered to heal a rabbi who had been bitten by a snake, but the rabbi refused because the student intended to heal him in the name of Jeshu Ben Pandira (Tosefta, Seder Kodashim, Tractate Chullin, 2:23).

Here, the name may link the Ben Pandera and the Jeshu strands; but if so, the combination only serves to complicate the picture and multiply the discrepancies. How many names can one man have?

In summary, these three strands, taken singly or together, present a picture that is garbled at best. If any of these three strands actually refers to the Jesus of Christianity, it is surprising that there is no mention, even a disparaging one, of a resurrection or a movement that survived his death. The Talmud is so vast that passages in it could be open to endless speculation, but these appear to be the three most popular references cited by those wishing to find non-Christian corroboration of Jesus's existence.

Its oral origins, late date of final editing, and garbled content, however, render it an unpersuasive source document.

Pagan Sources

Epictetus (circa 110 CE)

Epictetus or one of his students wrote, "If madness can produce this attitude (of detachment) toward these things (death, loss of family and property), and also habit, as with the Galileans, can no one learn from reason and demonstration that God has made everything in the universe, and the whole universe itself, to be unhampered and self-sufficient, and the parts of it for the use of the whole?"[12] If the author meant Christians when he wrote "Galileans," then he provides documentation of nothing more than that he had heard of Christians.

Pliny the Younger (circa 112 CE)

Pliny the Younger served as governor of a Roman province in Turkey. He wrote a letter to Emperor Trajan asking how he should deal with Christians. He wrote of some, "I asked them if they were Christians. If they confessed, I asked a second and third time, threatening with punishment: I ordered those who persevered to be led away." He wrote of others, "Following my lead they first invoked the gods and offered incense and wine to your image, which for this purpose I had ordered brought in with the images of the gods, and afterward cursed Christ. It is said that those who are really Christians cannot be forced to do any of these things. Others named in the indictment said they were Christians but presently denied it; they had been Christians but had stopped, some two years, others many years ago, a few twenty years past. All of them reverenced your image and the images of the gods and cursed Christ. They testified that this was the whole of their crime or error, that they had met regularly before dawn on a fixed day and recited an antiphonal ode to Christ as to a god." Emperor Trajan replied, assuring Pliny that he had proceeded properly (Letters 10.96-97).[13] Again, these writings simply document the existence of Christians.

Tacitus (circa 117 CE)

The Roman historian Tacitus in the *Annals* explains that after a great fire in Rome, many suspected Emperor Nero because he wanted to clear swaths of real estate for his grandiose building schemes. In order to deflect suspicion, Nero scapegoated the Christians: "To obliterate the rumor Nero substituted as guilty, and punished with the most refined tortures, a group hated for its crimes and called 'Christians' by the mob. After Christus, the founder of the name, had been punished by death through the procurator Pontius Pilate, the hateful superstition was suppressed for a moment but burst forth again not only in Judea, where this evil originated, but even in the City, where all things horrible and shameful flow together and are celebrated" (Annals 15:44).[14] Tacitus was not likely quoting Roman records because, had they existed, they would have used the individual's name (Jesus) rather than a theological title given to him by his followers (messiah/christ). He was probably repeating information he had heard secondhand.

Suetonius (circa 120 CE)

Suetonius was a Roman historian best known for his *Lives of the Caesars*. That work made two references to Christianity. First, during the reign of Claudius: "Since the Jews were constantly rioting under the leadership of Chrestus, he (Claudius) expelled them from Rome" (Life of Claudius, 25.4). Second, during the reign of Nero: "Punishments were inflicted on the Christians, a group of men with a new and harmful superstition" (Life of Nero, 16. 2).[15] "Chrestus" probably refers to Jesus and the unrest is an indication of conflict between Jews and Jewish Christians, a distinction a Roman outsider would not likely have understood. Neither passage by Suetonius reveals anything about the lives of Jesus or his apostles.

Sources that are late but nevertheless cited by apologists

Thallus (between 50-180 CE)

Thallus wrote a history of the world from the fall of Troy to the mid first century CE. No copies survive, but it is claimed he mentioned a midday darkness.

The Christian historian Julius Africanus in a book entitled *Chronography* (circa 220 CE) referred to Thallus. He wrote, regarding the time of Jesus's death, "On the whole world there pressed a most fearful darkness; and the rocks were rent by an earthquake, and many places in Judea and other districts were thrown down. This darkness Thallus, in the third book of his History, calls, as appears to me without reason, an eclipse of the sun."[16] In other words, according to the Christian Africanus, the non-Christian Thallus confirmed that the world was covered by darkness at the time of Jesus's death.

Very little is known of Thallus, the timing of his writing, or his sources. He might simply have been repeating beliefs readily found within the gospels. After all, a supernatural darkness in the middle of the day would have been noticed by others besides Christians and Thallus. But it is mentioned nowhere in Seneca's *Natural Questions* (circa 65 CE), a book devoted to scientific reporting, or in Pliny the Elder's encyclopedia *Natural History* (circa 80 CE) or in Ptolemy's *Almagest* (circa 150 CE), a book devoted to astronomy.[17]

Phlegon of Tralles (circa 140 CE)

Phlegon wrote a history called *Chronicles of the Olympics*. Little remains of his writing, but he is quoted by Eusebius and referred to by two other Christian writers, Julius Africanus and Origen.

According to Eusebius in a book called *Chronicle* (circa 320 CE), Phlegon wrote, "In the fourth year of the 202nd Olympiad, an eclipse of the sun happened, greater and more excellent than any that had happened before it; at the sixth hour, day turned into dark night, so that the stars were seen in the sky, and an earthquake in Bithynia toppled many buildings of the city of Nicaea."[18]

Julius Africanus in his *Chronography*, mentioned above, also referred to Phlegon. He wrote, "Phlegon records that, in the time of Tiberius Caesar, at full moon, there was a full eclipse of the sun from the sixth hour to the ninth—manifestly that one of which we speak. But what has an eclipse in common with an earthquake, the rending rocks, and the resurrection of the dead, and so great a perturbation throughout the universe? Surely no such event as this is recorded for a long period. But it was a darkness induced by God, because the Lord happened then to suffer."[19]

Origen (circa 250 CE) referred to Phlegon also. He wrote, "Phlegon, in the thirteenth or fourteenth book, I think, of his Chronicle even grants to Christ foreknowledge of certain future events . . . and he testified that it turned out in accordance with what Jesus had said." Later, he wrote, "And concerning the eclipse in the time of Tiberius Caesar, during whose reign Jesus appears to have been crucified, and about the great earthquakes that happened at that time, Phlegon has also made a record." Finally, "Phlegon . . . related that these events happened at the time of the Savior's passion."[20]

Even if all of these statements about Phlegon were accurate, the most that can be said is that a man writing circa 140 CE mentioned a midday darkness and maybe mentioned Jesus. This tells us nothing. By that date, the entire New Testament had been written, and the gospel of Mark had been in circulation for three generations.

Lucian of Samosata (circa 170 CE)

Lucian was a satirist who made fun of mountebank philosophers and Christians in *The Passing of Peregrinus*. He never used the words "Jesus" or "messiah" or "christ," but he referred to a founder of Christianity. Recounting the career of a huckster named Peregrinus, he wrote, "It was then that he learned the wondrous lore of the Christians, by associating with their priests and scribes in Palestine. And—how else could it be?—in a trice he made them all look like children, for he was prophet, cult-leader, head of the synagogue, and everything, all by himself. He interpreted and explained some of their books and even composed many, and they revered him as a god, made use of him as a lawgiver, and set him down as a protector, next after that other, to be sure, whom they still worship, the man who was crucified in Palestine because he introduced this new cult into the world."[21] It is clear from the late date of the writing and the obvious satire that Lucian does not provide factual evidence for anything.

Celsus (circa 180 CE)

Celsus wrote a book entitled *The True Word*, which criticized Christianity extensively. No copies survive, but it was heavily quoted by the Christian writer Origen in *Against Celsus* (circa 250). At one point, Celsus asserted that Jesus was the illegitimate son of a Roman soldier named Ben Panthera (Book One, chapter

32). This is interesting because there is a character of the same name in the Talmud (discussed previously). Due to the late date of the writing and the fact that Celsus cites no source for his assertion, however, it merits no higher status than that of scurrilous gossip.

Mara Bar-Serapion (between 70-200 CE)

A man named Mara Bar-Serapion wrote a flowery letter to his son, giving advice on life. At one point, he wrote, "For what else have we to say, when wise men are forcibly dragged by the hands of tyrants, and their wisdom is taken captive by calumny, and they are oppressed in their intelligence without defence? For what advantage did the Athenians gain by the murder of Socrates, the recompense of which they received in famine and pestilence? Or the people of Samos by the burning of Pythagoras, because in one hour, their country was entirely covered with sand? Or the Jews by the death of their wise king, because from that same time their kingdom was taken away? For with justice did God make recompense to the wisdom of these three: For the Athenians died of famine; and the Samians were overwhelmed by the sea without remedy; and the Jews, desolate and driven from their own kingdom, are scattered through every country. Socrates is not dead, because of Plato; neither Pythagoras, because of the statue of Juno; nor the wise king, because of the laws which he promulgated."[22]

Not much is known about this writing other than the immediate observation that many of the facts are wrong. Athens was not destroyed by famine after the death of Socrates. Pythagoras was not executed. Samos was never covered by sand or by the sea.

It is possible that the Jew's "wise king" is meant to be Jesus, but that is certainly not made clear. While the author mentions Socrates and Pythagoras by name, he does not mention Jesus at all. Yet Jesus would have been much closer to his own day than Socrates or Pythagoras. Moreover, the wording fits Jesus poorly as he did not promulgate or enact laws but rather taught and healed. In any event, even if the author was referring to Jesus, the uncertain date of the writing and the vagueness of the information tell us nothing more than that he had heard of him.

NOTES

Introduction

1. Pew Research Center's Forum on Religion and Public Life, Global Religious Landscape, December 2012, http://www.pewforum.org/2012/12/18/global-religious-landscape-exec/, August 11, 2013.
2. Pew Research Center, "Global Christianity: A Report on the Size and Distribution of the World's Christian Population," December 19, 2011, [http://www.pewforum.org/Christian/Global-Christianity-traditions.aspx?src=prc-section], April 17, 2013.

Chapter 1: The World

1. World Health Organization, Malaria Fact sheet N°94, April 2012, reviewed March 2013, [http://www.who.int/mediacentre/factsheets/fs094/en/], April 17, 2013.
2. For this notion of the moral obligations of a human with super-powers, I am indebted to Richard Carrier in his excellent book, Why I am not a Christian, Philosophy Press, Richmond, CA, 2011, pages 18-19.

Chapter 2: The Fall

[1] Encyclopedia of Creation Myths, David Adams Leeming, ABC-CLIO Inc., Santa Barbara, CA, 1994, pages 241-242.

Chapter 3: Original Sin

[1] Jaroslav Pelikan, Jesus Through the Centuries, Yale University Press, New Haven, CT, 1985, pages 72-73.

Chapter 4: The Satan

[1] Peggy L. Day, An Adversary in Heaven: Satan in the Hebrew Bible, Scholars Press, Atlanta, GA, 1988, Harvard Semitic Monographs, edited by Frank Moore Cross; pages 147-150 provide a summary.
[2] Elaine Pagels, The Origin of Satan, Random House, New York, NY, 1995, pages 39-42.
[3] Jeffrey Burton Russell, The Devil: Perceptions of Evil from Antiquity to Primitive Christianity, Cornell University Press, Ithaca, NY, 1977, pages 174, 217-218. Russell also provides an alternative explanation for the contradiction between 2 Samuel and 1 Chronicles regarding the census: by the time Chronicles was written, 4th century BCE, its compilers could no longer tolerate the original meaning, which was that god was the source of all good and all evil.
[4] Ibid., pages 185-204.
[5] Ibid., pages 218-219, 255.

Chapter 6: Afterlife

[1] Catechism of the Catholic Church, Part 1: The Profession of Faith; Section Two I. The Creeds; Chapter Three I believe in the Holy Spirit, Article 11 "I believe in the resurrection of the body", I. Christ's Resurrection and Ours, Line 997, [http://www.vatican.va/archive/ENG0015/_P2H.HTM#-1AB], April 17, 2013.

[2] Westminster Confession, Chapter 32, paragraph 2, Christian Classic Ethereal Library, [http://www.ccel.org/ccel/schaff/creeds3.iv.xvii.ii.html], April 17, 2013.

Chapter 7: Revelation

[1] J.P. Moreland, "Apologetics 315," [http://www.apologetics315.com/2009/06/sunday-quote-jp-moreland-on-gods.html], December 20, 2013.

Chapter 8: Faith

[1] Tertullian, On the Flesh of Christ, Chapter 5, New Advent, The Fathers of the Church, [http://www.newadvent.org/fathers/0315.htm], April 17, 2013.

Chapter 9: Judgment

[1] Origen, Contra Celsum, Book 6, Chapter 78, translated by Henry Chadwick, Cambridge University Press, London, 1953, page 391.

Chapter 10: Hell

[1] Neil Gillman, The Death of Death: Resurrection and Immortality in Jewish Thought, Jewish Lights Publishing, Woodstock, Vermont, 1997, pages 83-97. See also Jeffrey Burton Russell, op. cit., page 186.
[2] Robert Charles Zaehner, The Dawn and Twilight of Zoroastrianism, GP Putnam's Sons, New York, NY, 1961, page 58.
[3] The Jewish Study Bible, Jewish Publication Society, Adele Berlin and Marc Zvi Brettler editors, Oxford University Press, New York, NY, 2004, pages 1640-1642. For a good discussion of the

reasoning behind the dating see also, Neil Gillman, op. cit., pages 85-86.
4   Russell, op. cit., page 186.
5   Ibid., page 119.

Chapter 12: The Incarnation

1   Elaine Pagels, The Gnostic Gospels, Random House, New York, NY, 1979, pages 11-17.
2   Barton Ehrman, Lost Scriptures: Books That Did Not Make It Into The New Testament, Oxford University Press, New York, NY, 2003, page 20.
3   Elaine Pagels, The Gnostic Gospels, op. cit., pages xviii-xix.
4   Kenneth Scott LaTourette, A History of Christianity, Harper & Row, New York, NY, 1953, pages 154-157.
5   Ramsay Macmullen, Christianizing the Roman Empire (A.D. 100-400), Yale University Press, New Haven, CT, 1984, page 93.
6   Kenneth Scott LaTourette, op. cit., page 70.

Chapter 13: Holy Spirit

1   Clement of Rome, 2 Clement, Chapter 14, Ante-Nicene Fathers: The Writings of the Fathers Down to A.D. 325, editors: Alexander Roberts; James Donaldson, Sir; A. Cleveland Coxe; Allan Menzies; fourth edition, Hendrickson Publishing, Peabody, MA, 1994, 1885, Volume Nine, page 255.
2   Justin Martyr, First Apology, Chapter 33, Ante-Nicene Fathers: The Writings of the Fathers Down to A.D. 325, op. cit., Volume One, page 174.
3   Kenneth Scott LaTourette, op. cit., page 163.
4   Ibid., page 303.

Chapter 14: Morality

[1] Jefferson Davis, speech to Senate, "Slavery in the Territories," February 13, 1850, printed in Jefferson Davies, Constitutionalist: His Letters, Papers, and Speeches, Volume One, page 286, edited by Dunbar Rowland, Mississippi Department of Archives and History, 1923.

[2] Confucius, The Analects XV, 23, translated by Arthur Waley, George Allen & Unwin Ltd., London, 1938.

[3] "Is Faith Good for Us?" by Phil Zuckerman, Free Inquiry, August-September 2006. See also, "Cross-National Correlations of Quantifiable Societal Health with Popular Religiosity and Secularism in the Prosperous Democracies: A First Look" by Gregory S. Paul, Journal of Religion & Society, Volume 7, 2005.

[4] John G. Gager, The Origins of Anti-Semitism: Attitudes Toward Judaism in Pagan and Christian Antiquity, Oxford University Press, New York, NY, 1983, pages 39-54. According to this analysis, Jews were generally well regarded in the Hellenistic world. During the Roman period, there were instances of violence such as the Alexandrian riots of 38-41, but these were the result of political factionalism, not animus against Jews for being Jews. Most instances of anti-Jewish comments in Roman literature were the result of a general xenophobia among conservative Romans reacting to the influx of "un-Roman" ideas into the major cities of the empire.

[5] Tertullian, De Oratione, quoted in Robert Michael, Anti-Semitism and the Church Fathers, in Jewish-Christian Encounters over the Centuries, edited by Marvin Perry and Frederick M. Schweitzer, Peter Lang Publishing, New York, NY, 1994, page 111.

[6] Eusebius, Sermon on Resurrection, quoted in Robert Michael, op. cit., page 110.

[7] Augustine, Contra Faustum, Book 12, paragraph 12, New Advent, Fathers of the Church, [http://www.newadvent.org/fathers/140612.htm], April 17, 2013.

8   Luther's Works, Volume 47, The Christian in Society IV, edited by Franklin Sherman, general editor Helmut T. Lehman, Fortress Press, Philadelphia, PA, 1971, page 172.
9   Ibid., pages 268-270.
10 Norman Davies, Europe: A History, Oxford University Press, Oxford, 1996, pages 846-847. For a comprehensive summary, see Phyllis Goldstein, A Convenient Hatred: The History of Antisemitism, Facing History and Ourselves, Brookline, MA, 2012.
11 Adolf Hitler, Mein Kampf, translated by Ralph Manheim, Houghton Mifflin Company, New York, NY, 1971, page 65 (originally published in 1925).

Chapter 15: Purpose

1   Catechism of Catholic Church, [http://www.vatican.va/archive/ENG0015/_INDEX.HTM], April 17, 2013.
2   Westminster Confession, Center for Reformed Theology and Apologetics, [http://www.reformed.org/documents/index.html?mainframe=http://www.reformed.org/documents/westminster_conf_of_faith.html], April 17, 2013.
3   Rick Warren, The Purpose Driven Life, Zondervan, Grand Rapids, MI, 2002, page 53.

Chapter 16: The Church

1   John Henry Cardinal Newman, An Essay on the Development of Christian Doctrine, Longmans, Green and Company, New York, NY, 1949, page 7.
2   Barton Ehrman, Did Jesus Exist? The Historical Argument for Jesus of Nazareth, HarperCollins Books, New York, NY, 2012, pages 309-313.
3   2 Maccabees, Holy Bible, Catholic Edition, New Revised Standard Version, Harper Catholic Bibles, HarperOne, San Francisco, CA, 1989, page 701.

Chapter 17: Prayer

1. Herbert Benson, MD, "Study of the Therapeutic Effects of Intercessory Prayer (STEP) in cardiac bypass patients: A multicenter randomized trial of uncertainty and certainty of receiving intercessory prayer," American Heart Journal, April 2006; volume 151 number 4, pages 934-942, [http://www.ahjonline.com/article/S0002-8703(05)00649-6/abstract], April 17, 2013.

Chapter 18: Miracles

1. Divyavadana (Divine Stories) Part One, Classics of Indian Buddhism, translated by Andy Rotman, Wisdom Publications, Somerville, MA, 2008, pages 268-270.
2. Ibid., pages 270-287.
3. The Qur'an, English Translation and Parallel Arabic Text, translated and with an Introduction and Notes by M. A. S. Abdel Haleem, Oxford University Press, Oxford, 2004; Sura 17 Al-Isra (The Night Journey), verse 1, page 283.
4. Summarized Sahih Al-Bukhari, translated by Dr. Muhammad Muhsin Khan, Maktaba Dar-us-Salam, Riyadh, Saudi Arabia, 1996; Volume 5, Number 227, pages 737-743. The volume and number refer to original edition; the page number refers to the summarized version.
5. Book of Mormon, Testimony of the Three Witnesses; Testimony of the Eight Witnesses, The Church of Jesus Christ of Latter-day Saints, Salt Lake City, Utah, 1981, first published in 1830.
6. The Qur'an, op. cit.; Sura 13 Al-Ra'd (Thunder), verse 7, page 251.
7. Summarized Sahih Al-Bukhari, op. cit., Water: Volume 7, Number 543, pages 15-16; Corpse: Volume 4, Number 814, page 16; Moon: Volume 4, Number 830, page 709.

Chapter 19: Prophecies

1. Barton Ehrman, Jesus Interrupted: Revealing the Hidden Contradictions in the Bible, Harper Collins, 2009, New York, NY, page 50.

Chapter 20: Second Coming

1. Albert Schweitzer, The Quest of the Historical Jesus, Macmillan, New York, NY, 1910. See, for example, pages 358-368.
2. Flusser, David, "Apocalypse." Encyclopaedia Judaica. Ed. Michael Berenbaum and Fred Skolnik. 2nd ed. Vol. 2. Detroit: Macmillan Reference USA, 2007. 256-258. Gale Virtual Reference Library. Web. 4 July 2012. [http://go.galegroup.com/ps/i.do?id=GALE%7CCX2587501182&v=2.1&u=imcpl1111&it=r&p=GVRL&sw=w].

Chapter 21: Baseline

1. T. J. Cornell, The Beginnings of Rome: Italy and Rome from the Bronze Age to the Punic Wars, Routledge, London, 1995, pages 57-68. See also original sources: Ovid, Fasti, Books 2 and 3; Dionysius of Halicarnassus, Roman Antiquities, Book 2, Chapter 63; Cicero, Treatise on the Laws, Book 1.
2. Ovid, Metamorphoses, Book 4; Pindar, Pythian Ode 10; Homer, Iliad Book 14; Edith Hamilton, Mythology, Back Bay Books / Little, Brown and Company, New York, NY, pages 197-208.
3. Ovid, Metamorphoses, Book 9; Euripides, Herakles; Sophocles, Trachiniae; Pindar, Olympian 10.5; Edith Hamilton, op. cit., pages 224-243. Also: Elizabeth Vandiver, Classical Mythology, The Teaching Company, Chantilly VA, 2000, pages 81-86.
4. Susan K. Roll, Toward the Origins of Christmas, Kok Pharos Publishing House, Kampen, The Netherlands, 1995, page 110.

5 Michael Grant, History of Rome, Charles Scribner's Sons, New York, NY, 1978, pages 391-392. See also Roll, op. cit., pages 113-114.
6 Susan K. Roll, op. cit., page 111.
7 M.J. Vermaseren, Mithras, the Secret God, Chatto and Windus Ltd., London, 1963; birth: page 75; salvation: page 103.
8 Ibid., pages 27-28.
9 Brian Moynahan, The Faith: A History of Christianity, Doubleday, New York, NY, 2002, page 94, for first mention. For possible earlier belief, see Roll, op. cit., page 108.
10 Osiris: Geraldine Pinch, Egyptian Mythology, Oxford University Press, New York, NY, 2002, pages 178-179. Also Bojana Mojsov, Osiris: Death and Afterlife of a God, Blackwell Publishing, Malden, MA, 2005, especially pages xix-xx. Baal: Michael David Coogan, Stories from Ancient Canaan, The Westminster Press, Philadelphia, 1978, pages 75-115. Also: Tryggve N.D. Mettinger, The Riddle of Resurrection: Dying and Rising Gods in the Ancient Near East, Almqvist & Wiksell International, Stockholm, 2001, pages 57-81. Tammuz: Glenn S. Holland, Religion in the Ancient Mediterranean World, The Teaching Company, Chantilly VA, 2005, pages 72-76. Also: Mettinger, op. cit., pages 185-214. Dionysus and Persephone: Edith Hamilton, op. cit., on Dionysus pages 64-76; on Persephone pages 57-64. Also: Elizabeth Vandiver, op. cit.; on Dionysus pages 50-55; on Persephone pages 36-44. Asclepius: Emma J. Edelstein and Ludwig Edelstein, Asclepius: Collection and Interpretation of the Testimonies, Volumes I and II, The John Hopkins University Press, Baltimore, MD, 1945. See particularly testimonies 2, 31, 32, 56, 75, 237, 238, 262, and 524.
11 For mystery religions in general, see Robert Turcan, The Cults of the Roman Empire, Blackwell Publishing, Malden, MA, 1992. See also, Marvin W. Meyer, editor, The Ancient Mysteries: A Sourcebook, HarperCollins Publishers, New York, NY, 1987.

12   Joseph Campbell, The Transformations of Myth Through Time, Harper & Row, New York, NY, 1990, pages 189-209. See also, Glenn S. Holland, op. cit., pages 181-191.

13   Herodotus, The History, Book 2, 171, translated by David Grene, University of Chicago Press, Chicago, IL, 1987, page 205. Note: Around 300 BCE, under Ptolemaic auspices, the cults of Osiris and Apis were syncretized into the worship of one deity, Serapis. This Hellenized version of Osiris, along with his consort Isis, was the form in which the Egyptian mystery came to Rome.

14   Cicero, De Legibus (On the Laws), Book 2, 36, quoted by Edith Hamilton, op. cit., page 55.

15   Livy, Rome and the Mediterranean, Books 31-45 of The History of Rome From Its Foundation, translated by Henry Bettenson, Penguin Books, London, England, 1976, pages 401-415.

16   Plutarch, Consolatio ad Uxorem, paragraph 10, as published in Volume VII of the Loeb Classical Library edition, 1959, [http://penelope.uchicago.edu/Thayer/E/Roman/Texts/Plutarch/Moralia/Consolatio_ad_uxorem*.html#ref42], April 18, 2013.

17   Ezekiel was written circa 590-570 BCE and First Isaiah circa 730-700 BCE. This dating is my approximation, based on the Jewish Study Bible, op. cit. For Isaiah, see pages 780-784. The assumption is that chapters 1-39 were written by First Isaiah and that later chapters were written by Second, or possibly Third, Isaiah. For Ezekiel, see pages 1042-1044.

18   Justin Martyr, First Apology, Chapter 21, Ante-Nicene Fathers: The Writings of the Fathers Down to A.D. 325, op. cit., Volume One, page 170.

19   Justin Martyr, Dialogue with Trypho, Chapters 69-70, Ante-Nicene Fathers: The Writings of the Fathers Down to A.D. 325, op. cit., Volume One, pages 233-234.

Chapter 22: Paul

[1] Raymond E. Brown, An Introduction to the New Testament, Bantam Doubleday Dell, New York, NY, 1997, page 534 and note 64, for 1 Corinthians 15:3-5 and 11:23-26. See Barton Ehrman, Did Jesus Exist?, op. cit., page 111, for Romans 1:3-4.

Chapter 23: Oral Tradition

[1] This is the traditional alliterative trilemma, though it's not clear Lewis coined it. Nevertheless, this is among his arguments in C. S. Lewis, Mere Christianity, HarperCollins, San Francisco, CA, 2001 (original publication in 1952), page 52.

[2] Raymond E. Brown op. cit.; regarding the gospels, Brown adds the following: Mark was written "most likely between 68 and 73" (page 127). Matthew was written 80-90 "give or take a decade" (page 172). Luke was written circa 85 "give or take 5 to 10 years" (page 226). Regarding John, "Those who think that the Gospel was redacted (edited) by another hand after the main writer composed it may place the body of the Gospel in the 90s and the additions of the redactor ca. 100-110 (page 334). Regarding Paul's letters: 1 Thessalonians circa 50-51 (page 457), Galatians 54-55 (page 468), Philippians 56 but possibly as late as 63 (page 484), Philemon 55 but possibly as late as 63 (page 503), 1 Corinthians 56-57 (page 512), 2 Corinthians 57 (page 452), Romans 57-58 (page 560).

[3] Ibid., page 7.

[4] Ibid., pages 158-159.

[5] Barton Ehrman, Jesus Interrupted, op. cit., page 287, footnote 4.

[6] Raymond E. Brown, op. cit., page 158.

[7] Ibid., pages 208-211.

[8] Ibid., page 204.

[9] Scholarly opinion is divided. The view presented here is my understanding of Raymond E. Brown, op. cit., pages 368-371.

10. Catherine Hezser, Jewish Literacy in Roman Palestine, Mohr Siebeck, Tubingen, Germany, 2001, pages 23, 35, and 496.
11. Barton Ehrman, The New Testament: A Historical Introduction to the Early Christian Writings, Oxford University Press, New York, NY, 2000, pages 47-49.
12. Raymond E. Brown, op. cit., page 114.

Chapter 24: Canon

1. Jaroslav Pelikan, Whose Bible Is It? A History of the Scriptures Through the Ages, Penguin, New York, NY, 2005, pages 45-46.
2. Daniel J. Harrington, The Old Testament Apocrypha in the Early Church, in The Canon Debate, Lee Martin McDonald and James A. Sanders, editors, Hendrickson Publishers, Peabody, MA, 2002, page 198.
3. Raymond E. Brown, op. cit., page 762, "give or take a decade."
4. Helmut Koester, quoted in Elaine Pagels, Gnostic Gospels, op. cit., regarding Thomas, page xvii; also see Barton Ehrman's reference to research by April DeConick in Did Jesus Exist?, op. cit., page 82; L. Michael White, From Jesus to Christianity, HarperCollins Books, New York, NY, 2004, page 299, regarding Peter.
5. Barton Ehrman, From Jesus to Constantine: A History of Early Christianity, The Teaching Company, Chantilly, VA, 2004, pages 74-75.
6. Barton Ehrman, Lost Scriptures, op. cit., page 31.
7. Ibid., page 33.
8. Irenaeus, Against Heresies, Book 3, Chapter 11, paragraph 8, Ante-Nicene Fathers: The Writings of the Fathers Down to A.D. 325, editors: Alexander Roberts; James Donaldson, Sir; A Cleveland Coxe; Allan Menzies; fourth edition, Hendrickson Publishing, Peabody, MA, 1994, 1885, Volume One, page 428.
9. The Wisdom of Solomon (Barton Ehrman, Lost Scriptures, op. cit., page 331), The Apocalypse of Peter (Ibid., page 331), 1 and 2 Clement (Barton Ehrman, Jesus Interrupted, op. cit., page 211),

the Epistle of Barnabas (Ibid., page 203), The Shepherd of Hermas (Ibid., page 211), Didakhe (Bruce Metzger, The Text of the New Testament: Its Transmission, Corruption, and Restoration, Oxford University Press, Oxford, 1964, page 187).

10. Barton Ehrman, Forged: Writing in the Name of God—Why the Bible's Authors Are Not Who We Think They Are, Harper Collins, New York, NY, 2011, page 18-19. Ehrman counts over one hundred writings by Christians prior to 400 CE that one or more other Christians have claimed were forgeries.
11. Ibid., pages 92-93.
12. Ibid., pages 66-77.
13. Ibid., James, pages 192-198; Jude, pages 186-188.
14. Ibid., page 23; see also, Jesus Interrupted, pages 112-113 and 134-135.
15. Harry Y. Gamble, The New Testament Canon: Its Making and Meaning, Fortress Press, Philadelphia, PA, 1985, pages 68-72.
16. Harry Gamble, The New Testament Canon: Recent Research and the Status Quaestionis, in The Canon Debate, op. cit., pages 289-290.
17. Elaine Pagels, Revelations: Visions, Prophecy, and Politics in the Book of Revelation, Viking, New York, NY, 2012, pages 161-162.
18. Ibid., page 145.
19. Barton Ehrman, Lost Scriptures, op. cit., pages 339-341.

Chapter 25: Gospel Composition

1. Richard Carrier, Not the Impossible Faith: Why Christianity Didn't Need a Miracle to Succeed, Lulu.com, 2009, pages 161-212.
2. Bertrand Russell, Why I am Not a Christian, Simon and Schuster, New York, NY, 1957, page 19.
3. Barton Ehrman, Did Jesus Exist?, op. cit., page 184.
4. See New International Version (NIV) Holy Bible, Zondervan, Grand Rapids, MI, 2011, page 810, Matthew 27:16-17 and accompanying note.

[5] James Strong, The New Strong's Exhaustive Concordance of the Bible, Thomas Nelson Publishers, Nashville, TN, 1996, page 48.

[6] Richard Carrier as quoted by Robert M. Price in The Incredible Shrinking Son of Man: How Reliable is the Gospel Tradition?, Prometheus Books, Amherst, NY, 2003, pages 326-327.

[7] A. J. B. Higgins, The Christian Significance of the Old Testament, Independent Press Ltd., London, 1949, page 88.

[8] Cyrus the Great, Herodotus, The History, Book One, sections 108-113; Oedipus and Jason, Edith Hamilton, op. cit., pages 375-376 and pages 161-162; Horus, Geraldine Pinch, Egyptian Mythology, op. cit., pages 178-179. Also Bojana Mojsov, op. cit., especially pages xix-xx.

[9] Richard Carrier, Not the Impossible Faith, op. cit., page 179. Carrier provides an excellent critique of Luke's historiography. See pages 177-187.

[10] Raymond E. Brown, op. cit., page 263.

[11] Ibid., page 321.

[12] Ibid., page 292 note 33; see also Gafni, Isaiah. "Theudas." Encyclopaedia Judaica. Ed. Michael Berenbaum and Fred Skolnik. 2nd ed. Vol. 19. Detroit: Macmillan Reference USA, 2007. 703-704. Gale Virtual Reference Library. Web. 22 June 2012, [http://go.galegroup.com/ps/i.do?id=GALE%7CCX2587519802&v=2.1&u=imcpl1111&it=r&p=GVRL&sw=w)].

[13] Sarah B. Pomeroy, Stanley M. Burstein, Walter Donlan, Jennifer Tolbert Roberts, Ancient Greece: A Political, Social, and Cultural History, Oxford University Press, New York, NY, 2008, page 141.

[14] Encyclopedia of Classical Philosophy, edited by Donald J. Zeyl, Greenwood Press, Westport, CT, 1997, page 305.

[15] Cleanthes, Hymn to Zeus, line 12, translated by Johan C. Thom in Cleanthes' Hymn to Zeus: Text, Translation, and Commentary, Mohr Siebeck, Tubingen, Germany, 2005, page 40.

[16] Gershenson, Daniel E. "Logos." Encyclopaedia Judaica. Ed. Michael Berenbaum and Fred Skolnik. 2nd ed. Vol. 13. Detroit: Macmillan Reference USA, 2007. 174-175. Gale Virtual Reference Library.

Web. 10 June 2012, [http://go.galegroup.com/ps/i.do?id=GALE%7CCCX2587512726&v=2.1&u=imcpl1111&it=r&p=GVRL&sw=w].

17 Amir, Yehoyada, and Maren Niehoff. "Philo Judaeus." Encyclopaedia Judaica. Ed. Michael Berenbaum and Fred Skolnik. 2nd ed. Vol. 16. Detroit: Macmillan Reference USA, 2007. 59-64. Gale Virtual Reference Library. Web. 10 June 2012, [http://go.galegroup.com/ps/i.do?id=GALE%7CCCX2587515715&v=2.1&u=imcpl1111&it=r&p=GVRL&sw=w].

18 Gershenson, Daniel E. "Logos." Encyclopaedia Judaica. op. cit.

19 De Agricultura (On Husbandry) 51, The Works of Philo Judaeus, The contemporary of Josephus, translated from the Greek, by Charles Duke Yonge, London, H. G. Bohn, 1854-1890. [http://www.earlychristianwritings.com/yonge/book11.html], April 18, 2013.

Chapter 26: Gospel Preservation

1 Barton Ehrman, The New Testament, op. cit., page 443.
2 Ibid., page 403.
3 Barton Ehrman, on the first fragment, known as P52, see Misquoting Jesus, The Story Behind Who Changed the Bible and Why, HarperCollins Publishers, New York, NY, 2005, page 88. On complete books, see The New Testament, op. cit., page 156.
4 Origen, Commentary on Matthew 15:14, as quoted by Bruce Metzger in 'Explicit References in the Works of Origen to Variant Readings in New Testament Manuscripts', Biblical and Patristic Studies in Memory of Robert Pierce Casey, edited by J. Neville Birdsall and Robert W. Thomson, Herder K. G., Freiburg, Germany, 1963, pages 78-79.
5 Jerome, Epistle LXXI, To Lucinius, as quoted by Bruce Metzger, in The Text of the New Testament, op. cit., page 194.
6 Barton Ehrman, Misquoting Jesus, op. cit., page 73.
7 Ibid., pages 65-68.
8 Bruce M. Metzger, op. cit., page 229.

9   Barton Ehrman, Misquoting Jesus, op. cit., pages 80-83. See also NIV textual note on page 2582.

10   Barton Ehrman, Misquoting Jesus, op. cit., pages 157-161.

Chapter 27: Misrepresentation

1   This is based on the language analysis of Uri Yosef, Isaiah 7:14—Part One: An Accurate Grammatical Analysis, and Part Two: Refuting Christian Apologetics, 2011, [http://thejewishhome.org/counter-index.html], April 18, 2013.

Chapter 29: Corroboration

1   Only fragments survive, but the ninth century Christian writer Photius, in his review of Justus's history, criticized Justus for omitting discussion of Jesus. "Justus's style is very concise, and he omits a great deal that is of the utmost importance. Suffering from the common fault of the Jews, to which race he belonged, he does not even mention the coming of Christ, the events of His life, or the miracles performed by Him." Photius, Bibliotheca, 33. [Justus of Tiberias, Chronicle of the Kings of the Jews], Early Church Fathers—Additional Texts, Edited by Roger Pearse, Photius of Constantinople, The Bibliotheca or Myriobiblion, [http://www.tertullian.org/fathers/index.htm#Photius_of_Constantinople], April 18, 2013.

2   Robert M. Grant, Second Century Christianity: A Collection of Fragments, 2nd Edition, Westminster John Knox Press, Louisville, Kentucky, 2003, page 25.

3   Eusebius, The History of the Church from Christ to Constantine, translated by G. A. Williamson, Penguin Books, Baltimore, MD, 1965, page 107.

4   Barton Ehrman, Lost Scriptures, op. cit.; for dating Acts of John, page 94. For dating Acts of Thomas, page 122. For dating of Acts of Peter, L. Michael White, op. cit., page 402.

⁵ Barton Ehrman, Lost Scriptures, op. cit., Acts of Peter, pages 135-154.

Chapter 30: Resurrection

¹ Catherine Hezser, op. cit., pages 23, 35, 496.
² CIA, The World Factbook, Field Listing Literacy: https://www.cia.gov/library/publications/the-world-factbook/fields/2103.html], April 18, 2013.
³ Pew Forum on Religion & Public Life, Many Americans Not Dogmatic About Religion Reincarnation, Astrology and the "Evil Eye", December 10, 2009, [http://pewresearch.org/pubs/1434/multiple-religious-practices-reincarnation-astrology-psychic], April 18, 2013.
⁴ Alan F. Segal, Paul the Convert: The Apostolate and Apostasy of Saul the Pharisee, Yale University Press, New Haven, CT, 1990, page 56.
⁵ Caroline Walker Bynum, The Resurrection of the Body in Western Christianity, 200-1336, Columbia University Press, New York, NY, 1995, page 22.
⁶ Edith Steffen and Adrian Coyle, 'Sense of Presence' Experiences in Bereavement and their Relationship to Mental Health: A Critical Examination of a Continuing Controversy, in Mental Health and Anomalous Experience, Craig Murray, editor, Nova Science Publishers, New York, NY, 2012, pages 33-56. For an older but comprehensive discussion of relevance to this issue, see Dale C. Allison Jr., Resurrecting Jesus: The Earliest Christian Tradition and its Interpreters, T&T Clark International, New York, NY, 2005, pages 272-290 and 364-375.
⁷ Edith Steffen and Adrian Coyle, op. cit., page 47.
⁸ J.P. Moreland, quoted in Lee Strobel, The Case for Christ, Zondervan, Grand Rapids, MI, 1998, pages 250-251.
⁹ Tractate Yehamot 16:3 a-e, cited in Jeffery Jay Lowder, Historical Evidence and the Empty Tomb Story: A reply to William Lane

Craig, in Beyond the Empty Tomb: Jesus Beyond the Grave, op. cit., pages 289 and 304 note 121.
10   Richard Carrier, Beyond the Empty Tomb, op. cit., pages 108-109.

Chapter 31: Legend

1   John P. Meier, The Circle of the Twelve: Did It Exist During Jesus's Public Ministry? Journal of Biblical Literature, 116/4, 1997, page 660. See also Dale C. Allison Jr., Resurrecting Jesus: The Earliest Christian Tradition and its Interpreters, T&T Clark International, New York, NY, 2005, page 234.
2   Barton Ehrman, Did Jesus Exist? op. cit., pages 111 and 130. This belief appears also in Acts 13:32-33, which repeats another early oral creed, "We tell you the good news: What God promised our ancestors he has fulfilled for us, their children, by raising up Jesus. As it is written in the second Psalm: 'You are my son; today I have become your father.'" Notice the word "today."

Chapter 32: Growth

1   Rodney Stark, The Rise of Christianity, Princeton University Press, Princeton, NJ, 1996, pages 1-13.
2   Ibid., pages 184-188.
3   Barton Ehrman, Jesus Interrupted, op. cit., pages 80-82.
4   Origen, Contra Celsum, Book 3, Chapter 44, translated by Henry Chadwick, op. cit., page 158.
5   Rodney Stark, op. cit., 179-180.
6   Tertullian, Apologetic, Chapter 50, Christian Classics Ethereal Library, http://www.ccel.org/ccel/schaff/anf03.iv.iii.l.html, July 12, 2013.
7   Brian Moynahan, op. cit., pages 106-107.
8   Rodney Stark, op. cit., pages 73-82.
9   Ibid., 122-126.
10 Ramsay MacMullen, op. cit., pages 49-50.

[11] Ibid., page 96.
[12] LaTourette, op. cit., pages 97-98 and Ramsay Macmullen, op. cit., page 99.
[13] Ibid., LaTourette, pages 97-98 and Macmullen, page 89.

Conclusion

[1] Ernest Becker, The Denial of Death, The Free Press, 1973, New York, NY, pages 150-155.

Appendix 3: The Suffering Servant of Isaiah 53

[1] Origen, Contra Celsum, Book 1, Chapter 55, translated by Henry Chadwick, op. cit., pages 50-51.
[2] Michael L. Brown, Jewish Interpretations of Isaiah 53, in Darrell L. Bock and Mitch Glaser, The Gospel According to Isaiah 53: Encountering the Suffering Servant in Jewish and Christian Theology, Kregel Publications, Grand Rapids, Michigan, 2012, pages 62-63.
[3] Gerald Sigal, Isaiah 53: Who is the Servant?, Xlibris, Bloomington, IN, 2007, pages 37-75.
[4] Although the interpretation presented here is my own, it draws upon analysis by Richard J. Clifford, Fair Spoken and Persuading: An Interpretation of Second Isaiah, Paulist Press, New York, NY, 1984, pages 173-181.
[5] Jewish Study Bible, op. cit., pages 782-783.
[6] Simon Sebag Montefiore, Jerusalem: The Biography, Alfred A. Knopf, New York, NY, 2011.
[7] Gerald Sigal, op. cit., page 167.
[8] Michael L. Brown, op. cit., pages 72-75.
[9] Gerald Sigal, op. cit., page 195, note 5.
[10] Ibid., pages 205-206.

Appendix 4: Descents and Resurrections

1. Geraldine Pinch, op. cit., pages 178-179. Also Bojana Mojsov, op. cit., especially pages xix-xx.
2. Michael David Coogan, op. cit., pages 75-115. Also: Mettinger, op. cit., pages 57-81.
3. Glenn S. Holland, op. cit., pages 72-76. Also: Mettinger, op. cit., pages 185-214.
4. Edith Hamilton, op. cit., pages 64-76. Elizabeth Vandiver, op. cit., pages 50-55. There are multiple versions of the Dionysus story. Among the most complete is that found in Nonnus, Dionysiaca, Books 5-9.
5. Ibid., Hamilton, pages 57-64 and Vandiver, pages 36-44.
6. Emma J. Edelstein and Ludwig Edelstein, op. cit.

Appendix 5: Canon

1. Barton Ehrman, Forged, op. cit., page 229.
2. Raymond E. Brown, op. cit., pages 610 and 620.
3. Ibid., pages 108-114.
4. Barton Ehrman, Jesus Interrupted, op. cit., pages 130-134.
5. Ibid., page 131.
6. Barton Ehrman, Forged, op. cit., page 19.
7. Ibid., regarding James, pages 192-198; regarding Jude, pages 187.
8. Barton Ehrman, Jesus Interrupted, op. cit., pages 113, 134-135; see also his Forged, op. cit., 186-88.
9. Barton Ehrman, Forged, op. cit., pages 186-188.
10. Ibid., page 23; see also, Jesus Interrupted, pages 112-113 and 134-135.
11. Barton Ehrman, Jesus Interrupted, op. cit., pages 134-135; see also Forged, op. cit., page 223.
12. Barton Ehrman, Forged op. cit., pages 66-77.
13. Ibid., pages 67-68 and 199-200.
14. Elaine Pagels, Revelations, op. cit., pages 2, 8-9, 103-112.

[15] Barton Ehrman, God's Problem, HarperCollins Publishers, New York, NY, 2008, pages 255-258 and note 8 on page 284. See also Raymond E. Brown, op. cit., pages 802-805.

Appendix 6: Corroboration

[1] Clement, One Clement, Chapter 26, Ante-Nicene Fathers: The Writings of the Fathers Down to A.D. 325, op. cit., Volume Nine, page 237.
[2] Barton Ehrman, Did Jesus Exist? op. cit., pages 101-104.
[3] Ibid., pages 98-101.
[4] Robert M. Grant, op. cit., page 43.
[5] Barton Ehrman, After the New Testament: The Writings of the Apostolic Fathers, The Teaching Company, Chantilly, VA, 2005, pages 57-60.
[6] The Epistle of Barnabas, Early Christian Writings, Church Fathers, http://www.earlychristianwritings.com/text/barnabas-lightfoot.html, May 3, 2013.
[7] Josephus, Antiquities of the Jews 18.3.3, translated by William Whiston, Kregel Publications, Grand Rapids, MI, 1960, pages 379-380.
[8] Robert E. Van Voorst, Jesus Outside the New Testament: An Introduction to the Ancient Evidence, William B. Eerdmans Publishing Company, Grand Rapids, Michigan, 2000, page 92.
[9] Josephus, Antiquities of the Jews, 20.9.1, translated by William Whiston, op. cit., page 423.
[10] John P. Meier, A Marginal Jew: Rethinking the Historical Jesus, Bantam Doubleday Dell Publishing, New York, NY, 1991, page 206.
[11] Babylonian Talmud, Seder Nezikin, Tractate Sanhedron, Folio 43a, edited by Rabbi Dr. Isidore Epstein, [http://www.come-and-hear.com/sanhedrin/sanhedrin_43.html], April 18, 2013.
[12] Robert M. Grant, op. cit., page 3.
[13] Ibid., pages 4-6.
[14] Ibid., page 6.

[15] Ibid., pages 6-7.
[16] Julius Africanus, Chronography, 18.1, The Extant Fragments of the Five Books of the Chronography of Julius Africanus, Writings of Julius Africanus, Text edited by Rev. Alexander Roberts and James Donaldson and first published by T&T Clark in Edinburgh in 1867, [http://www.mb-soft.com/believe/txua/africanu.htm], April 18, 2013.
[17] Richard Carrier, The Spiritual Body of Christ and the Legend of the Empty Tomb, in Beyond the Empty Tomb, op. cit., pages 176-177.
[18] Early Church Fathers—Additional Texts, Edited by Roger Pearse, Jerome's Chronicle Being Eusebius' Chronicle, Part II, Translated from Latin by Roger Pearse, [http://www.tertullian.org/fathers/jerome_chronicle_03_part2.htm], April 18, 2013.
[19] Julius Africanus, op. cit., 18.1.
[20] Origen, Contra Celsum, Book 2, Chapters 14, 33, and 59, translated by Henry Chadwick, op. cit., pages 81, 94, and 112.
[21] Early Christian Writings, Lucian, translated by A.M. Harmon, 1936, Published in Loeb Classical Library, [http://www.earlychristianwritings.com/lucian.html], April 18, 2013.
[22] Spicilegium Syriacum: Containing Remains of Bardesan, Meliton, Ambrose and Mara Bar Serapion, edited and translated by William Cureton, Rivingtons, London, 1855, pages 73-74.

INDEX

A

Abraham, 89, 139-42, 177, 235
Achilles, 128
Acts, 81, 99, 131, 141, 145-47, 153, 158, 165-67, 185, 193, 195-96, 199, 201-5, 210, 261, 266, 294-96
   noncanonical (Peter, John, and Thomas), 153, 195-96
Adam and Eve, 23-30, 34-36, 51, 77, 85, 229
adoptionism, 172, 213
Adventures of Huckleberry Finn, The, 165
Aeneas, 128
afterlife, 21-22, 41-43, 45, 47, 52, 56, 59, 63-64, 85, 96, 104, 123, 132-33, 252, 280, 287
Ahriman, 33, 64
Ahura Mazda, 33, 64, 86
Allah, 110, 138

Amos, 122, 242, 244
Ananda, 110
angels, 30-32, 75, 111, 121, 154, 156, 187, 213
Anglican, 101
anomalous experiences, 79-81, 295
Anselm, 36, 223
Antiquities of the Jews, 190, 267-68
anti-Semitism, 91-93, 283
apocalypticism, 33, 121-23, 127, 133, 147, 149-50, 154, 157, 200-202, 248, 286
apostle (*see also* disciple), 55, 81, 112, 121, 137, 145, 166, 185-88, 190, 192-96, 204, 209, 260, 265, 271
Arianism, 73, 75
ascension, 128, 167, 200, 203, 210, 225
Asclepius, 132, 194, 255, 287
assumption of Mary, 76
Assyrians, 133, 202, 231, 235, 238

301

Athanasius, 157-58
atonement, theories of, 5, 34, 36-38, 40, 72, 86, 100, 104, 230, 234, 243
atonement sacrifice, 212, 230, 243
Augustine (early church leader), 27, 93, 283

B

Baal, 108, 132-33, 253, 287
Babylon, 234, 236, 241-42, 247, 261
Babylonian Exile, 33, 118, 231, 236-38
Babylonians, 132-33, 202, 231-32, 235, 243, 246
baptism, 102-3, 142, 212-15, 259
Bar Kochba Revolt, 232, 237
Barnabas, 153-55, 199, 266
Basilides, 266
Ben Stada, 269, 271
birth (*see also* virgin birth), 15, 46, 91, 128, 130-31, 134, 176, 212-14, 224-25, 252, 287
blindness, 161, 178
blood sacrifice, 36, 39-40, 56
book of Acts, the. *See* Luke-Acts
book of Daniel, 65, 133, 152, 256
Book of Mormon, 101, 111, 285
brain, 44-45, 80
Brown, Raymond E., 258, 289-90, 292, 298-99
Buddhism, 58, 80, 110-11, 160, 203, 285

C

Cardinal Newman. *See* Newman, John Henry
career, 60, 86, 92, 109, 128-29, 135, 192, 195, 213, 238, 268, 276
Carrier, Richard, 11, 162, 164, 205, 279, 291-92, 296, 300
Catholic church, 35, 41, 76, 280, 284
Catholics, 5, 89, 102-4, 256
Celsus (philosopher), 60, 216, 276-77
census, 32, 166, 280
children, 20-21, 27, 54, 66, 83-84, 92, 217, 223, 249, 276, 296
China, 60, 91, 116, 220
Christ. *See* Jesus Christ
Christian god, 14, 20, 22, 36, 50-52, 59, 61, 66, 72, 80, 82, 86, 106, 108, 112, 119, 135, 217
Christianity, 4-5, 13-16, 19-20, 22-34, 36-38, 40-42, 44, 46, 48, 50-60, 62-66, 68, 70, 72-74, 76, 78, 80-82, 84-86, 88, 90-92, 94-96, 98-100, 102, 104-6, 108-10, 112, 114-20, 122, 127-28, 130-36, 138, 140, 142, 146, 148, 150-52, 154, 156-58, 160, 162, 164, 166, 168-70, 172, 176, 178, 180, 182, 184, 186, 188, 192, 194, 196, 198, 200,

202-7, 210, 212, 214-26,
229-30, 232, 234, 236, 238,
240, 242, 244, 246, 248,
250-51, 254, 256, 258, 260,
262, 264-66, 268-74, 276,
278, 280, 282, 284, 286-88,
290-92, 294-96, 298, 300
Christians, 13, 20, 23, 26-28,
30-32, 35, 37, 39-40, 42-44,
50-51, 55, 58, 66-68, 71,
77-78, 80-84, 87, 91-93, 96,
99, 101-2, 108-9, 120, 131,
138-39, 141, 152-53, 155,
157, 164-65, 192, 196-97,
211, 215-19, 224, 230, 234,
237, 241, 244, 249, 264,
266-67, 272-74, 276, 291
Chronicles, 32, 37, 66, 141, 177,
257, 275, 280, 294
church, 4, 15, 48, 74-76, 79,
99-101, 103, 120, 145, 154,
158, 181, 210, 225, 262-64,
281, 283-85, 290, 294, 299
church leaders, 36, 75, 77-78, 86,
93, 103, 153, 155, 170, 222,
258-59, 268
Cicero, 132
Clement of Alexandria, 192, 195,
263, 266
Colossians, 84, 155, 258-59
Columbian Exchange, 116
conception, 29, 64, 212-14
confirmation bias, 106-7, 116
Confucianism, 87

confusion tradition, 206
conscience, 83, 87
consciousness, 44-46, 225-26
Constantine (emperor), 74-75,
218-19, 290, 294
consubstantiality, 75, 79
conversions, 136, 138, 146, 203,
210, 218-19
Corinthians, 136-37, 139, 154,
181, 201, 204-5, 209, 230,
258-59, 289
corporate guilt, 122
cosmic drama, 14, 70, 226, 229
cosmic dualism, 33, 122-23
Council of Nicaea, 75, 79, 214, 275
Councils (Chalcedon,
Constantinople, Nicaea, Toledo,
and Trent), 75, 79, 102, 275
covenant, 122, 141, 235, 239, 266
credentials, 53, 55, 137, 204
crucifixion, 154, 201, 205, 241,
244-45, 247, 271
culture, 24, 49, 54, 80, 93, 109,
113, 116, 200, 202, 231
Cyrus the Great, 163, 232, 239, 292

D

Damascus, 137, 166
darkness, 64-65, 86, 179, 274-75
David, 39, 119, 177, 183-84,
231, 239
death, 14-15, 19, 22-23, 26, 28,
35-38, 41-42, 44-45, 47, 73,

75-76, 83, 86, 93, 115, 123, 132, 138, 141-42, 161, 163, 190, 196, 201-2, 205, 207, 210, 212, 218, 225, 234, 246-48, 250, 253, 271-73, 277, 281, 287, 297
deity, 20, 22, 48-49, 51, 55, 57, 66, 80-81, 83, 87, 89, 100, 104, 106, 127, 173, 206, 214, 288
delayed parousia, 261
demons, 190, 194, 248
Deuteronomy, 27, 37, 52, 64, 66, 69, 83, 107, 141, 174-75, 230, 235, 247
devil, 32, 35, 92-93, 280. *See also* Satan
Didache, 154
Dionysus, 132-34, 254, 287
Dioscouri, 128, 134
disciple, 61, 74, 84, 110, 118, 120, 138, 147, 149, 161-62, 182, 185, 187, 202-3, 205-6, 248
divine, 36, 46, 58, 72, 75, 79-80, 128, 144, 212-14, 217, 222, 225, 241, 253
divine dictation, 156
Divyavadana, 110, 285
Doubting Thomas, 149, 187, 189
dyophysitism, 72, 75-76

E

early church, 15, 74, 138, 153, 172, 198, 264, 266, 290

earth, 49-50, 60, 114, 120, 131, 139, 150, 156, 164, 216, 222, 225, 235, 240, 252-54, 262, 265
earthquake, 20, 110, 187, 274-75
Eastern Orthodox, 5, 13, 76
education, 112, 202
Ehrman, Barton, 11, 169, 258, 282, 284, 286, 288-91, 293-98
Elect, the, 56, 93
Elijah, 113-14, 200
Elisha, 113-14
Emmaus, 187, 189, 207
empty tomb, 139, 149, 171, 207, 263
Ephesians, 56, 84, 155, 258-59, 264
Epictetus (Greek philosopher), 192, 272
Epistle of Barnabas, 154-55, 291, 299
eternity, 22, 46, 57-58, 63, 65, 85-86, 95-96, 214
ethical monotheism, 143, 229
eucharist, 102-3, 131, 135, 139, 226
Eusebius, 93, 145-46, 157, 195, 265, 268, 275, 283, 294
exiles, 177, 232, 237, 245-46, 251
eyewitnesses, 144-46, 150, 164-65, 198, 203
Ezekiel, 16, 37-40, 118-19, 133, 141, 242, 246, 249-50, 257, 288

F

faith, 14, 51, 53-61, 73-74, 85-86, 89, 91, 102-3, 107, 133, 136, 139-40, 143, 157, 174-76, 197, 206-7, 211, 219, 221-24, 243, 259, 264, 266, 280-81, 287
faith-in-Jesus test, 56-57, 59, 61, 65-66, 103, 223
famine, 255, 277
Feast of the Pentecost, 81, 120-21, 205
filioque, 79, 100
1 Clement, 153-55, 190, 263
First Council of Constantinople, 79
First Isaiah, 133, 236, 242-43, 251, 288
free will, 20, 31, 45, 49, 51-52, 66, 83

G

Galatians, 137, 140, 142, 154, 166, 204, 210, 289
Galileans, 166, 272
Galilee, 145, 186-87, 191, 200, 211
Gandhi, 56
Ganesh, 209
Gehenna, 65, 133
Gemara, 269
genealogy, 177, 183-84, 188, 212
general revelation, 61-62
Genesis, 25, 27, 31, 33, 84-85, 139-41, 200, 219, 235
gentiles, 130, 137, 139-40, 142-43, 203, 240, 261
germ theory of medicine, 116
Gilgamesh, 128
glossolalia, 81
gnosticism, 73-74, 264, 266
god-fearers, 143
golden rule, 83, 87-88
gospel, 60-61, 99, 109, 113, 121, 128, 137, 139, 142, 146-47, 149-50, 153-54, 159-61, 163, 169, 182, 185-86, 190, 194-95, 198-99, 239, 242, 262, 264, 289
gospel of John, 19, 53, 55, 59, 74-75, 86, 92, 103, 112, 117, 123, 146-50, 153, 155, 158, 167-68, 170-72, 182, 187, 189-90, 205, 207, 209, 211-12, 214, 216, 222, 229-30, 240, 243-48, 250, 260-62, 264
gospel of Mark, 16, 63, 74-75, 84, 105-6, 113, 115, 117-18, 120-21, 123, 129, 139, 144-46, 148-49, 160, 162-63, 165-66, 171, 182, 186-87, 191, 193-94, 199-200, 202, 206, 212-14, 216, 230, 240, 245, 248, 261, 266, 276, 289
gospel of Mary, 74

gospel of Matthew, 52, 59,
    61, 74-75, 78, 84, 91-92,
    100, 103, 105-6, 112, 118,
    120-23, 144-46, 148, 150,
    160-61, 163-66, 176-78,
    182-86, 190-91, 200, 206,
    209, 211-14, 216, 229-30,
    240, 243, 245, 248, 261,
    265, 269, 289
gospel of Peter, 14, 84, 138,
    153-55, 158, 187, 194-96,
    209-10, 261, 264, 266
gospels, noncanonical (Thomas,
    Philip, Truth, and Mary), 74,
    153
gospel writers, 116-17, 131, 159,
    164, 239
grace, 56, 102-3

H

hadith, 110, 114, 144
Han Dynasty, 60, 116
heaven, 20, 33, 42, 46-47, 53,
    55-56, 59, 63, 66-67, 75-77,
    91, 95, 104, 106-7, 110, 113,
    121-22, 134, 136-37, 150,
    164, 167, 171-72, 212, 216,
    222, 253, 262, 280
Hebrews, 38, 53, 115-16, 152, 154,
    158, 179-80, 230, 258, 269
hell, 42, 59, 63-67, 86, 91, 93,
    95-96, 104, 107, 222, 224,
    281

Hercules, 129, 134
hero archetype, 128-29, 163
Herod, 163, 166, 191, 201
Herodotus, 132, 288, 292
Hinduism, 52, 58, 80, 108, 156,
    223
Hitler, Adolf, 93, 284
holy ghost, 68-69, 78, 171. *See
    also* holy spirit
holy spirit, 78-81, 213, 259-60,
    280, 282
human beings. *See* humans
humankind, 22, 24, 28, 30,
    34-35, 37-38, 49, 56, 60, 63,
    65, 72, 85-87, 90-91, 94-97,
    102, 130, 141-42, 206, 225,
    234, 240, 244, 254-55, 260
human nature, 28-29, 37, 87,
    234, 264
humans, 19-22, 24, 26-27, 29,
    35, 37, 39, 41-42, 46, 49,
    52, 54, 56, 60, 65, 72-73, 77,
    86-90, 94, 97, 99, 103, 106,
    111, 113, 116, 121, 127,
    132, 134-35, 141, 151, 156,
    166, 173, 175, 188, 208,
    223, 225, 241, 249, 255
hymn, 139, 209, 214, 292

I

Ignatius, 192, 264
Iliad, The, 163, 286
immaculate conception, 76-77, 100

incarnation, 72-73, 75-77, 86, 212, 225, 252, 282
India, 54, 60, 116
industrial revolution, 116
inspiration, 138, 147, 155
Iran, 54. *See also* Persian
Irenaeus, 146-47, 154, 261, 266, 268, 290
Iroquois, 23-24
Isaiah, 39, 69, 118, 122, 133, 175-79, 233-43, 245, 247-51, 288, 292, 294, 297
Islam, 58, 110, 220
Israel, 31, 39, 64, 83, 93, 121-22, 133, 139, 141-42, 174, 185, 200, 230-31, 235-36, 239-42, 244-46, 248-49
Israelites, 27, 33, 35, 60, 83, 122, 175, 244, 251

J

Jacob, 175, 235-36, 240
James, 16, 56, 102-3, 107, 138, 155, 158, 186, 196, 204-5, 209-10, 259-60, 265, 268, 291, 298
Jehovah's Witnesses, 13
Jeremiah, 39, 118-19, 122, 151, 184, 236, 242, 244, 248, 250, 257
Jerome, 170, 293
Jerusalem, 39, 104, 110, 117-18, 137-38, 164, 166, 187, 191, 195, 207, 210-11, 232, 234, 236-37, 242-43, 245, 248, 297
Jesus. *See* Jesus Christ, 5, 22, 24, 28-29, 34-40, 42-43, 48, 54-57, 59-63, 65-66, 68-69, 72-80, 83-86, 88, 91-92, 99-100, 102-23, 127-50, 153-55, 157-68, 171-72, 174, 176-80, 182-88, 190-96, 198-210, 212-14, 216, 222-23, 225-26, 229-30, 233-34, 237-51, 258-71, 273-78, 280, 284-86, 289-90, 294, 296
Jesus Christ, 5, 22, 24, 28-29, 34-40, 42-43, 48, 54-57, 59-63, 66, 68-69, 72-80, 83-86, 88, 91-92, 99-100, 102-23, 127, 129-42, 144-50, 153, 155, 157-68, 171-72, 174, 176-80, 182-88, 190-96, 198-210, 212-14, 216, 222-23, 225-26, 229-30, 233-34, 237-51, 258-71, 273-78, 280, 284-86, 289-90
 death of, 28, 34, 37-38, 99, 191, 194, 204, 207, 230, 244, 274
 divinity of, 139, 208, 212, 214, 230
 followers of, 29, 140, 149, 201-2, 205, 207, 222, 230, 258-59
 life of, 115, 146, 190, 196, 222

resurrection of, 43, 131, 164, 201-3, 249, 263
sacrifice of, 35, 102, 139, 141, 244
teachings of, 92, 103, 121, 149
Jesus movement, 92, 133, 139, 198, 204, 207
Jewish Bible / Old Testament, 28, 31-32, 85, 92, 141, 229-30
Jews, 33, 58, 92-93, 99, 115, 118, 122, 133, 137, 139-40, 142-43, 148-49, 152, 161, 190-91, 202, 204, 216-18, 222, 229, 231-32, 235, 237, 239, 246-47, 260-61, 266-68, 273, 277, 283, 294, 299
Jibrael, 110
Job, 27, 31-32, 64
John (apostle), 145-47, 149, 155, 157-58, 195-96, 260, 262, 265
John Mark, 145
John of Patmos, 157-58, 261
John the Baptist, 121-22, 200, 205, 213-14
Joseph, 162, 183-84, 213
Josephus, 163-64, 192, 267-69, 293, 299
Judaism, 15, 30, 33, 40, 82, 133, 137, 152, 168, 200, 215-18, 249, 283
Judas, 166, 185-86, 193
Judea, 191, 210, 231-32, 273-74
judgment, 42, 59, 61, 64-65, 84, 88, 103-4, 123, 133, 136, 222-23, 250, 281

Julius Africanus, 274-75, 300
justice, 36, 65, 123, 225, 277
Justin Martyr, 79, 134-35, 146, 261, 282, 288

K

King Minos, 128
kings, 27, 113, 115, 117, 176, 200, 233, 244, 253, 257, 294
knowledge, 7, 23-24, 50, 57, 61, 73-74, 221, 249
Koran, 110, 114, 138, 144, 147, 156

L

law, the, 27, 56, 60, 83-84, 102, 133, 137, 139-43, 152, 174-76, 179, 184, 204-5, 222, 235, 249-50, 260, 268, 277
legend, 113, 144, 152, 180, 208-9, 211, 213, 296, 300
Leviticus, 27, 37-38, 40, 84, 230
Lewis, C. S., 144, 289
literacy, 112, 148, 156, 200, 220, 290
Livy, 191, 288
logos, 168, 214, 292-93
Lord (*see also* Jesus Christ), 31, 38, 64, 83, 93, 107, 114, 136-37, 141, 162, 176, 179, 230, 235, 238-40, 242-43, 248, 258, 265-66, 275

Lucian of Samosata, 276
Luke-Acts, 16, 52, 63, 78, 84-85, 117, 123, 145-46, 148, 150, 160, 163-67, 172, 178-79, 182-84, 186-87, 189, 191, 194, 200, 206, 211-14, 229-30, 240, 243, 245, 266, 269, 289
Luther, Martin, 93, 284

M

Maccabean Revolt, 104, 151-52, 200, 232, 284
Mandeans, 205
manuscripts, 146, 161, 169-72, 268
Mara Bar-Serapion, 277
Mary, 76, 78, 166, 183-84, 187, 201, 207, 209, 213, 216, 225
Mecca, 110
miracles, 81, 92, 109-14, 186, 190, 193-94, 196, 265, 285, 291, 294
miracle scale factor (MSF), 194
Mishnah, 269, 271
mission, 195, 236, 239-41
Mithras, 130-32, 217, 287
Mohammed, 110-11, 114, 137-38, 144
Moloch, 65
monophysitism, 73, 75-76
monotheism, 30, 68, 133, 143, 215-16, 222, 229, 235

morality, 24, 61-62, 64, 82-83, 85-91, 93, 102-3, 218, 283
Mormonism, 101, 111, 215, 285
Moroni, 111
Moses, 27, 110, 142, 164, 174, 191, 235, 266
murder, 37, 91, 277
Muslims, 52, 58, 84, 108, 138, 221, 237
mystery religions, 130, 132-34, 142, 222, 254-55, 287
mythicism, 193

N

Newman, John Henry (Cardinal), 101, 284
New Testament, 14, 28, 63, 74-75, 84, 99, 101, 115, 117, 137, 151, 153-54, 157-58, 162, 169, 173-74, 178, 181, 188, 194, 196, 229, 238, 258, 276, 282, 289-91, 293, 299

O

offerings, burnt, 38-39, 179
offspring, 58, 128, 235, 238, 248-49, 254
Old Testament, 27-28, 31-32, 37-39, 60, 63-64, 78, 83, 85, 92, 115-17, 119, 122, 141, 151-53, 162-63, 174-76, 183,

198, 229-30, 233, 235-36, 249, 256, 266, 292
Olorun, 54
once-and-for-all sacrifice, 38-39, 119
oral tradition, 110, 144-45, 147-50, 159, 163, 192, 207, 263-64, 269, 289
Origen (Christian writer), 194, 196, 268, 275, 281, 293, 296-97, 300
original sin, 26-29, 31, 76-77, 280
Osiris, 132, 252, 287-88

P

pagans, 127, 130, 216-17, 219, 283
Palestine, 14, 63, 118-19, 145-46, 203, 211, 232, 276
Papias, 145-46, 192, 264-65
paraclete, 260-61
paradise, 64-65, 84, 86
Pascal's Wager, 57-58
Passover, 182, 269-70
Paul, 99, 102-3, 129, 136-43, 145-46, 154, 158, 160, 166, 174-75, 181-82, 185, 193, 201, 204, 207-12, 214, 222, 239, 258-59, 261-63, 266, 289, 295
Paul-James contradiction, 102-3
penal theory, 35-36, 39
Persephone, 132, 254-55, 287

Perseus, 129-30, 134, 163
Persian, 33, 64, 130, 232, 239
Peter (apostle), 100, 145-46, 155, 160, 165, 187, 194-95, 209-10, 261, 266
Pharisees, 205, 295
Phlegon of Tralles, 275
Pilate, 161-62, 182, 201, 267-68
Plato, 168, 277
Pliny the Elder (Roman scholar), 164, 192, 272-74
Pliny the Younger (Roman author), 272
politics, 13, 204, 221, 261, 291
Polycarp, 147, 192, 264
pope, 99
population, 13, 60, 62, 215-16, 218, 231-32, 279
prayer, 37, 80, 96, 104-8, 114, 116, 152, 160, 221, 248, 285
prayers for the dead, 104, 152
priests, 39, 92, 99, 115, 233, 235, 276
problem of disagreement, 89
prophecy, 39, 115-19, 121, 128-29, 133, 138, 163, 176-77, 180, 229, 235, 238, 242, 251
prophecy cycle, 235, 238, 251
Protestant Reformation, 36, 100-102, 152
Protestants, 5, 13, 35, 41, 48, 56, 77, 89, 100-104, 152, 256
Proverbs, 37, 52, 141, 168

Psalms, 32, 38, 116, 141, 162-63, 168, 179, 244, 246, 256
punishment, 21, 26, 31, 35, 40, 52, 63-64, 85, 90, 122-23, 235, 244-46, 272-73
purgatory, 104, 152
Pythagoras, 277-78

Q

Q (*Quelle*), 148
Quadratus of Athens, 192, 265

R

rabbi, 152, 160, 188, 199, 201, 230, 271, 299
ransom theory, 35
received oral tradition, 137-38
religions, 4-5, 13-14, 24, 52, 54-55, 58, 71, 79-80, 82, 85, 89-90, 97, 107, 109, 111, 114, 123, 127-28, 130, 135, 154-55, 190-91, 198, 207, 215, 219, 224-25, 287
resurrection, 5, 38, 42-44, 74, 92, 109, 120, 123, 127-28, 131-34, 142, 171, 186, 198-205, 207, 210, 212, 214, 222, 225, 252-53, 255, 263, 271, 275, 280-81, 283, 287, 295, 298
retreat to the possible, 21, 61
revelation, 14, 47-52, 84, 122, 135, 137-38, 143, 153, 157-58, 221, 258, 261-62, 281, 291, 298
Revelations, noncanonical (Peter, Ezra, and the Shepherd of Hermas), 153
righteous minority interpretation, 118, 233-34, 237-38, 240-43, 245-51
Roman Catholic, 5, 13, 79, 100, 151
Romans, 26, 35, 66, 102, 129-30, 139-40, 142, 154, 174-75, 181, 191, 195, 205, 214, 229-30, 232, 237, 289
Rome, 14, 100, 128, 131-32, 157, 194, 196, 220, 261, 263-64, 268, 273, 282, 286-88
Romulus, 128-30, 163
Russell, Bertrand, 7, 160, 291

S

sacraments, 102, 215, 226
sacrifice, 35-40, 56, 65, 72, 85-86, 89, 102, 119, 139, 141, 179, 182, 223, 230, 234, 239, 243-44, 247, 251
Sadducees, 200, 205
salvation, 51, 62, 73-74, 86, 91, 99, 102-4, 131, 137, 139, 176, 240, 258, 287
salvation by faith, 74, 133, 136, 139
Samuel, 32, 66, 83, 184, 257, 280
Satan, 30-33, 135, 280
satisfaction theory, 35-36

Schweitzer, Albert, 121, 286
science, 50, 54, 107, 112, 164
scientific method, 116, 220
scribes, 170, 198, 268, 276
scripture, 15, 30, 32, 37, 50, 69, 73, 76, 92, 100-101, 104, 138-42, 148, 150-51, 153-57, 160, 162-63, 173-74, 179-80, 187, 211-12, 220, 229, 235, 270, 290
2 Clement, 79, 154, 282
Second Council of Ephesus, 75
Second Isaiah, 40, 236-37, 239, 242-43, 246, 251, 297
2 Maccabees, 104, 151-52, 284
Seneca, 164, 191, 274
sense of presence, 201-2, 206
Septuagint, 152, 177, 256
Sheol, 64-65, 133, 222
Shepherd of Hermas, 153-55, 291
sins, 35, 37-40, 66, 76-77, 104, 122, 140-41, 175, 213, 250
slavery, 84-85, 91, 165, 283
slaves, 16, 84-85, 149, 217, 231
Smith, Joseph, 101, 111
Socrates, 160, 277-78
sola fide, 102
sola scriptura, 100-101
Solomon, 31, 151, 177, 183-84, 231, 290
Son of Man, 120-21, 249
souls, 41-42, 44-47, 52, 65, 69, 97, 102, 133, 224, 230
spirituality, 226

Sravasti, 110
Stoicism, 216
substitutionary sacrifice, 35, 40
Suetonius (Roman author), 192, 273-74
suffering, 14, 19-23, 26, 28, 39, 41, 64, 86-87, 89-90, 95, 118, 122-23, 201, 222-23, 225, 233-34, 237-39, 241, 243-45, 250-51, 266
sun, 65, 110, 120, 130-31, 253, 274-75
synagogues, 93, 178, 230, 276
Synods (Hippo, Laodicea), 157-58
synoptics, 148-50, 182, 246

T

Tacitus, 192, 273
Talmud, 192, 269, 271, 277
Tammuz, 132-33, 253-54, 287
temple, 31, 39-40, 152, 160, 162, 219, 230, 232, 234, 246-47, 259
ten commandments, the, 27, 83
Tertullian (Christian writer), 55, 93, 194, 196, 218, 268, 281, 283, 296
Thallus, 274
Therapeutic Effects of Intercessory Prayer (STEP) study, 107, 285
Thessalonians, 136, 154-55, 259
Third Isaiah, 39, 119, 236
Thomas, 55, 74, 149, 153, 187, 195, 265, 290, 294

Timothy, 77, 84, 155-56, 182, 259, 264
Titus, 155, 259
tomb, 154, 164, 186-87, 207, 240
Tosefta, 271
transfiguration, 120-21
transgressions, 26, 36, 38, 234-35, 244, 250
tribes, 25, 118, 185-86, 231, 240, 267
trinity, 68-72, 77-78, 101, 172, 223, 241, 249
truth, 57, 89-90, 117, 194, 196, 210, 221, 230, 261, 267
Twain, Mark, 46

U

underworld, 167, 253-55
Unitarians, 101
universe, 33, 94-96, 168, 224, 272, 275

V

values, 40, 88, 97-98, 109, 224, 226, 264
Venus, 128
vicarious sacrifice, 40, 85, 223, 234, 239, 244, 251
virgin birth, 78, 83-84, 128-29, 176, 213, 269
Vishnu, 54, 80
visions, 39, 202, 204, 291

Vulgate, 170

W

Washington, George, 119
winter solstice, 127, 130-31, 134
wisdom, 70, 151, 168, 243, 277, 285, 290
witnesses, 111, 147, 165, 187-88, 195, 201, 210-11, 270, 285
worship, 51-52, 58, 65, 131, 148, 182, 217, 235, 276, 288

X

xenoglossy, 81

Y

Yahweh, 27-28, 32, 108, 122, 139-41, 161, 175-76, 179, 222, 225, 231-32, 234-35, 242-43, 245, 249
Yeshu, 270-71

Z

Zechariah, 32, 39, 117-19
Zeus, 36, 60, 128-29, 134, 199, 254-55, 292
Zoroastrianism, 33, 63-65, 86, 122, 134

Made in the USA
San Bernardino, CA
27 July 2020